The Prizes
of WAR

The Prizes
of WAR

THE NAVAL PRIZE SYSTEM IN THE
NAPOLEONIC WARS, 1793–1815

RICHARD HILL

Royal Naval
MUSEUM
PUBLICATIONS

SUTTON PUBLISHING

First published in the United Kingdom 1998 by
Sutton Publishing Limited · Phoenix Mill
Thrupp · Stroud · Gloucestershire · GL5 2BU
in association with the Royal Naval Museum

British Library Cataloguing in Publication Data
A catalogue record for this book is available from the British Library

ISBN 0 7509 1816-0

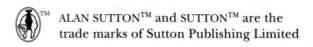

ALAN SUTTON™ and SUTTON™ are the
trade marks of Sutton Publishing Limited

Typeset in 10/12pt New Baskerville.
Typesetting and origination by
Sutton Publishing Limited.
Printed and bound in Great Britain by
Biddles Ltd, Guildford and King's Lynn.

Contents

List of Plates and Maps

The plates are between pages 108 and 109.

Maps

Abbreviations

ADM	Public Records Office, Admiralty papers
C. Rob.	Robinson, *Reports*
Dods.	Dodson, *Reports*
Edw.	Edwards, *Reports*
HCA	Public Records Office, High Court of Admiralty papers
LG	The *London Gazette*
MM	The *Mariner's Mirror*
NC	The *Naval Chronicle*
NMM	National Maritime Museum
RNM	Royal Naval Museum, Portsmouth

In abbreviated citations the volume number of a multi-volume work is placed before the author or title. For cases cited in the Robinson's, Dodson's and Edwards' *Reports*, the date given in square brackets is that of the court hearing, not of the capture.

Chronology

1793	January	Louis XVI executed
	February	France declares war on Britain and Holland. Britain proclaims general reprisals. Reign of Terror in France
	Summer	First Coalition formed against France: Britain, Dutch Republic, Russia, Austria, Spain, Portugal, Sardinia, Naples
	August	British occupy Toulon. British expedition to Flanders under the Duke of York
	October	Marie Antoinette executed
	November	British expedition (Jervis-Grey) to the Caribbean
	December	British evacuate Toulon
1794	May	Successful French counter-attacks in Flanders. British successes in the Caribbean checked by French resistance, fever and insensitive handling of booty
	June	Battle of the Glorious First of June. Howe defeats French fleet but grain convoy reaches France. British forces occupy Corsica
	July	Nelson loses sight of right eye at Calvi. End of the Reign of Terror in France. French victories on European mainland
	Autumn	Further British expedition (Abercromby-Christian) to the Caribbean
1795	February	Holland invaded and forced to join France against Britain
	April	Prussia makes peace with France. British position in Caribbean severely weakened due to reverses and disease
	May	German states make peace with France
	July	Spain makes peace with France
	August	Britain seizes Cape of Good Hope from Holland. Directory established in France

	September	General reprisals declared against Holland. Dutch settlements in Indian Ocean seized by Britain
	October	Third Partition of Poland
1796	Spring	Napoleon's Italian Campaign. Further British reinforcement of Caribbean and partial restoration of conquests
	Summer	British operations on west coast of Italy fail to give decisive help to Austrians. Austria withdraws from the Coalition
	September	Spain signs treaty with France
	October	Spain declares war on Britain
	November	British begin evacuation of Corsica
	December	British fleet withdraws from the Mediterranean
1797	January	French attempt on Ireland thwarted. Napoleon's victories continue in Italy
	February	Spanish fleet defeated by Jervis at St Vincent. Jervis made Earl St Vincent, Nelson knighted
	April	Royal Navy mutiny at Spithead
	May	Mutiny at the Nore
	July	Unsuccessful assault on Santa Cruz, Tenerife. Nelson loses right arm
	October	Dutch fleet defeated by Duncan at Camperdown
1798	January	Squadron under Commodore Lawford intercepts Swedish convoy, leading to the *Maria* case
	Spring	France begins forming a flotilla for the invasion of England
	April	Strong British squadron under Nelson returns to the Mediterranean. French expedition led by Napoleon sails from Toulon for Egypt
	June	French capture Malta
	July	French land in Egypt
	August	French fleet defeated by Nelson at the Battle of the Nile. Nelson created Viscount
	October	Sir William Scott succeeds Sir John Marriott as Judge of the High Court of Admiralty. Further French expedition to Ireland under Bompart frustrated by squadron under Sir John Warren
	December	Capture of the *Eenrom* by HMS *Brilliant*
1799	Spring	Formation of the Second Coalition: Britain, Austria and Russia. Nelson embroiled with Lady

		Hamilton and in Sicilian and Neapolitan intrigue. Many Spanish and Dutch possessions in the Caribbean fall into British hands
	Summer	Sidney Smith's defence of Acre: tide turns against French force in Egypt
	May	*Eenrom* condemned in High Court of Admiralty and appealed. British victories in India. Tippoo Sahib killed
	August	Surrender of Dutch fleet to Mitchell at Den Helder
	October	Capture of Spanish treasure ships *Santa Brigida* and *El Thetis*
	November	Napoleon returns to Paris. Directory overthrown
	December	Further visit-and-search incident off Gibraltar involving Danish frigate. Napoleon elected First Consul
1800	June	Battle of Marengo. Austrians defeated by Napoleon
	July	Danish convoying frigate *Freja* fires on British boarding boat in southern North Sea
	September	British forces occupy Malta. Second Coalition collapsing
	November	Russia, Sweden and Denmark form Armed Neutrality to counter British assertion of belligerent rights. Nelson returns to England
1801	February	Pitt the Younger succeeded by Addington as Prime Minister. Lord St Vincent First Lord of the Admiralty. France and Austria sign Peace of Luneville
	March	British fleet under Lord Keith lands Abercromby's army in Egypt. Battle of Alexandria. Abercromby defeats French but is killed
	April	Nelson defeats Danes at Battle of Copenhagen
	Summer	Dissolution of Armed Neutrality
	October	Truce followed by Peace of Amiens (March 1802)
1802		British refusal to evacuate Malta
	March	Court of Appeal in Prize Causes upholds condemnation of the *Eenrom*
	August	Napoleon appointed First Consul for life. St Vincent institutes commissions to enquire into naval maladministration

1803	May	Britain declares war on France. Letters of Reprisal issued against France and Holland. Initial swoop yields many prizes. France begins forming a flotilla for the invasion of England. Strategic blockades of Brest (Cornwallis) and Toulon (Nelson). Commercial/strategic blockades of Dutch and northern French ports
1804	January	Marsden succeeds Nepean as Secretary of the Admiralty. Strengthening of French puppet régime in Spain. Small-scale operations against invasion flotilla continue all year
	May	Pitt succeeds Addington as Prime Minister. Napoleon crowned Emperor. Melville succeeds St Vincent as First Lord
	August	Alexander Cochrane begins watch on Ferrol
	October	Attack on four Spanish treasure ships
	November	Squadron in the western approaches to Gibraltar under Sir John Orde
	December	Spain declares war on Britain
1805	February	Cruise of Thomas Cochrane in the *Pallas*
	March	Villeneuve's squadron escapes from Toulon
	April	Villeneuve with Spanish reinforcement leaves Cádiz for West Indies. Nelson pursues. Orde falls back on Channel Fleet
	May	Barham succeeds Melville as First Lord
	July	Villeneuve returns to Ferrol after battle with Calder's squadron, thence to Cádiz
	August	Napoleon abandons plans for invasion of England
	October	Battle of Trafalgar. Nineteen French/Spanish ships taken in British victory. Nelson killed. Napoleon forces surrender of Austrian force at Ulm
	December	Napoleon defeats Russian/Austrian armies at Austerlitz
1806	January	British force under Popham retakes Cape of Good Hope. Death of Pitt. Grenville/Fox administration
	February	Grey succeeds Barham as First Lord. Duckworth defeats French squadron at Battle of Santo Domingo

	April	Britain declares two-tier blockade of French and Dutch coasts. *Leander* off New York causes death of an American seaman
	June	Popham's expedition against the River Plate
	September	Grenville succeeds Grey as First Lord
	October	Napoleon defeats Prussians at Jena and Auerstadt
	November	Berlin Decree institutes Napoleon's Continental System
1807	January	British Order in Council issued interdicting trade to French-controlled ports without licence
	February	Drawn Battle of Eylau between French and Russians. Abolition of the British slave trade
	March	British attempt to persuade Turkey against France fails. British fifty-gun ship *Leopard* forces US frigate *Chesapeake* to submit for recovery of British deserters
	April	Mulgrave succeeds Grenville as First Lord. Rose appointed Treasurer of the Navy, Barrow Second Secretary
	June	Napoleon defeats Russians at Friedland. Wellesley Pole succeeds Marsden as Secretary of the Admiralty
	July	Treaty of Tilsit between France and Russia
	August	Gambier's expedition to Copenhagen neutralizes Danish fleet and frustrates a further Northern coalition
	Autumn	British forces seize Dutch and Danish possessions in East and West Indies
	November	British Order in Council reinforces licence system. Thomas Cochrane in *Imperieuse* captures Maltese privateer *King George*, initiating his quarrel with and investigation of the Malta Vice Admiralty Court
	December	Napoleon issues Milan Decree in retaliation to British Order in Council
1808	February	Occupation of further French possessions in West Indies. French Brest squadron takes refuge in Basque Roads
	June	Joseph Bonaparte proclaimed King of Spain
	July	*Seahorse* takes Turkish *Badere Zaffer* in Aegean
	August	Sir Arthur Wellesley lands in Portugal for Peninsular Campaign. Wellesley defeats French

		at Vimeiro. Convention of Cintra concluded by Dalrymple with terms favourable to the French in Portugal. British squadron under Saumarez in the Baltic to support Sweden against Denmark and Russia
	October	Sir Arthur Wellesley returns to Britain
1809	January	French privateering activity increases in the Channel
	February	Martinique and Cayenne captured by forces under Alexander Cochrane
	April	Attack on French fleet in Basque Roads by explosion vessels under Thomas Cochrane. Capture of *Le Niemen* by *Amethyst* and *Arethusa*. General uprising in Spain against French rule, assisting British littoral operations as well as Peninsular Campaign
	May	Wellesley occupies Oporto
	July	Wellesley defeats French at Talavera. Battle of Wagram: Napoleon gains Pyrrhic victory over Austrians. British expedition mounted against Walcheren. British forces seize Senegal. Gambier acquitted by Court Martial for inactivity at Basque Roads
	October	Wellesley created Viscount Wellington. Croker succeeds Pole as Secretary of the Admiralty
	December	Walcheren evacuated. Wellington retires to Lines of Torres Vedras. Napoleon divorces Josephine
1810	January	British capture Guadeloupe
	February	British seize Amboina and other Dutch possessions in East Indies
	April	Napoleon marries Marie Louise of Austria. Littoral operations on French and Italian coasts in the Mediterranean intensified. Réunion captured
	May	Yorke succeeds Mulgrave as First Lord
	July	Napoleon extends full French suzerainty to Holland and Hanse towns
	August	Napoleon imposes heavy tariffs on non-European produce. British naval force defeated in attempt on Mauritius
	September	Battle of Busaco. Wellington defeats Masséna but remains in Portugal. Poor British harvest

		accelerates recession and increases pressure for repeal of Orders in Council
	October	Littoral operations extended to Adriatic
	December	Capture of Mauritius by British joint army and navy forces. Increasing tension between Napoleon and the Tsar over clandestine British exports to the Continent
1811	January	French main fleets bottled up in North Sea harbours, Brest and Toulon. Napoleon begins planning Russian Campaign
	February	Thomas Cochrane's raid on the Vice Admiralty Court at Malta
	March	British campaign against Java begins. Napoleon's son born to Marie Louise
	May	Incident between USS *President* and HMS *Little Belt* increases UK/US tension. Wellington defeats Masséna at Fuentes d'Onoro
	September	Surrender of all Dutch forces in Java
	November	Wellington withdraws to Portugal. Inquiry into costs and fees in Vice Admiralty Courts, demanded by Parliament, initiated in Doctors' Commons
1812	January	Wellington captures Ciudad Rodrigo
	March	French squadron escapes from Lorient to rejoin Brest fleet. Otherwise French bottled up as before. Melville succeeds Yorke as First Lord
	April	Badajoz captured with heavy British loss
	June	Liverpool Prime Minister. Repeal of British Orders in Council too late to prevent American Declaration of War. Numerous British littoral operations on French, Spanish and Italian coasts. *Grande Armée* crosses the Niemen
	July	Wellington defeats Marmont at Salamanca
	August	Early American success in single-ship actions continues to end of the year (*Constitution/Guerrière, United States/Macedonian, Constitution/Java*). Numerous American prizes, privateer and merchant, taken by the British
	September	Battle of Borodino. Napoleon wins Pyrrhic victory over the Russians and continues to Moscow

	October	Retreat from Moscow begins
	November	Wellington retires behind the Douro

1813 March Hoste defeats superior French/Venetian frigate force at Lissa. Russia and Prussia conclude alliance against France

May USS *Chesapeake* captured by HMS *Shannon*. Napoleon begins First Saxon Campaign against the Allies, culminating in six-week armistice

June Wellington defeats French at Vitoria

August Prussia, Russia and Austria re-enter the war

September Americans defeat British at Battle of Lake Erie

November Running engagement between British and French battle fleets off Toulon. French retire to base. Napoleon's European Campaigns end in failure at Leipzig

1814 March USS *Essex* taken after fifteen months' cruise in the Pacific

April Abdication of Napoleon and exile to Elba

May Treaties of Paris. Most British conquests returned to France and Holland

August Cockburn burns Washington. Alexander Cochrane conducts spoiling raids on American East coast

December American War ends

1815 February Napoleon escapes from Elba. Hundred Days begins. Fleet re-mobilized

June Battle of Waterloo. Napoleon defeated by Wellington and Blücher

July Napoleon boards HMS *Bellerophon*

October Napoleon arrives in St Helena

Introduction

The north-south arm of the Bench Corridor in the Middle Temple, linking the Bench Apartments with the incomparable Elizabethan Hall, is dominated by Phillips' portrait of Sir William Scott, Lord Stowell. It shows a man ripe of wisdom and judgement, if a little rheumy, who looks out over the panelled passage in the Inn of Court he adorned during the French Revolutionary and Napoleonic Wars, the period of this book.

As the Inn's Chief Executive I used to, and as an Honorary Bencher still do, bow as I pass this picture, for William Scott was not only a great Admiralty Judge but a man with a deep and broad understanding of the sea and of the way of a sailing ship in it, and a man of immense skill in the clear use of the English language: both qualities which command my admiration.

The genesis of this book lies then with Scott. Rambles through the Middle Temple Library, when there was time, led to the books containing his judgments: fascination was inevitable. His contribution to International Law was my first interest: as Judge of the High Court of Admiralty it was the Law of Nations he administered and he developed it in ways some of which have come down to this day. A paper on that topic, given to the Middle Temple Historical Society in the 1980s, was well received.

But there was more. Scott was dealing after all with flesh and blood issues. Every one of the many thousand captures made during the great wars of the time, every single one, had to be adjudicated in a properly constituted court, and not until it was judged to be lawful prize could the captors reap the benefit. This was the Course of Admiralty, the basis of a system which if not legally regulated would be mere state-sanctioned robbery. The people affected by this process were the officers and men of His Majesty's Ships, masters and crews of privateers, owners, masters and crews of the captured ships and cargoes: fortunes were sometimes at stake, livelihoods often. Did the law understand them; did they understand the law? It was often, heaven knew, complicated enough and it was under constant development, particularly when overlaid by government policy. Did government understand always the effect of its orders and instructions? How were operations influenced by the law?

Further questions arose about the way the system was administered. If captains had handled their own prize matters, the war would have come to a grinding halt. Numerous middlemen were necessary and their reputation, then and subsequently, was often unsavoury; was this justified? Were captors regularly fleeced of their just rewards? Were court officials corrupt or predatory? All these seemed to be charges levelled at the time, reproduced in passing by historians years later.

Seeking answers to such questions about the prize system appeared to be a reasonable objective for study when, after retirement, I looked for some topic that would repay research – provided of course that it had not already been covered by historians. Enquiries showed, to my astonishment, that no comprehensive study of the prize system, its relation to operations and its effects on those who participated in it existed. Even with experience now of the daunting scale of the task, it is still a surprise that no one has so far attempted it.

That then was the ground I set out to cover. The layout of the book fell quite easily into three sections. Because of the importance of the law, pervading as it did every activity connected with Prize, the first section inevitably deals with Law and Operations. These were found to be interlinked in a multitude of ways, not always well defined, often as matters of perception rather than precise instruction. The second section goes on to look at the Middlemen: the Agents, who had such a key role to play on behalf of captors, and the officers of the Court – from Judges through Proctors and Advocates to Registrars and Marshals, for all took their fees. Finally, the book looks at the Spoils, both globally for several categories of capture and recapture and individually in certain cases that seemed to have a particular point to make, ending with an overview of the attitudes of the naval community to the prize system, followed by a chapter of summary and conclusions.

If the sequence of the book is logical, and I very much hope it is, there was nothing sequential about the research. I quickly decided that although the study was to be comprehensive – in that it would seek to touch on every major interaction between strategy, the law, operations, the machinery of the courts, the finances of the captors and the whole ethos of the system – it could not seek to be definitive. To treat and record all the available material must have taken a single researcher the best part of twenty years. That kind of timescale was not open to me.

Some self-imposed limitations were relatively easy to apply. The spoils, for example, were very well documented in thousands of Agents' accounts for the High Court of Admiralty in London. There seemed little point in taking more than a 12 per cent sample which in statistical terms was bound to be robust enough to supply the necessary conclusions, provided that the sample covered the whole period 1793–1815 and was not atypical, and that was relatively easy to ensure.

These accounts were in the Public Records Office at Kew, but that was not the only use made of that wonderful organization. Ships' Logs,

Commander-in-Chiefs' order books and journals, and Admiralty circulars were all consulted freely. However, on one set of documents I can I believe claim an unusual depth of study: the correspondence between Doctors' Commons, seat of the High Court of Admiralty, and the Admiralty Office itself yielded a great deal of information, some of which may alter previously accepted readings of the history of the period, as well as insights into characters at the heart of the system including Scott himself.

On one important set of cases and circumstances the Public Records Offices files were less than comprehensive, and that was in the work of the Vice Admiralty Courts that were set up to adjudicate on foreign stations. These cases were not reported in volume form and only in appeal cases do records exist. There is quite a lot on the administration of these Courts in the Doctors' Commons files, and correspondence on one or two celebrated cases goes into great detail, but I have to say that time did not allow any further research. Nevertheless I hope enough has been included to give a fair picture of these Courts' operation and reputation, as well as the colourful characters who swagger in and out of the archives.

Indeed one of the charms of the study, which I hope is transmitted to readers, is the way personalities – both famous and less well known – keep popping up in the records, often demonstrating traits that were not fully expected. That element is not confined to the public records. One other major, in this context indispensable, source was the *Naval Chronicle*, a magazine not entirely dissimilar from today's *Naval Review*, which I edit. Not only does the *Chronicle* contain all the war news, it is immensely valuable in indicating the flavour of the time, the concerns of the more thoughtful elements of the Navy and the language, so clear and well constructed yet so forceful, that was used.

Such language is a characteristic of my third major contemporary source, the Reports of the judgments of Sir William Scott in the High Court of Admiralty. Like all Law Reports they cover only the cases thought most interesting by the reporter, but these were exceptionally experienced reporters who chose well and they had the other great advantage of using Scott's language to a very large degree. But, maddeningly to a researcher trying to establish links with other contemporary documents, they often do not specify the capturing vessel or the date or position of capture.

This leads on, though, to a further limitation that I have deliberately put on the scope of the book. A number of Scott's cases – it is not always clear which, for the reason given above – dealt with captures by British privateers, those ships authorized by government 'Letters of Marque' to operate against enemy shipping. While I have reviewed such cases when they were of leading legal importance or affected naval operations or attitudes, I have not sought to analyse the returns of privateering operations, for two reasons: the fragmented nature of the records, and the fact that privateers accounted for a relatively small proportion of total British effort in the field of British trade warfare during these wars.

Any researcher needs a few strokes of luck to lighten his task and illuminate corners that would otherwise be dark. I had several. The first was the appearance in 1995 of an MA thesis by Lynne Townley, then a student and now a barrister of Middle Temple, on Scott and his influence on prize law. This most impressive piece of work is vastly detailed in its coverage and has been constantly at my elbow. Lynne Townley does not claim to be a naval historian, as I do not claim to be a legal analyst, and I hope that my work complements hers by bringing some of her excellent legal assessments into the field of naval operations. She has commented most helpfully and encouragingly on Part 1 of the book, and my thanks are due to her for that too.

My second stroke of luck was the work, some already published, on prize agency by Tony Gutridge and on the Scottish dimension by Michael Dun. This pointed down some very productive paths, as did Geoffrey L. Green's *The Royal Navy and Anglo-Jewry 1740–1820.* Dr Nicholas Tracy's *Attack on Maritime Trade* was another essential stimulus and I was grateful for his early support.

Finally, I struck exceptionally lucky in the choice early on of a case to which some deeper analysis might be extended – *The Eenrom.* This turned out to be 'The Case That Had Everything': a difficult neutral capture; a well-known name in the captor, Henry Blackwood of the *Brilliant;* a story of skulduggery well before the capture; conspiracy and false papers; a magisterial judgment by Scott; an appeal involving quite grand personalities in the Danish Royal Court; numerous movements of the prize and its cargo, and transactions involving two of the top agents of the day; and a final settlement that must have been financially satisfying to the captors. Sufficient detail was available on all these points to make a fascinating story that bobs up at various places in the book.

I have had unstinting help from Allison Wareham at the King Alfred Library of the Royal Naval Museum, Portsmouth, from Jenny Wraight in the Admiralty Library and from the staff of the National Maritime Museum. The archive department at NatWest Bank kindly provided unique agency papers. Gillian Hughes was most helpful in copying and sending some relevant War Office records. Lord Digby most kindly gave me a day at Minterne Magna among the archives of his illustrious ancestor Henry, and Commander the Hon. Michael Cochrane was most helpful in discussions about Alexander and Thomas of that family – though he may not be happy at a shaft or two directed particularly at the more famous Thomas.

The Portsmouth Royal Naval Museum has been indispensable to the book in many ways other than its library facilities. Matthew Sheldon has put together much archive material and, most importantly, arranged for the preparation of visual material, mostly from their excellent print collection. Under the aegis of the Museum's Director, Campbell McMurray, Dr Chris Howard Bailey has consistently encouraged the project and provided the necessary liaison with the publishers, to whom I must also record my thanks, particularly Jonathan Falconer and Alison Flowers.

Finally, those to whom thanks are especially due are Dr Nicholas Rodger and Captain Tony Sainsbury, both of whom read the whole text and made immensely valuable as well as encouraging comments, and my wife Patricia and daughter Anna, trusted critics who did the same, reassured me that most of it was readable, and pointed out some places where I had been carried away by technicalities.

Which leads, I suppose, to a final point. The prize system bridged several diverse disciplines and systems of thought: critically, those of the judge, the captor and the agent. Each had his own agenda and the way they interacted is the principal fascination of the topic. But each generates its own language. I have tried to avoid too much talking-down to the reader – the language, after all, as the great novels of Patrick O'Brian remind us, is part of the essence of the time. I have therefore provided a glossary to which readers can refer, and hope this is comprehensive enough to meet most needs. In the text it has often been thought best to let the personalities who figure in the book use their own words – which, great characters as so many of them were, they were well able to do.

Richard Hill
Bishop's Waltham, 1998

Prologue

On 28 December 1798 HMS *Brilliant*, twenty-eight guns, Captain the Hon. Henry Blackwood, could look back on a tough, difficult and financially unproductive eighteen months' work.

The ship's company had been deeply involved in the Mutiny at the Nore in May and June 1797.[1] On 12 June the ship's log[2] says 'the *Brilliant* came up to the Little Nore, where the officers again took command and those concerned in the mutiny was sent on shore'. Within a month the ship was on convoy and cruising duty in the North Sea, not the easiest of environments for a twenty-year-old frigate. Britain had been at war with France since 1793; Holland had recently, perforce, joined her as an ally. The North Sea and the Dutch coast were a war area and instructions to 'cruise for the protection of the trade and the annoyance of enemy privateers' had real point; on 1 September 1797 *Brilliant* was in action against the *Intrepid* privateer of Dunkirk and a lugger, which was driven on shore. But she could claim no capture.

Further frustration must have followed when the ship arrived at the Great Nore on 16 October, after five weeks working out of Lerwick in the Shetlands, and heard the news of the Battle of Camperdown. On 11 October Admiral Duncan's fleet had comprehensively defeated the Dutch under de Winter. So the chance of prizes and military glory again eluded the *Brilliant*. To complete the irony, Duncan also arrived at the Nore on the 16th.[3] The *Brilliant*'s log made no mention of the celebrations, but ship's logs are not meant to be chatty.

Winter at the Nore may have given some respite from weather but it was scarcely likely to have sweetened the atmosphere, with the backwash of that year's mutiny and resultant courts martial. Perhaps it was something of a relief to captain and crew to be sent in the spring of 1798 to Cork, even though that inevitably meant convoy duty.

From the *Brilliant*'s log it is clear that the North American convoy she escorted in April and May of 1798 was a very typical one. The convoy escort commander had constantly to be on the alert for privateers (one was chased off on 27 April and again the next day) and larger enemy forces (worrying intelligence was received from a schooner on 2 May that 'three cut down ships and two frigates of the French were cruising off the outer banks of Newfoundland'). Strays from the merchantmen in the convoy had to be rounded up and convoy discipline preserved. In the event, St John's, Newfoundland was safely reached in late May.

1

A convoy back to Vigo in late June and early July, going with the prevailing winds and in summer, was an easier task. Now came possible reward: *Brilliant* was instructed to cruise off Tenerife, and this might be thought a good hunting ground for prizes. But the luck was out. Two French frigates, the *Vertu* and *Regenerée*, were in Tenerife and their sortie was perilous for *Brilliant*. On her own, outgunned and outnumbered, she escaped only by the most spirited combination of gun action and manoeuvre, and at the expense of most of her anchors and boats, cast away to lighten and speed the ship. The action was professional and courageous enough to earn a note in the standard histories and the *Dictionary of National Biography*[4] and no doubt at the time it got admiration from Blackwood's crew who had no wish to spend time in captivity in France or Spain, but it did nothing to supplement their income.

The same lack of fortune dogged the ship for most of the rest of the year. She had her chances: a French convoy was encountered by *Flora* and *Brilliant* on 9 August but the escort was well handled and *Flora*, the senior officer, thought it too strong for them. Chase of a French lugger on 8 and 9 September proved abortive. October was spent cruising in longitude 50° West and days passed with no sight of anything. The frustration on board is almost palpable from the log entries. A brief respite in St John's, Newfoundland, in November, was followed by a further passage with a convoy across the Atlantic.

But on 28 December, perhaps the luck had changed at last. The log reads:

> Fresh gales and hazey. Saw a strange sail to windward gave chace Boarded her made her a Prize and detained her supposing her to be a Dutch Indiaman under Danish colours called the *Eenrom*.

Behind that laconic entry lay a process that can be gathered from many contemporary accounts of similar actions, though no further detail exists of this one. The sighting of a strange sail to windward, reported either by the officer of the watch or a sharp-eyed lookout, would have brought Blackwood on deck if he had not already been there. He would have ordered more sail to be set for the chase; a frigate, even to leeward, would easily fore-reach on a laden merchantman. When close enough to identify the chase's Danish colours, Blackwood was faced with his first major decision: whether simply to speak with this ostensible neutral and allow her to proceed, or to investigate by visit and search. Something about the *Eenrom*'s appearance and conduct – position and course, configuration, cut of the sails, even the name which had a Dutch ring – must have convinced Blackwood he should order boarding.

When within hail, then, the *Eenrom* would be bidden to bring to. She would not argue; though armed as a matter of course, single merchant ships seldom resisted boarding for the purpose of search, certainly not by a frigate with her crew at quarters and the guns run out, as the *Brilliant*'s under Blackwood surely would have been. The ships would lie perhaps within pistol shot, broadside to broadside, hove to, backed topsails slatting in the Atlantic swell. It was no situation for a merchant ship to show fight.

One of the *Brilliant*'s cutters, oars pulled by experienced seamen, would take the boarding party to the *Eenrom* (there are countless contemporary despatches describing prodigious endurance by boats' crews and, in spite of the 'fresh gales', such work would be routine for *Brilliant*'s cutter's crew). The boat would be armed and the crew ready for trouble. The boarding officer, probably one of the frigate's lieutenants, might himself not be armed if strict protocol was observed. He was well covered by his supporting party and boat's crew.

Language could be a difficulty: neither Danish nor Dutch was generally understood and the difference between the two not readily apparent. But English tended to be the common language of the sea and there were educated men on board the *Eenrom*, no doubt with enough English to answer the routine questions about port of departure, destination, cargo, ownership and nationality, and to produce the ship's papers: certificates, log and cargo manifests. And, as it subsequently appeared, a genuine English-speaker turned up, an American seaman of the *Eenrom*'s crew and (drawn aside perhaps) he had some interesting things to say.

The boarding officer was not satisfied. Something was not right about the *Eenrom*. All the papers and officers' replies to his enquiries pointed to Danish ownership, operation and destination: yet all his instincts – aided perhaps even at this stage by asides from the American sailor – suggested a Dutch connection. When the boat returned to the *Brilliant* he must have reported his suspicions to Blackwood.

So the *Brilliant* detained her prize. But there was much to be gone through before Blackwood or his ship's company could see any product from it. Not least, the law must be satisfied. This book, in its investigation of the influence of the prize system on naval operations and naval life during the wars of 1793–1815, will revisit the *Eenrom* case at various points, to give one concrete example of the way the system worked.

NOTES

1.   William Laird Clowes, *The Royal Navy: A History from the Earliest Times to 1900*, vol. 4 (Chatham, 1997), p. 174.
2.   PRO ADM 51/1245.
3.   Clowes, *The Royal Navy*, p. 391.
4.   Robert Gardiner (ed.), *Nelson against Napoleon* (Chatham, 1997), p. 54.

PART ONE

LAW AND OPERATIONS

CHAPTER ONE

Roots and Rationale

A ship is a lonely object, occupying a relatively tiny area in a very wide expanse of sea. It contains in that small space a variety of valuable assets: its own hull, its crew, equipment, armament if any, stores and cargo, if any. It is an attractive target for predators. Thus, from early times the capture of ships by other ships was a feature of sea life and attempts were made to subject it to regulation by law. The reason was no different from the usual one for establishing law: to impose order on an activity which, if left uncontrolled, would result in chaos, the Hobbesian nightmare of every person seeking to exercise their own tyranny.

But law concerning the sea was not so easy to formulate as domestic laws covering such things as theft and murder. For a start, the sea had always been a highway for vessels of many nationalities or (since nationality was a somewhat vague idea anyway) allegiances. Any effective law had to be international in scope, but there were no international tribunals capable of judging, much less enforcing, it, so national courts (such as there were) had to do the business. Second, there were predators out there: piracy, often on an opportunist basis by vessels which at other times conducted ordinary trading,[1] was widespread. Victims would seldom be confined to a single nationality. Finally, there was the question of inter-state war and the principles of law which might govern that situation.

In medieval times numerous attempts were made to codify the law of capture at sea in a way that was internationally acceptable. These were generally incorporated in instruments of broader scope that included rules for many other forms of maritime conduct. Probably the most coherent, as well as one of the earliest, was the *Consolato del Mare*, formulated in the Mediterranean in the eleventh century.[2] In the Atlantic, the Rolls of Oleron appeared only a little later and were

5

sponsored by Eleanor of Aquitaine and subsequently Richard I of England.[3] The Black Book of the Admiralty, appearing in England a hundred years later,[4] incorporated many of the provisions of the Rolls. There was far more consistency than inconsistency between these various formulations, which made the international development of the principles of law more certain, even though – as will be seen throughout this book – the detail often remained a matter for controversy.

Thus by the beginning of the sixteenth century some international basis for the law had been achieved. How did it answer the requirement for the preservation of good order and redress of wrong?

Redress of individual wrong rested still on the principle of reprisal. A sovereign could grant to a citizen who had been wronged by a national of another country – whether pirate or defaulter of another kind – Letters of Reprisal,[5] by which he could lawfully seize property of that nation in redress. Such authorization could be extended to other nationals in the same cause; in 1414 Henry V issued Letters to 'All and Singular Admirals' to seize ships of Leyden in order to recover a debt owing to John de Waghen.[6] This procedure could operate in time of peace or in the more usual condition of not-peace-not-war.

But the principle of reprisal could be extended to the redress of alleged national wrong, such as could result in a state of war. It is noticeable that even at this stage the Letters are of 'Marque and Reprisal'. Letters of Marque pure and simple (though in this period, as Oscar Wilde said of Truth, they are rarely pure and never simple) were much more in the province of war. In 1405 Henry IV issued 'Letters of Marque against all the King's enemies' to two masters of Bristol ships.[7] The document goes on to say that what they have captured they may 'have and keep for their proper use': and this raised an important principle that recurs throughout all the history of prize warfare.

When formal war existed, the rules in fact became simpler than in other times. All ships of a belligerent, whether 'King's Ships' or private ships operating under Letters of Marque, were entitled to capture property of *enemy character*. This included enemy ships and cargo belonging to the enemy on board those ships, and also enemy cargo on board neutral ships. So much was established in the *Consolato del Mare*.[8] In war, this captured property became in legal terms a Droit of the Crown. Thus, it took a positive act by the Crown, either by Letter of Marque, Act or Proclamation, to grant away the proceeds to the captor.

Throughout the sixteenth century there was steady progress in Europe towards the formation of tribunals charged with judging prize matters. Jurisdiction in such cases had been granted on numerous occasions in previous centuries, but it had been haphazard and temporary, certainly in England.[9] The sixteenth-century flavour was typified by Sir Edward Howard's 1512 statement: 'No prises shall be made or taken but such as shall be lawfull and may be justified'.[10] The structure of the courts took most of the rest of the century to follow the principle, but by 1586 an Admiralty Court was established in England under a judge with the evocative name of Julius Caesar and its first formal condemnation (that is to say, judgment that a capture constituted lawful prize) was made in 1589. England could not, however, claim priority; in the Netherlands prize courts had been operating since the mid-1570s.[11]

During the seventeenth century many aspects of the system became increasingly formalized. The nature of naval forces changed: they became relatively highly organized national fighting forces, in place of the gatherings, in time of need, of armed private vessels round a nucleus of King's Ships. The nature of Letter-of-Marque ships changed: they became generally known as privateers, the notion of private reprisal fell away and they operated under the patronage of Crown or Commonwealth. The nature of overseas commerce and trade changed: it was greatly expanded by all the European nations, it was fostered by the settlement of colonies, large and influential companies were formed to develop it and national laws established to protect it.

But most of all, the nature of war changed. It became more organized; the distinction between war and peace was more clearly defined, declarations of war being more common than previously; its aims were often better articulated than in previous centuries. One aim in particular concerns us here, and is wrapped up in the concept of mercantilism.

Dictionary definitions of mercantilism are not much use. 'The mercantile spirit' or 'commercialism'[12] are inadequate to describe what is now meant by the term. Mercantilism, in the period under study, comprised several elements: the possession of substantial overseas trading and productive interests; the protection of those interests by restrictive legislation in peace and armed cover in war; and offensive action in war against similar interests held by the enemy. In those terms, a principal aim of war increasingly became that of ruining one's opponent while preserving one's own economy.

It was in this context that prize became not just an adjunct of war but one of the prime instruments of strategy.[13] If enemy commerce could be crippled, colonies cut off, outposts harried or occupied and war supplies curtailed, then a favourable peace was likely to be the outcome. Certainly there might be other motives; Cromwell's Western Design had religious as well as mercantilist roots;[14] but the mercantile drive was there, increasingly pushed by influential business and landowning interests as their wealth increased throughout the seventeenth and eighteenth centuries.

The law developed along with the strategy. The Admiralty Court, repelling an attack from the common-law courts in the early seventeenth century on its sole jurisdiction in maritime matters, grew in strength and reputation under a succession of distinguished judges of whom the most remarkable was Sir Leoline Jenkins, who held office from 1668 to 1685.

This was no ordinary court of English common law; the international nature of the law surrounding prize decreed another approach. The lawyers who practised in Doctors' Commons, as it was called (its buildings were just to the east of where Ludgate Circus now stands but no trace of them remains) were called civilians because it was civil law – as opposed to criminal or precedent-led common law – which was administered. All were doctors of law, their education owing more to the Universities of Oxford or Cambridge than to the Inns of Court, though all belonged to an Inn as well.[15] Consequently, they might be thought of as more learned than the general run of common lawyers; this did not necessarily mean they had greater skill in adversarial court work, for much of the work was on paper, as will be seen.

As the wars of the seventeenth and eighteenth centuries unfolded, the law of prize developed, as it was bound to do. One statute and several legal concepts were the principal features of this development.

The statute was the Convoys and Cruizers Act of 1708.[16] This has been rightly described as 'the greatest step forward in the whole of prize legislation'.[17] However, it is noteworthy that the first five articles are not about prize but about the protection of trade, with details laid down of cruising stations at what would now be called choke points, instructions to local commanders as to the regulation of traffic and escort, records to be kept, and so on. The twin ideas of protecting the country's own trade while 'annoying' that of the enemy were firmly in place.

When the Act did reach the business of Prize, the jurisdiction of the High Court of Admiralty was confirmed as to 'all manner of captures, seizures, prizes and reprisals of all ships, vessels and goods that are or shall be taken and to adjudge and condemn the same according to the Course of Admiralty and the law of nations'. The 'Course of Admiralty' was a shorthand way of describing the legal processes governing capture and condemnation of prize. It is a phrase which constantly recurs in literature and correspondence. A Commission or Proclamation – not necessarily a declaration of war – was required to put the jurisdiction of the Admiralty Court into effect.

The Act then went on to matters of much more immediate concern to mariners. It laid down that the captors, whether naval vessels or privateers operating under letters of marque, were entitled to all the net proceeds of a condemned prize. In effect it signed away the Droit of the Crown which had been variously exercised by monarchs over previous centuries: Elizabeth I had been inclined to take half, Cromwell a third, but now that was no longer to be. It did indeed require a proclamation to bring the arrangement into effect at the start of hostilities, but that became standard procedure. One or two anomalies remained; they could

8

be important in individual cases; these will become apparent as this book proceeds.

The Act went on to cover arrangements for taking into service warships and privateers captured from the enemy; bounty for such captures, based on the number of men in the enemy crew at the start of the action, a basis which had replaced the earlier 'gun money' that gave little return or incentive; payment of customs duties on certain items of prize cargo (the state would get some cut, after all); the right of captains and other individuals to appoint agents to handle their prize affairs; the entitlement of Greenwich Hospital (founded a few years before to accommodate, in John Evelyn's words, 'worn out seamen')[18] to take up any unclaimed shares of prize money; and orders for the handling of prize goods, in particular the provision that bulk was not to be broken until the cargo had been condemned as lawful prize. This was the simplest criterion for the checking of pillage or outright robbery by the crew of the capturing ship and had long formed part of the rule of law, but its incorporation into the basic Act governing Prize was of prime importance.

The effects of the Convoys and Cruizers Act were many, but nowhere were they more profound than in the incentive they gave for men to join the naval service. It was true that the proportions laid down for the sharing out of prize money greatly favoured seniority; captains were to get three-eighths of the whole, with one of those eighths going to the flag officer if 'directing' the operation (flag officers usually made sure they were, in form if not in practice), while subordinates got shares of the remainder on a carefully laid down scale. But the lure of prize, even for foremast jacks, remained strong, spurred by the occasional spectacular capture such as that of the Spanish treasure ship *Hermione* in 1762 when each able seaman received more than £300.[19] Without this incentive, the number of volunteers would have been far less than it was; and even pressed men found some consolation in the possibility of prize money.[20] As for the officers, the prospect certainly attracted many who would otherwise not have considered the profession.

While privateers do not feature prominently in this study, it is worth mentioning here that the rules governing them were more flexible. Their prizes had to be adjudged lawful in exactly the same way as those of warships, and the regulations governing the handling of prize ships and cargoes were no less stringent, but the sharing of the proceeds was left to the owners and captains of the privateers themselves.

The law, however, as it developed in the Admiralty Court, was rightly more concerned with matters of principle: what did and did not constitute lawful prize?

The knottiest problem concerned the rights of belligerents towards neutrals. This had been recognized from very early times and was addressed in Chapter XXIII of the *Consolato del Mare*, and it was those principles that were followed in an important statement of the law as interpreted in England, confusingly called the Report on the Silesian Loan, in 1753.[21] Briefly, the Law Officers of the Crown there set out the principle that the goods of an enemy on board the ship of a neutral might be taken, while the goods of a neutral on board the ship of an enemy should be restored. This ran counter to the frequently asserted contention by neutrals that the flag covered the cargo and made it inviolable – the doctrine of 'free ships free goods', of which more will be heard.

There remained the question, also covered in the 1753 report, of contraband. That such a thing as contraband – literally, a violation of custom[22] – existed was not in doubt; in war, it could be held to constitute any articles destined for the enemy (though still in the ownership of a neutral) which might be useful to the enemy in his war effort. But where was the line to be drawn? Continental, and notably French, jurisdictions tended to restrict contraband to munitions and armaments – pikes, muskets, gunpowder. British courts cast the net much more widely. However, the 1753 report referred only in passing to what might and might not be classed as contraband and clearly wished to leave it to the court to decide in each instance. Such definition occupied a large part of the Admiralty Court's work in the period later in the eighteenth century and into the nineteenth. It must have been a headache for those who were trying to operate the system at sea: the more so as the 1753 report ominously says at one point '. . . if a seizure is made without probable cause, the captor is adjudged to pay costs and damages'.[23] That was the reverse of the glittering coin of the prize system.

Naturally, in order to discover whether a neutral vessel was carrying cargo belonging to the enemy, or contraband goods destined for him, it was necessary for the warships of a belligerent to visit and search that vessel and inspect its papers and cargo. This right was implied in the *Consolato del Mare*, and recognized in English and French ordinances in the sixteenth century.[24] However, its simple application was overlaid by numerous treaties in the seventeenth and eighteenth centuries, particularly concerning the states of northern Europe, which had a great interest in commerce in the wars occupying their neighbours to the south. Sweden and Denmark, often with the support of other powers, were most forward in claiming that when merchant vessels were under the convoy of their warships, empowered to give assurance of the innocence of their cargoes, then no belligerent right of visit and search existed. Britain's policy was to insist on the maintenance of the right unless there was specific treaty provision to the contrary between the parties involved.[25] But here again, her cruisers might be expected to have some tricky problems to solve in actual encounters at sea.

Finally, a heavy weapon in the legal armoury was Blockade. This has been defined as 'the interception by sea of the approaches to the coasts or ports of an enemy with the purpose of cutting off all his overseas communications. Its object is not only to stop the importation of supplies but to prevent export as well.'[26] Blockade applied to all traffic, whether enemy or neutral (or, come to that, friendly; trading with the enemy by British ships had been known). By the end of the eighteenth century, when blockade had been frequently practised for over a century, it was recognized that it was a draconian instrument and therefore had to satisfy strict criteria: it must be declared as an act of state, must be effective over the whole of the declared area and must be continuous. Again, the responsibility of commanders, and of the naval forces under them, in exerting blockade were likely to be onerous, particularly when sail and oars were the only motive power available.

Those, then, were the bones of the system of what may be called prize warfare when war broke out between revolutionary France and Britain in 1793. It was a war that would go on, with one intermission from 1801 to 1803, until the final defeat of Napoleon in 1815; a war in which sea power has always been acknowledged to be a highly significant, many would contend a decisive, factor; certainly a war in which the economies of Britain and the Continent were regarded by the protagonists as being of the utmost importance. The prize system was an integral component of this economic warfare; the law was its regulator, the naval and privateer forces of the protagonists its instruments, the spoils its principal incentive, the civil and court officials, agents and middlemen its essential lubricants. To explain how these fitted together is the task of the rest of this book.

NOTES

1. Susan Rose in J.R. Hill (ed.), *Oxford Illustrated History of the Royal Navy* (OUP, 1995), p. 13.
2. Lynne Townley, 'Sir William Scott, Lord Stowell and the Development of Prize Law in the High Court of Admiralty 1798–1828, with Particular Reference to the Rights of Belligerents' (unpublished thesis, University of Birmingham, 1995), p. 74.
3. C. John Colombos, *International Law of the Sea*, 6th edn (Longman, 1967), pp. 32–3.
4. R.G. Marsden (ed.), *The Law and Custom of the Sea*, vol. I (Navy Records Society, 1915), p. 118; Lt-Cdr Peter Kemp RN, *Prize Money* (Gale and Polden, 1946), p. 3.
5. N.A.M. Rodger, *The Safeguard of the Sea* (Harper Collins, 1997), p. 199.
6. Marsden, *The Law and Custom of the Sea*, vol. I, p. 126.
7. Ibid., p. 114.
8. Townley, 'Sir William Scott, Lord Stowell and the Development of Prize Law', pp. 101ff.

9.   Colombos, *International Law of the Sea*, pp. 14–15.

10.   E.S. Roscoe, *History of the English Prize Court* (Lloyd's, 1924), p. 14.

11.   I.J. van Loo, New Researchers' Conference, Liverpool, 15 March 1997.

12.   *Shorter Oxford English Dictionary* (OUP, 1973), p. 1308.

13.   David French, *The British Way in Warfare 1688–2000* (Unwin Hyman, 1990), p. 56.

14.   Christopher Hill, *God's Englishman* (Pelican, 1972), p. 152.

15.   G.D. Squibb, *Doctors' Commons: A History of the College of Advocates and Doctors of Law* (Clarendon Press, Oxford, 1977), pp. 42, 213.

16.   6 Anne c. 65, in C. Robinson, *Collectanea Maritima* (White and Butterworth, 1801), pp. 188ff, and Statutes at Large 1706–7, p. 227. The Act received Royal Assent in 1707 but the Prize Provisions did not come into force until 26 March 1708.

17.   Kemp, *Prize Money*, p. 14.

18.   John Evelyn, *Diary*, 17 February 1695.

19.   Christopher Lloyd, *The Nation and the Navy* (Cresset Press, 1954), p. 109.

20.   D.B. Ellison, *Pressganged* (Ellison's Editions, 1994), p. 30: the letters of George Price alias Green illustrate the point clearly.

21.   Marsden, *The Law and Custom of the Sea*, vol. II, pp. 348ff.

22.   Colombos, *International Law of the Sea*, p. 675n.

23.   Marsden, *The Law and Custom of the Sea*, vol. II, p. 352.

24.   Colombos, *International Law of the Sea*, p. 754.

25.   Townley, 'Sir William Scott, Lord Stowell and the Development of Prize Law', pp. 155ff.

26.   Colombos, *International Law of the Sea*, p. 714.

CHAPTER TWO

Five Years In

In 1798, the war against revolutionary (not yet Napoleonic) France had been in progress for five years. British strategy in 1793 had followed lines that had been traditional and generally successful throughout the eighteenth century. A coalition with most of the other European powers, alarmed by the French Revolution and even more by the subsequent Terror, would it was hoped contain France on the mainland of Europe, with a reasonable prospect of helping the sizeable monarchist forces still in France and her colonies to restore the monarchy. Meanwhile, British sea power would make captures of French territory overseas – notably in the Caribbean – and exert a stranglehold on French maritime trade. In both its strategic aim, the weakening of the French republican régime to the point where it had to succumb, and its mercantilist objective, the capture of enough French assets to finance the allies' war and ruin the French economy, this strategy had been unsuccessful.

Although Howe had won the signal victory of the First of June 1794 against the French battle fleet, Montagu had failed to capture the crucial grain convoy covered by it, so that the republican régime could still be seen by the French population as able to support it. Royalist insurrections at Toulon and in the Vendée, though stiffened by British forces, had been put down.

In the West Indies, many of the amphibious operations had misfired. Partly this was due to too optimistic a view of Britain's ability to mount and project large-scale expeditions to coincide with the (relatively) healthy campaigning season. By arriving too late in the year, forces several times, after initial success, succumbed catastrophically to fever and the gains amounted to very little. In the first expedition, however, there was another factor: the grasping after plunder of the senior officers, Admiral Jervis and General Grey, alienated the French population, even those who had royalist leanings,[1] and played into the hands of republican leaders like Victor Hugues or insurrectionists like Toussaint l'Ouverture. Even the British government realized that the commanders had overstepped the mark and their takings were pegged back (Jervis perhaps learnt a lesson, as may be seen in subsequent chapters) but the damage had been done. Grey in fact was never employed overseas again.[2]

Meanwhile, French victories on the continent had confounded the Coalition, which by 1797 had fallen to pieces, with some members, notably Spain and Holland, moving perforce to the French side and others making peace with France.

There had been some successes, even though Britain's overall situation was not favourable. By defeating the Spanish and Dutch fleets at St Vincent and Camperdown respectively in 1797, Britain had reduced the threat of an invasion of Ireland or even the mainland. Moreover, the mercantilist side of the war continued; by joining the French, the Dutch laid open their more vulnerable East Indies colonies as well as the Cape of Good Hope to assault and, closer to home, their shipping suffered as did that of the French.

The Spaniards may well have caught a nastier cold than either of their new allies. In the *Aurora* between 11 January 1797 and 16 September 1798, Captain Henry Digby captured fifty vessels in the Eastern Atlantic, thirty-nine of which were Spanish.[3] Many papers of this outstanding frigate captain survive and we shall come across him again; it needs saying here only that he seems to have deserved his luck, for his standing orders for the conduct of his ship are a model of firmness and humanity which could serve as an example today.[4]

So, even though Collingwood in 1795 was writing 'This is not a war of profit: much gain is not to be expected in it',[5] there were plenty of exceptions; and when he went on to say 'I believe that is as little a consideration with sailors as with any class of people', he was perhaps judging by his own very high standards and his own strategic perception. To those with the vision, it was a different sort of war, a war (as became evident subsequently between 1803 and 1805) of national survival, but the mercantilist thread remained strong and the incentive of prize money still mattered greatly, even through the dark days of the collapse of the First Coalition and the 1797 mutinies at Spithead and the Nore. It is worth noting that the system of prize money and the scale of its distribution did not figure at all in the demands of the Spithead mutineers, and only marginally in those of the more politically minded mutineers at the Nore.[6]

There are good reasons though, unconnected with the course of the wars, for choosing 1798 as a first breathing point in this survey of the prize system. They are researchers' and historians' reasons, but valid nonetheless.

The first and perhaps most important is the appointment to the High Court of Admiralty of a singular man who will figure prominently in this study: who indeed would threaten to dominate it if allowed to. This was William Scott, later Lord Stowell. He succeeded Sir James Marriott, who had held the office for twenty years and had acquired a reputation for idiosyncratic judgments and overstatement and thereby for lack of legal knowledge and balance. These may not have been entirely deserved; Marriott after retirement compiled some scholarly collections.[7] But there is little doubt he was at the end of his tour as a judge in 1798.

Scott was a natural successor. He was born in 1745, son of a Newcastle coal merchant. The rebellion of that year, with effects uncomfortably close to Newcastle, caused him to be born in the county of Durham where his mother had moved for safety. Some years later this circumstance helped Scott, who in 1761 won a scholarship to Corpus Christi College, Oxford reserved for Durham men.[8] He pursued a largely academic career until 1780, having been made Camden Reader in Ancient History in 1774 and obtaining his Doctorate of Law in 1779.

He had long since been a student member of the Middle Temple, which he joined in 1762, and began to keep terms in 1777. These, with the few formal exercises that were all that remained of the once rigorous regimen of the Inns of Court, qualified him for Call to the Bar in 1780, and he thereupon joined Doctors' Commons with the intention of practising there. A 'year of silence', not unlike the modern system of pupillage for barristers, followed but thereafter Scott became quickly established in a court that was busy with work from the War of American Independence, still in progress. He was a part of intellectual and coffee-house London too: a good friend of Dr Johnson, he was named an executor of his will.[9]

Not only Scott's ability as a civilian lawyer and advocate, but his seniority, conspired to bring him to the top of his chosen profession. The other significant names in Doctors' Commons at the turn of the century – John Nicholl, James Henry Arnold, French Laurence, Maurice Swabey, Christopher Robinson – had all joined after Scott, between 1785 and 1796.[10] Thus Scott was a natural choice for the critically important post of King's Advocate, which he assumed in 1789. Given his success in that position, which was marked, his elevation to the High Court Bench was almost assured. It was as if he had come into his own.

His confidence as he did so is apparent from many sources. It shows almost at once in the correspondence between Doctors' Commons and the Admiralty.[11] There, Scott's strong, rapid, instantly recognizable handwriting stands out among the more clerkly inputs of Gostling the Admiralty Procurator or Heseltine the King's Proctor. These were concerned more with administration: sometimes weighty matters to be sure, but not to be compared with Scott's statements on policy and legal principle.

Very soon after assuming office he was called on to give a view on a knotty problem concerning prize jurisdiction in Ireland on Droits of Admiralty,[12] and the magisterial tone is at once clear:

> . . . all droits are equally prize though the beneficial interest in one case goes to the Lord Admiral, in another to the individual captors, and in another to the King *jure coronae* . . . [there is] a misapprehension very common among sailors that Droits are of a nature totally differing from that of prize, whereas they are essentially the same.

This was instructive, though firm enough. Much tougher was Scott's reaction to an incident after the capture of the Spanish treasure ships *El Thetis* and *Santa Brigida* (both are variously spelt in the records) by *Naiad, Ethalion, Triton* and *Alcmene* (Captain Henry Digby again, in a new command) in 1799. The treasure was loaded into forty-four wagons and transported, under an army guard, from Plymouth to London[13] to be sold to the Bank of England for the enormous sum of £661,206 13s 9d.[14] In 1999 that would be worth £120 million. It was a hugely popular success and headline news. But technically bulk had been broken and Scott had to make a point: it was 'a high misdemeanour punishable with severe penalties . . . Neither the captors nor their agents have acted with sufficient caution.'[15] Scott's remonstrance was written personally to Evan Nepean, the Secretary of the Admiralty and one of the most powerful men in Britain. The new Judge of the High Court of Admiralty was showing himself as lacking neither in confidence nor authority.

He was fortunate in inheriting an established system and a well-run-in court. The latest Prize Act, significantly entitled 'An Act for the Encouragement of Seamen',[16] had been in force since 1793 so was reasonably up to date; the necessary Proclamations as to powers of lawful seizure in the course of the war (still labelled as 'Reprisal') were in date; and the procedures to be followed on taking a prize were laid down. These included, before the case could come to court, the age-old stipulations about not breaking bulk (with some dispensation for perishables), the need to take the prize in to a port where there was some British authority, and the requirement to take statements from the master, mate and one other person from the captured ship.

These were called the Standing Interrogatories, and remained an integral part of the system for the whole of the period considered in this book.[17] There were thirty-two groups of questions and they were skilfully drafted; they covered nationality of the owner, the officers and of the ship itself; the nature, provenance and destination of the cargo, and the instructions under which she was sailing. If honestly answered, they would give sufficient evidence to the court to determine questions of enemy character and contraband. However, evasion was common; and the ship's papers, cargo manifests and even correspondence were invariably seized and brought into evidence to determine whether there were inconsistencies.

All this evidence would then be brought into court on production of a monition by the captor; if the lawfulness of the prize was to be contested, a claim had to be entered by the owner of ship or cargo, or other interested party, within a specified time. Uncontested cases – typically, those where enemy character was undoubted, the place and conditions of capture were subject to no legal restriction and there was no dispute as to the entitlement of the captor or captors – could result in rapid condemnation. Contested cases would take longer to come to court, though by the standards of the late twentieth century the delays in first hearing were not excessive, being generally a few weeks. But a requirement for further and better particulars, naturally arising in cases of doubt, could drag the case on; and there was a right of appeal to the Lords Commissioners of Appeal in Prize Causes, which like any appeal procedure could stretch into years.

Most of the evidence would be on paper and it was rare for witnesses to be examined in person. Indeed, it would have been highly detrimental to the conduct of the war if seagoing officers had had to give evidence in court and the costs of keeping officers of the captured ships, or other claimants, in attendance would have been high. There were, of course, no juries in this civil jurisdiction. Thus the atmosphere of Doctors' Commons tended to be that of scholarly inquiry and polite argument rather than the rough-and-tumble of the Common Law. It may well have been that which attracted Scott, with his strongly academic bent, towards this branch of the law in the first place.

He was, by all accounts, no orator himself,[18] and as a judge he almost at once formed the habit of writing out his judgments and reading them in court. This has been a key element in our knowledge of his unique contribution to the law, for it enabled a quite new dimension to be brought in to the recording of the Admiralty Court's business.

The man responsible for the reporting of Admiralty cases in the first ten years of Scott's tenure was Christopher Robinson, himself a member of Doctors' Commons and the successor to Sir John Nicholl as King's Advocate in 1809. Robinson's reports for the years 1798 to 1808 occupy six volumes and contain every case either of serious contention or of formulation and clarification of the law of prize. They are probably the most valuable single source of our knowledge of the subject in this period. They are more remarkable in that they had no precursor; there were spasmodic reports of cases heard under Marriott and Hay his predecessor,[19] but they amount to no more than a taster of what went on and suggest far less method and continuity than was now applied by Scott. Robinson's work was carried on by Edwards in one volume, from 1808 to 1811, and by Dodson in two volumes from 1811 to 1828.

So the Course of Admiralty – that convenient short title for the whole process of capture, monition, claim, condemnation (or restoration) and appeal, leading to sale and distribution – was well reported from 1798 onwards. Fortuitously, the systematic recording of the course of the naval war began in that year as well. The *Naval Chronicle*, a private venture by the publisher Gold, appeared monthly from that year to well after the end of the war and quickly became indispensable reading for all officers with any pretension to advancement. A typical issue would include a biographical memoir of some naval worthy (living or dead), a lively correspondence section in which few punches were pulled, 'philosophical' papers discussing technical ideas for the naval service, hydrographic information, reports on proceedings in Parliament touching naval business, the more important Proclamations governing the course of the war and shifts in alliances and 'Reports on Service' which were extracts from the *London Gazette*, mainly about naval actions both large and small. From time to time, reports on proceedings in the Admiralty Court would be included, but they seem to have depended on the availability of someone to do the reporting and, with some exceptions which will be covered later, bear little relevance to the legal or operational importance of the cases.

This is but a small blemish. The *Naval Chronicle* is a key source not only for accounts of the progress of the war but for material to help in analysing naval mood and preoccupations, not least the navy's attitude to and knowledge of the prize system in all its complexities.

Of course, 1798 was a hinge year for many reasons other than the systematic recording of naval operations in support of the prize system. It defined Napoleon Bonaparte as the dominant figure in the world scene; after his Egyptian expedition, with its lofty visions, he could not look back.[20] It established Horatio Nelson not only as Britain's foremost fighting admiral but as a strategic commander; his victory at the Nile was the product of politico-military insight and not merely of professional expertise.[21] Most of all, it ensured that the war would be prolonged and decisive in a way that no eighteenth-century war had been or sought to be. Beside these vast events the taking of individual prizes, whether merchants or vessels of war, might seem in hindsight to have been a relic of the outgoing century; but it remained a chosen instrument of sea power and, as will be seen, it had its effects.

NOTES

1. Michael Duffy, *Soldiers, Sugar and Seapower* (Clarendon Press, 1987), p. 106.
2. Ibid., p. 113.
3. Papers in the possession of Lord Digby.
4. Ibid.
5. E.A. Hughes (ed.), *The Private Correspondence of Admiral Lord Collingwood* (Navy Records Society, 1957), p. 65.
6. Dudley Pope, *Life in Nelson's Navy* (Chatham, 1997), p. 150.
7. Lynne Townley, 'Sir William Scott, Lord Stowell, and the Development of the Prize Law in the High Court of Admiralty 1798–1828' (unpublished thesis, University of Birmingham 1995), Bibliography.
8. Ibid., p. 37.
9. Henry J. Bourguignon, *Sir William Scott, Lord Stowell* (Cambridge University Press, 1987), p. 39.

10.   G.D. Squibb, *Doctors' Commons: A History of the College of Advocates and Doctors of Law* (Clarendon Press, Oxford, 1977), p. 194.

11.   PRO ADM 1/3894.

12.   See Chapter 8.

13.   See E.M. Broadley and R.G. Barthelot, *Three Dorset Captains at Trafalgar* (John Murray, 1906), for an account of the procession.

14.   Digby, n. 3.

15.   ADM 1/3894.

16.   33 Geo. III c.66.

17.   1 C. Rob, 381ff.

18.   Bourguignon, *Sir William Scott, Lord Stowell*, p. 50. Bourguignon's evidence here is drawn from W.C. Townsend, *Lives of Twelve Eminent Judges* (London, 1846), vol. II, p. 295, and this presumably is the source of a similar assertion in the *Dictionary of National Biography*. There is no known counterclaim that Scott was an accomplished orator.

19.   Townley, 'Sir William Scott, Lord Stowell, and the Development of the Prize Law', p. 28, n. 114.

20.   J. Holland Rose, *The Life of Napoleon I*, vol. I (Bell, 1920), p. 215.

21.   Carola Oman, *Nelson* (Sphere Books edn, 1968), p. 248; A.T. Mahan, *The Life of Nelson*, vol. I (Sampson Low, 1897), pp. 334–6.

CHAPTER THREE

Trouble with Neutrals

An Admiralty circular of 7 September 1795, addressed to Commanders in Chief at Portsmouth, Plymouth and the Downs, as well as to Lord Howe in the Channel Fleet,[1] gave a frank statement of a perennial dilemma:

> . . . among the captures of neutral ships . . . there appears to be many cases where such ships are not laden with military stores or provisions, and where there is no ground to support the suspicion of enemy's property, which has occasioned much expence and inconvenience to government . . . the only ground on which they ought to be stopped is a reasonable suspicion of their being enemy's property; and . . . in all those cases the captors must take on their own risk the proof of such suspicion . . .

It was no wonder that cruising captains were cautious about taking risks of this sort, for it was on them alone that the liability fell. Later on, some machinery was devised for meeting the costs of captains who had made captures in good faith on suspicion that a neutral was not all he seemed,[2] but it appears that at this stage in the war the restoration of a neutral vessel or cargo could put a captain in severe financial difficulty.

When he came to the Admiralty Bench in 1798, Sir William Scott's first priority appears to have been to clarify the law regarding neutrals. By the nature of the English court system, he could not do this except in the context of the cases that came before him; but these were not far to seek. His very first case, *The Vigilantia*,[3] concerned national character; this, he ruled, was generally determined by the place of residence of the owner, but special circumstances might negate the general rule, such as the traffic on which the ship was engaged.

This case is interesting as it illustrates Scott's methods. He did not, as some earlier analysis suggested,[4] create law on the hoof. His judgments, particularly when they addressed matters of principle, were generally based on profound knowledge of what had gone before; he had not only his own extensive experience in Doctors' Commons (in *The Vigilantia*, for example, he had argued as King's Advocate a very similar case in 1794),[5] but the accumulated experience of the Court through the latter half of the eighteenth century, embodied in notebooks carefully kept and annotated and known to have been in Scott's personal possession. They are now held in the Rare Books Room of the Middle Temple Library.[6]

But *The Vigilantia* ruling, even if it had been widely promulgated, could have been of little help to a boarding officer in a rolling, pitching, hove-to merchantman, with a master and crew professing little knowledge of English, ship's papers and cargo manifests in foreign languages, and an impatient captain across the water in the detaining frigate or sloop wanting to know if it was 'prize or no prize'. In the end, nine times out of ten the decision would be a matter of nous born of experience: a nose for the suspicious, governed by caution as to what would happen if the prize was taken and it proved wrong.

No doubt on many occasions caution would prevail and the potential prize would be allowed to proceed. It was not for nothing that St Vincent wrote to Grenville in 1806: 'where one captain makes fortune by the capture of neutrals, ten are ruined; [no one else] bearing any part of the onus'.[7] St Vincent was prone to heavy exaggeration, but he had a point.

A graphic account of the kind of dilemma that could be encountered was given by William Henry Dillon, later Vice Admiral of the Red, in his *Narrative of my Professional Adventures*.[8] In the West Indies on 15 September 1801, Dillon as First Lieutenant of the *Aimable* boarded the American vessel *Alert* with a cargo of quicksilver. The supercargo (it was usual for merchant ships to carry such a person to be in charge of the cargo and commercial transactions connected with it at each port touched) was made out by Dillon to be a Frenchman, but it turned out he was a naturalized American. This raised doubt about the legality of the prize, but Dillon's captain, William Lobb, brought her in, along with another, the *Richmond,* which Dillon considered more valid. Sureties were raised on the *Richmond* in case of costs or damages and, sure enough, when the shore authorities examined the papers they warned that the *Alert* was 'a very doubtful case'.[9] Then, in a transaction which could certainly not have happened in home waters but was of the sort tolerated on the more easy-going Leeward Islands station, Dillon negotiated a document of acquittal and the *Alert* sailed away with no further questions asked.

A variation on the neutrality question concerned trading with the enemy. In the case of *The Hoop*[10] a ship was laden from Rotterdam ostensibly for Bergen but in reality for England. Since the Netherlands were under French control this amounted to enemy trade; and not even the fact that the Glasgow customs had advised that the trade was lawful exonerated the owners. Scott treated this as a leading case and analysed the whole question by reference to precedents from the War of the Austrian Succession, the Seven Years War and the War of American Independence. The cargo was condemned, but the expenses of the owners were paid out of the proceeds. Again, one is led to wonder what sort and detail of guidance would have helped the officers of a ship detaining a merchantman in such circumstances.

Rather more comfort might be available in another range of cases. These concerned neutral vessels seeking to take part, in wartime, in a trade that was barred to them in time of peace. The Navigation Acts that were such a common feature of the mercantilist system often did impose such a restriction on foreign vessels: trade with a colony was reserved, by domestic legislation, to the ships of the mother country. But there were in peacetime numerous variants, such as the system of 'free ports' in the British West Indies where trade was unrestricted.

In the mid-eighteenth century Britain had developed a doctrine to counter the natural tendency of neutrals to jump in, in time of war, to the colonial trades of belligerents, much to their own advantage. This doctrine was known as 'the Rule of the War of 1756' and could be simply stated as 'a neutral cannot legally engage, in wartime, in the trade of a belligerent not open to that neutral in peacetime'.[11] It was implicit in the wording of the Instructions to His Majesty's ships and Letters of Marque both of 6 November 1793 and 25 January 1798; the former instructed them to 'stop and detain *all* [my italics] ships loaden with goods the produce of any colony belonging to France . . . and bring the same, with their cargoes, to legal adjudication in our court of Admiralty', while the latter less stringently ordered the same to be applied to 'all ships laden with goods the product of any island or settlement belonging to France, Spain or the United Provinces [Holland], and coming directly from any port of the said settlements to any port of Europe not being a port of this Kingdom nor a port of that country to which such ships, being neutral ships, shall belong'.[12]

These were clear instructions, though at sea the earlier was easier to implement, because it was not selective, than the later. However, this was a national instruction to give force to a national proclamation and Scott's business was to enforce the law of nations. Consequently, in the first case before him which tested the Rule of 1756, he analysed the principles behind it in some detail. It did not greatly matter that this case, *The Emanuel*,[13] concerned a Danish ship taking part in the coasting trade of the Spanish mainland; that too was barred to the Danes in time of peace; Scott concluded that the Danish flag gave 'extraordinary assistance' to the enemy and refused the costs of freight, though the ship was restored.

Confusingly, the most fully recorded case concerning neutrals in the colonial trade proper was *The Immanuel*.[14] This was a Hamburg ship going to Santo Domingo, touching at Bordeaux on the way. The case was complicated by Toussaint l'Ouverture's insurrection in Santo Domingo, which had put him in control of the island at the time of the capture; the claimants argued that it was no longer strictly a colony. But Scott dismissed these arguments and returned to the principle: '. . . it is the

right of neutrals to carry on their accustomed trade . . . very different is
the case of a trade which the neutral has never possessed, which he holds
by no title of use and habit in time of peace, and which, in fact, can
obtain in war by no other title, than by the success of one belligerent
against the other . . . and this I take to be the colonial trade, generally
speaking'. A belligerent had the right, in war, to possess himself of the
opponent's colonies; what right, asked Scott, had a third party claiming
neutrality to 'step in and prevent the execution'? The Rule of 1756 was
'known and revered by every state of Europe' at the time of Blackstone.
As for marginal cases, 'the true rule to this Court is the text of the
Instructions'; what was not permitted by them was prohibited. Scott ruled
that goods shipped at Bordeaux were liable to confiscation, and freight
was refused but the ship was restored.

If word of this judgment got around the coffee houses of London,
Portsmouth, Plymouth and Bath and the great cabins of the fleet (there
is no record of its general promulgation and the published Reports of
Robinson did not appear till some years later), it must have been of some
comfort. At least the Instructions could be trusted to have the force of
law and so long as cruisers kept to them strictly they should have the
protection of the Court. And the Rule of 1756 was alive and well, so far as
the British Court of Admiralty was concerned – though one is entitled to
wonder how many frigate captains could have quoted it.

More difficult questions of interpretation surrounded Contraband.
There had been tension throughout the eighteenth century between the
continental powers, including the Scandinavian countries on the one
hand and Britain on the other, as to what constituted contraband: Britain
adopted a broad definition while other states sought a narrower one.
Such a division was natural; if Britain, having dominance over the sea
routes by which supplies of naval stores from Scandinavia reached the
main continental powers, could legally inhibit such traffic then it would
give her great advantage in war. There was a firm enough argument too
in legal principle: for in an age where sea warfare assumed great
importance, surely naval stores such as pitch, tar and hemp were in
essence warlike stores.

However, there were counter-arguments. First was legal precedent in
Britain; in the seventeenth century the great Admiralty judge Leoline
Jenkins had given his opinion that these very pitch, tar and hemp were
not contraband.[15] The more extensive definition had crept in during the
eighteenth century. Second was a more practical reason: those very
Scandinavian countries that might supply France and Spain with these
commodities would also be suppliers to Britain. It was necessary to keep
on friendly, or at least sound commercial, terms with them.

In consequence, British policy was to make treaties where possible with
potential suppliers which would give maximum advantage to Britain

while depriving the enemy to the greatest possible extent; and in the absence of such treaties, to exercise a broad definition of contraband with the sop, to the neutral, of a 'right of pre-emption': that is to say, to buy into British service at a fair price any contraband goods which were the product of the nation under whose flag the ship sailed.

Scott's judgments followed this policy and critics may well say that he was not so impartial in his interpretation of the law of nations in this matter as he was in some others;[16] he relied heavily on an appeal case in 1750, *The Med Guds Hjelpe*.[17] He was, however, consistent, and not without clemency. In the first such case that came before him, *The Sarah Christina*,[18] while condemning a contraband cargo aggravated by false papers, he spared the ship because she might have been put under duress.

Where doubt arose as to destination, too, he could be lenient; in *The Imina*[19] a ship on her way from Danzig to Amsterdam and diverted to Emden with a cargo of ship timber was restored for this reason. Significantly, though, Scott added that 'as it was absolutely incumbent on the captors to bring the cause to adjudication, from the circumstance of the apparently original destination, I think they are fairly entitled to their expences'.

This is an example of Scott's fairness and commonsense. His knowledge of sea affairs was apparent in a case soon afterwards, *The Franklin*.[20] This Prussian ship, with a cargo of hemp and iron, was taken 3 miles off Bilbao though her cargo was ostensibly for Lisbon. Scott admitted it was 'very difficult to detect a fraud of this species' on that coast, but 'the ship had ingulphed herself deep in the Bay of Biscay' and was steering east under an experienced captain. 'The month of November last year was particularly mild', and the master's explanations were insufficient. In this case, said Scott, 'the carriage of contraband with a false destination will work a condemnation of the ship as well as the cargo'.

It must have been of considerable comfort to cruising captains that the law was being broadly interpreted. One must, however, add the usual caveat: 'If they knew that was the case'. For little can be found in official guidance on the subject. While contraband is mentioned in numerous Proclamations[21] no definition of it can be found there and instructions by flag officers to their captains yield no more. Clearly, the younger captains would have sought guidance from those of more experience, and from their agents; moreover, many would as midshipmen or lieutenants have acquired some working knowledge. But here, as in many other aspects of the prize system, it seems to have been a matter of picking up the expertise as one went along.

That there was no formal requirement for knowledge of this nature is borne out by evidence, albeit negative, surrounding the Examination for Lieutenant – the only formal examination taken by an officer throughout his career. Both in the Certificate and in such examiners' notes as survive,[22] the whole emphasis is on the handling and navigation of a ship. Neither administration nor discipline seem to have been subjects for examination, much less prize procedures.

There was indeed one area in which rather more guidance became available, and that was in the matter of visit and search. As was mentioned above, this was a indispensable tool of the whole system; without this belligerent right, nothing could be achieved.

The leading case here was *The Maria*.[23] In January 1798 a Swedish convoy, escorted by a single frigate, was intercepted in the Channel by a British squadron under Commodore Lawford in the *Romney*. The convoy's cargo included pitch, tar, hemp, deals and iron and this brought in the question of contraband which was thoroughly covered by Scott in his judgment. But the heart of the matter was the right of visit and search, which was disputed by the Swedish authorities. The whole question was sharpened by the fact that some resistance had been offered by the escorting Swedish frigate – a matter of honour, argued the Swedish captain, who resented particularly the fact that some boardings had taken place at night when he could not see what was going on.

Scott's judgment in *The Maria* is possibly the most influential of his whole career. It certainly sets out his philosophy in a clearer and more categorical way than any other:

> I consider myself as stationed here, not to deliver occasional and shifting opinions to serve present purposes of particular national interest, but to administer with indifference that justice which the law of nations holds out without distinction to independent states.

Scott went on to question whether a neutral nation could legally maintain a 'pretension' by force to extinguish the right of a belligerent to make maritime captures in war. Given the circumstances of the case – one Swedish frigate making a token resistance to a British squadron – this might be thought pitching it rather high; but in law it was a valid proposition, particularly as the instructions to the Swedish commander specifically authorized the use of violence, albeit to be 'opposed against violence'. Scott's judgment, that the right of visit and search was inherent in belligerency, was founded upon authorities from the Black Book of Admiralty onwards, including French, Swiss and Spanish writers and at least one Swede, Puffendorff.

Scott went on to make an even more far-reaching observation. The fact of resistance, he maintained, rendered ships offering such resistance and ships under their protection subject to seizure as lawful prize. He founded this too on Ordinances that were by no means confined to Britain.

Sweden's contention was that once neutral vessels were under properly constituted convoy, they were no longer subject to visit and search; a statement by the convoy commander, with the full backing of his sovereign, that no contraband goods were being carried, should be sufficient to reassure any belligerent cruiser who would then not interfere further. This was not an easy argument to sustain in view of the proved presence on board the *Maria* of goods which by British definition were contraband; but of course differences of definition were one of the points of contention anyway. The case ended in condemnation of the ships in the convoy; their value was reported to be of the order of £600,000.

Another incident of the same kind, but this time concerning Denmark and taking place in the Gut of Gibraltar, occurred around Christmas 1799.[24] The frigate *Emerald*, seeking to board a Danish merchantman in the offing, had her boat fired on by a Danish frigate whose name was transcribed, probably inaccurately, as *Hawfrewen*; a British sailor in the boarding boat was wounded. Lord Keith, the British Commander in Chief in the Mediterranean, was in Gibraltar at the time. When the Danish frigate was brought in by superior force without further resistance so that the matter could be investigated, Keith had several exchanges with her captain by letter. It is clear that he found these unsatisfactory and frustrating. The Danish captain, Docrum, assured Keith on his honour that he had 'only fulfilled his instructions' which, however, he refused to produce. Keith deplored Docrum's disinclination to give any sort of security, stated that 'according to the law of nations every power at war has a right to examine and search all vessels on the seas' and that 'any degree of resistance . . . subjects [the ships convoyed] to confiscation'. Whether or not Keith had read *The Maria* judgment (which had been made some months before) he had certainly got the essence right. But it appears that the Gibraltar incident ended with the Danish ship allowed to sail without conceding any part of its position: an unsatisfactory outcome from the British point of view.

A more serious incident came seven months later when a British force in the Channel intercepted a Danish convoy off Ostend. The Captain of the *Freya*, the Danish escorting frigate, refused to allow boarding for visit and search; a British boat was fired on; and a general action ensued, with casualties on both sides, ending with the capture of the *Freya* and her convoy.[25] Protracted diplomatic activity followed, the British government showing great sensitivity to Danish concerns while maintaining its claimed belligerent rights.

This did not, however, prevent the formation of the Armed Neutrality by Russia, Sweden and Denmark in December 1800, a move which led to the British expedition to the Baltic and the Battle of Copenhagen in April 1801. Nelson's victory and subsequent diplomacy there, coupled with the assassination of the Tsar, caused the Armed Neutrality to collapse. The law of visit and search survived: belligerent rights continued to be exercised throughout this and many subsequent wars.

Visit and search, then, must have been a fairly common topic of discussion in naval circles as the world entered the nineteenth century, and in hindsight it is perhaps unsurprising that in the *Naval Chronicle* for September 1800,[26] there appeared a fairly full report of *The Maria* case with the preamble 'We think it will gratify our readers with an extract . . . on a question of highest importance to the country'. A long quotation from the judgment concluded with three salient points: the right of visit and search exists; a neutral sovereign cannot vary this belligerent right; and resistance to visit and search leads to confiscation.

This entry in the *Chronicle* is notable for being its first acknowledgement that matters of high legal principle really affected sea officers. Certainly there had been some reports of Admiralty Court cases before that,[27] but they were spasmodic and though by no means uninteresting, did not by any means cover all that a commanding officer might need or wish to know.

THE EENROM REVISITED: BRINGING A 'NEUTRAL' TO COURT

At the end of the Prologue we left HMS *Brilliant* in possession of the merchant vessel *Eenrom*, 'on suspicion of being a Dutch Indiaman under Danish colours', somewhere in the eastern Atlantic on 28 December 1798. Captain Henry Blackwood did not, as was often customary, put a prize crew on board and instruct them to sail the ship back to a British port. It appears that Blackwood thought the ship and cargo too valuable, and the questions of ownership and destination too complex, for such treatment. He kept the prize well under his lee until they made Lisbon together on 14 January 1799.

At Lisbon there was no Vice Admiralty Court; such courts were allowed only on British or British-controlled territory. It is known that there were British agents there; Henry Digby's records for his time in the *Aurora* give the names of several.[28] But Blackwood did not follow the usual course of engaging an agent to take the laid-down Interrogatories. Instead he had taken, before Arbouin the British Vice Consul, affidavits by many members of the *Eenrom*'s crew, sworn on the evangelist and duly attested.[29] Assuming that Blackwood knew the proper procedure – and he had been a post captain for over three years – why did he seek to vary it?

The answer can only be conjectural, but it seems likely that Blackwood, having had plenty of time since the capture to unravel the tangled skein of the *Eenrom*'s voyage from the East Indies, judged that the Interrogatories were insufficient to prove enemy character and that the depositions he now arranged would be necessary.

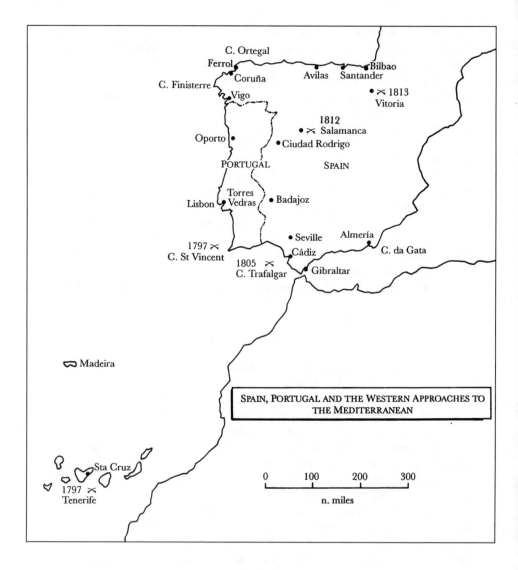

SPAIN, PORTUGAL AND THE WESTERN APPROACHES TO
THE MEDITERRANEAN

For, as these documents and the report of the subsequent case before
the Admiralty Court[30] show, the story was indeed a complex one. The
ship was owned by the firm Fabritius and Wever of Copenhagen. She
been away from Europe for over a year and had undertaken some cross-
trading voyages in East Asia. During that time her master, Poinsaing, and
the supercargo, Fabritius, a son of one of the owners, had been ill for
significant periods; at the time of the capture the ship was under the
command of Fronier the mate.

Her homeward voyage, with the stated destination of neutral
Copenhagen, had been full of incident. She had put in to Mauritius, at

that time a colony of France, under stress of weather and for repairs and had there disembarked some deteriorating cargo and embarked some items. She had then put in to Cape Town, which was under British occupation, and there the story acquired a more lurid tinge.

According to the affidavits, John Christian, a Goanese seaman on board the *Eenrom*, had deserted from the ship at the Cape. He was retrieved, possibly with the connivance of the British authorities there, but not before he had been interviewed by the British Commander in Chief. Once the ship was at sea, Christian was flogged with 200 lashes 'for trying to get the ship into trouble'. Christian's own evidence was corroborated by the deposition of Porter, an American-born seaman in the *Eenrom*, who said that Christian, 'one of the black mariners', had been flogged 'because he knew the cargo was Dutch property'. Porter also testified that Griffiths and Lawley, seamen, had told him the ship herself was Dutch property and had been 'put in prison because the supercargo was afraid they would give that information'.

In their own depositions Fabritius and Fronier resolutely maintained that the ship was Danish, the 'greatest part' of the cargo belonged to Fabritius and Wever, and the destination was Copenhagen. Somewhere in between came the evidence of Lund, who was a junior officer, perhaps third mate; he maintained the Danish character of the ship, making the point that the majority of the crew were Danish, but admitted that at the time the ship was fitting out in Copenhagen before departing for the voyage, Fabritius and Wever were in communication with different houses of commerce in Holland.

All this took place in Lisbon before the British Vice Consul. (Long afterwards, when the case came to Appeal, one of the Danish affidavits alleged that the boatswain of the *Brilliant* was present throughout the depositions, with his starting-stick.) The actual Interrogatories were not conducted until the *Eenrom* was brought back to Portsmouth in a British convoy, in February 1799. They were taken by James Primrose Maxwell, a well-established prize agent of the day, at the George Inn; witnesses included the Lord Mayor of Portsmouth.

The answers to the Interrogatories suggest that, however irregular it may have been, Blackwood's conduct in having depositions taken before the Vice Consul in Lisbon was prudent. Poinsaing (by then, apparently, recovered from his illness), Fronier and Grons, the second mate, all maintained the Danish character of ship, cargo and destination. It would have been difficult to shake their contention from the Interrogatories alone.

The case came before the Admiralty Court quite quickly and was concluded there on 21 May 1799. But a good deal had happened in the meantime, as Scott's masterly judgment shows. First, the regular application by the captors, through a monition by the King's Proctor, for condemnation had been followed by a claim for restoration by Fabritius junior. This claim was for the ship and, significantly as it turned out, half the cargo. Scott had then quite reasonably ordered that Fabritius should give an account of the ownership of the remainder of the cargo; the response had been far from clear: '[Fabritius] was sick and confined at Batavia, and obliged to entrust the actual shipment of the cargo to Mr. Inglehart, with whom he had not come to any final settlement before he had left that place'. And Inglehart was a Dutchman.

Scott in his judgment then disposed, as he was accustomed to do, of one or two extraneous points, concerning the alleged interest of a certain Marshal Blucker of the Danish court and the possible existence of bottomry bonds,[31] before returning to the main question of ownership. He detected numerous discrepancies between the evidence given in the Interrogatories, which claimed all the cargo belonged to Fabritius and Wever, and the claim now made by Fabritius junior. He expressed grave doubt about the instructions to the master and supercargo, which nowhere mentioned Inglehart:

> I am strongly induced to suspect that these were merely colourable instructions . . . [was it] the intention of the supercargo, in this part of the transaction, to mislead the British Courts of justice, and British cruizers, as to the property of the cargo? . . . this is no ordinary supercargo, he is the son of his employer, and appears to have been delegated with greater powers than supercargoes usually enjoy; his conduct must . . . be held to bind his principal with peculiar force.

But the clinching factor appears to have been the change in Fabritius's position – between an implied claim to own the whole cargo and the claim now made for only half – and the reason for it. For it emerged that Fabritius knew, and Scott knew that he knew, that in another recent case, *The Nancy*, the name of Inglehart had 'peeped out'[32] and indeed his concern in the cargo of the *Eenrom* had come to light. The plea that Fabritius' change of heart entitled him to favourable consideration was not accepted by Scott: '. . . if the Court is satisfied that the intention was to hold out to British cruizers a *noli me tangere* as to the whole . . . I cannot but think that it comes a little too late'.

So Fabritius' attempt at damage limitation failed. Scott condemned the ship and the whole of the cargo. His statement of principle is memorable:

> . . . it is a rule of this Court, which I shall ever hold, till I am better instructed by a superior Court, that if a neutral will weave a web of fraud of this sort, this Court will not take the trouble of picking out the threads for him, in order to distinguish between the sound and the unsound; if he is detected in fraud he will be involved in toto.[33]

What Scott did not do, at any point in the trial, was admit in evidence the statements so painstakingly taken in Lisbon. 'It has been pressed on the Court, by the captors, to receive the depositions there made by Mr. Fabritius and others; but the Court has declined to receive those depositions, as irregularly taken, and therefore cannot advert to them.'[34]

The case then went on appeal to the Lords Commissioners of Appeal in Prize Causes. From the documents[35] it is likely that the Lisbon depositions were admitted in evidence there. There were also several lengthy submissions from Marshal Blucker asserting his interest; they are a fine example of late eighteenth-century rank-pulling, for Blucker was an official of the Danish royal court and not above mentioning the regard of his sovereign in the matter. Sir John Nicholl, the King's Advocate, kept a notebook on appeal cases; it is interesting that the greater part of his brief note on this case[36] is devoted to the Blucker aspect. There was also an assertion from another source, not noted by Nicholl, that the Purser of the *Brilliant* had altered some of the Lisbon depositions. It was all to no avail. The Appeal Court affirmed Scott's judgment on 27 March 1802.

So the *Brilliant*'s prize was at last secure. We shall revisit it once more, in Part 3, to see what the spoils were. But at this stage it is worth reviewing some of the points that emerge concerning the relationship between His Majesty's Ships, neutrals and the law.

First one must pose about Blackwood the question asked more recently about certain American Presidents in the late twentieth century: how much did he know and when did he know it? A frigate captain with three years in post and five years as a lieutenant and commander before that,[37] most of them in a pretty intensive war, could be expected to have plenty of practical experience; but how much did he know of the law and how much did he need to know?

There was no manual of prize law. The Prize Act of 1793 might well be available to flag officers, but it was lengthy and there is no record of its general availability to captains. When the 1805 Prize Act[38] superseded it, copies were distributed to all ships[39] – perhaps an admission that knowledge was not all it should be. This may have been stimulated by the appearance in 1803 of a little book called *Horne's Compendium*[40] which in some 150 octavo pages sought to give a privateer or frigate captain all the rules he ought to know. We shall come across further examples of guidance to cruising captains and the admirals who commanded them, later on in this study. But nothing of this sort, it seems, would have been available to Blackwood in 1798.

There is no evidence that Blackwood knew anything about the *Eenrom* before the capture. It would have been well-nigh impossible for intelligence to have reached Britain from the Cape about suspicions concerning her, let alone for it to have penetrated to Newfoundland or for instructions to reach the *Brilliant* from there.

One is led to the conclusion that common knowledge and common sense, tempered by experience, were the principal means by which cruising captains could judge whether taking a neutral would lead to fortune or potential financial disaster. They were not lawyers; what could Blackwood know of the finer points of the Doctrine of Infection, which is one ingredient of *The Eenrom* case? Yet not only were they and their ship's companies affected by the outcomes of the law, they were also to a considerable degree enforcers of the law. To some extent their position was comparable with that of a policeman on the beat: they needed a grasp of the principles, a lot of experience and a good nose to smell a rat.

It is notable that in this case Blackwood's rat was not quite the same as the one smelt by Scott. Indeed, if it had not been for the appearance of Inglehart in another case, and the inconsistencies in their evidence, the claimants might have had the ship and cargo restored; and they were confident enough to go to appeal, though that might have had something to do with the *amour-propre* of Marshal Blucker. It had been a near run thing and Blackwood must have been mightily relieved that his hunch had come off.

NOTES

1.   PRO ADM 2/1079.

2.   See Chapter 8.

3.   1 C. Rob, p. 1 [1798].

4.   E.S. Roscoe, *A History of the English Prize Court* (Lloyd's, 1924), p. 55.

5.   Henry J. Bourguignon, *Sir William Scott, Lord Stowell* (Cambridge University Press, 1987), p. 142.

6.   Lynne Townley, 'Sir William Scott, Lord Stowell and the Development of the Prize Law in the High Court of Admiralty 1798–1828' (unpublished thesis, University of Birmingham, 1995), pp. 15–24 and App. 3.

7.   C.C. Lloyd (ed.), *The Naval Miscellany*, vol. IV (Navy Records Society, 1952), p. 487.

8.   Sir William Henry Dillon, Vice Admiral of the Red, *A Narrative of my Professional Adventures* (Navy Records Society, 1953), p. 421.

9.   Ibid., p. 424.

10.   1 C. Rob, p. 196 [1799].

11.   Townley, 'Sir William Scott, Lord Stowell and the Development of the Prize Law', p. 193.

12.   2 C. Rob, Appendix.

13.   1 C. Rob, p. 296 [1799].

14.   2 C. Rob, p. 186 [1799].

15.   Townley, 'Sir William Scott, Lord Stowell and the Development of the Prize Law', p. 275; C. John Colombos, *International Law of the Sea*, 6th edn

(Longman, 1967), p. 677.

16.   Bourguignon, *Sir William Scott, Lord Stowell*, p. 190.

17.   Lords [1750].

18.   1 C. Rob, p. 167 [1799].

19.   3 C. Rob, p. 167 [1800].

20.   3 C. Rob, p. 217 [1801].

21.   *Notifications, Orders and Instructions relating to Prize Subjects during the Present War* (Strahan, for Butterworth and White, 1810), pp. 5, 14, 19.

22.   J. Knox Laughton (ed.), *The Barham Papers*, vol. III (Navy Records Society, 1911), pp. 389–91; Brian Lavery, *Nelson's Navy* (Conway, 1989), p. 93; RNM 64/67, Certificate of John Binney, 8 June 1813.

23.   1 C. Rob, p. 340 [1799].

24.   ADM 1/400, 1/401.

25.   W.L. Clowes, *The Royal Navy: A History from the Earliest Times to 1900*, vol. 4 (Chatham, 1997), p. 427.

26.   IV NC, p. 206.

27.   II NC, pp. 213, 337; IV NC, p. 78.

28.   Papers in the possession of Lord Digby.

29.   HCA 42/217.

30.   2 C. Rob, p. 1 [1799].

31.   Ibid. at p. 5. For a definition of bottomry bonds, see Glossary.

32.   Ibid. at p. 2.

33.   Ibid. at p. 9.

34.   Ibid. at p. 14.

35.   HCA 42/217.

36.   HCA 30/466.

37.   David Syrett and R.L. DiNardo (eds), *The Commissioned Sea Officers of the Royal Navy 1660–1815* (Scolar Presds for the Navy Records Society, 1994), p. 36.

38.   45 Geo. III c.72.

39.   ADM 2/1081.

40.   Thomas Hartwell Horne, *A Compendium of the Statute Laws and Regulations of the Court of Admiralty relative to Ships of War, Privateers, Recaptures and Prize Money* (W. Clarke and Sons, 1803).

CHAPTER FOUR

Blockade

On 26 November 1799 Heseltine the King's Proctor wrote from Doctors' Commons to Sir Evan Nepean the Secretary of the Admiralty enquiring whether the whole of the coast of Holland was in a state of blockade as early as 10 March that year; or was the blockade confined to particular ports? 'Also whether notices of the blockade had then been communicated to the several cruizers on that station, by the Board of Admiralty, or whether the Commander in Chief had received instructions on that point to be by him communicated to the cruizers? Many causes . . . may be affected thereby.'[1] Nepean's note on the flyleaf, rapid and neat as ever, read: 'Prepare copies of the orders and send them in with this: and a letter to Mr Heseltine transmitting them.'

There is no hint of impatience in Nepean's note, nor was there need for it. Blockade was a complicated business and known to be; it was perfectly proper for the Court to seek clarification if there was the least doubt about the extent or rigour of a blockade. And in fact a very high proportion of the cases coming before the Court for judgment in the years 1798 and 1799 were of blockade, the decision resting on the answers to the three classical questions: had a blockade been notified by proper authority? Was it being effectively enforced? And had an attempt to break it actually been made? Naturally, all those who thought they had been unlawfully detained were, or claimed to be, neutrals; had they been under enemy flag or ownership, they would have been lawful prize anyway. But it must be remembered that when a blockade was properly in force, no vessel of whatever flag, whatever her cargo, could lawfully enter or leave a blockaded port or area.

It all sounds quite simple, and so it was – in principle. The cases as reported soon show that it was not so simple at all.

The first blockade case to come before Scott was *The Mercurius*.[2] In May 1798 a Hamburg ship with an American cargo was intercepted by a British cruiser and told Amsterdam was blockaded; her log read 'Hindered from the Texel'. But then she entered the Ijsselmeer with the apparent intention of reaching Amsterdam by that route and was promptly captured by the *Jalouse*. Scott condemned the *Mercurius* as lawful prize, but restored the cargo, holding that the owners could not have known of the blockade when it was loaded in Baltimore.

A curious sequel to this case is found in the Doctors' Commons files.[3] On 22 May 1799 Gostling the Procurator (effectively, the Admiralty's man at court) admitted that the *Mercurius* had been restored 'by mistake' and had had to be re-seized before the case could be tried properly. She had thereby become a Droit of Admiralty[4] coming under quite different rules for rewarding the captor. Nepean demanded to know who had authorized the restoration and Doctors' Commons owned up; so probably the crew of the *Jalouse* did not suffer.

The commander of a cruiser was less lucky in the case of *The Henrick and Maria*.[5] He had intercepted this ship bound to Amsterdam from Norway and had warned her not only not to proceed to Amsterdam but to keep clear of any Dutch port. But the blockade as declared did not extend to the whole of the Dutch coast: and Scott in his judgment said 'a declaration of a blockade is a high act of sovereignty, and a commander of a king's ship is not to extend it'. The *Henrick and Maria* was restored.

With blockading forces subject to stress of wind and weather, the effectiveness of blockade naturally came into question in various forms. How many ships were enough for proper enforcement; how were temporary absences from station to be treated? Scott here showed a degree of commonsense and nautical knowledge that mark him out as a man of much perception as well as experience.

In *The Neptunus*,[6] captured off the Vlie in September 1798, Scott distinguished between blockades *de facto* – in which notification was to be presumed by the very fact of cruisers lying off the blockaded port and stopping traffic both in and out – and blockades that were formally notified. In the former case, the lifting of the blockade was to be presumed as soon as the blockading force disappeared. In the latter, only public repeal of the blockade lifted it, unless the cruisers were driven off by force, in which case it ceased. The cruisers' temporarily being blown off station would not terminate a notified blockade.[7]

The notoriety of blockade was a thorny point, however, between Britain and the continental powers. France and Spain, particularly, demanded formal diplomatic notification before blockade could be recognized.[8] This did not much inhibit the British authorities, who probably regarded it merely as a reflection of the weaker strategic position at sea of the continental states. Thus Lord Keith, in the spring of 1800, had no compunction in declaring a blockade of Genoa while he was attempting to support the Austrian armies ashore in Liguria.[9] He was a Commander in Chief and his sovereign's representative.

Keith's journal for the few months of these operations is an interesting reflection of his preoccupations in this complex situation. His first priority was undoubtedly his lines of communication back to Gibraltar and England. There is much more about convoy arrangements than about blockade enforcement, cruising, prize-taking or even support of the Austrians – though that was clearly the ultimate objective and was fulfilled to the best of Keith's ability with the forces at his disposal.

The blockade of Genoa – which culminated in its brief occupation by Keith's squadron in June, before the 'mortifying Convention' following defeats ashore led to the Austrian evacuation of Piedmont – was enforced by up to five ships on carefully detailed cruising stations. Prizes were sent in to Leghorn, which was the British advanced base. But it is clear that however considerable Keith's prize money earnings might have been during his career as a whole,[10] they were not in the front of his mind at this time.

Meanwhile, problems concerning the blockades closer to home continued to arise. Mostly, they were on the margins: hard cases notoriously make bad, or at least difficult, law. It was not made any easier for the cruisers, or the Court, that the Admiralty's or Commander in Chiefs' instructions for blockade varied according to circumstances. These would include the special interests of certain neutrals and trades, the prevailing weather conditions and the ships available for enforcement. Sometimes the ships got it wrong.

For example, in *The Juffrouw Maria Schroeder*,[11] a Prussian ship sailing for Altona (now a district of Hamburg) from Rouen was taken when leaving Le Havre. The claimants pleaded that the blockade had been relaxed; the ship had been allowed to go in, apparently owing to the inattention or tacit permission of the cruisers, why was she not allowed to go out? The notification had said the blockade would be 'rigorous' but evidence was brought that it had not been consistently so and that Nepean himself had remonstrated with the commanders of the blockading forces about it. The cargo was condemned; Scott held that the shippers must have known of the fact of blockade and were taking a risk unjustifiable in law. On the ship, however, he took a more lenient view. She had come from Bordeaux where she might have had no knowledge of the blockade of Havre; the inattention of the cruisers off Le Havre when she entered the port entitled the master to favourable consideration. The ship was restored.

Scott was severe on the Royal Navy in this case:

It is in vain for governments to impose blockades if those employed on that service will not enforce them. The inconvenience is very great, and spreads far beyond the individual case; reports are eagerly circulated, that the blockade is raised; foreigners take advantage of the information; the property of innocent persons is ensnared, and the honour of our own country is involved in the mistake.[12]

It was in this case also that Scott came to grips with the distinction between blockades that had a mainly economic objective and those that were of a more directly strategic sort. The watch on Brest, for example, had been a feature of British strategy in all the wars since the days of

Anson, fifty years earlier. Its purpose was to bottle up the French fleet in its main Atlantic base, and so negate its freedom of action and ability to do mischief in a dozen ways, from the support of invasion of Ireland or even England, to establishing local dominance in remote areas, to effecting dangerous concentrations with other naval forces in the Mediterranean. Brest had no commercial, but great strategic, significance.

Scott recognized this: 'A blockade may be more or less rigorous, either for the single purpose of watching the military operations of the enemy, and preventing the egress of his fleet . . . or on a more extended scale, to cut off all access of neutral vessels to that interdicted place; which is strictly and properly a blockade, for the other is in truth no blockade at all, as far as neutrals are concerned'.[13] Scott's distinction is borne out by the actions of government, for no formal notification of a blockade of Brest appears to have been made before 1806 and then, as will be seen, the circumstances were quite different.

Another *Neptunus*[14] (there was an irritating lack of imagination in the naming of ships at about this time, though the law reporters sought to reduce confusion by naming the Master as well as the vessel in their reports) was restored in very much the same circumstances as the *Juffrouw Maria Schroeder*. The *Neptunus* had been 'examined and liberated by the captain of an English frigate' – not named – who told him Havre was not blockaded. The vessel and cargo were restored.

Naturally, many attempts at blockade-breaking were much less well founded than those of the *Juffrouw Maria Schroeder* or the *Neptunus* (No. 2). Moreover, some pretty frivolous claims came to court. The most usual was stress of weather or need for stores. Scott was scathing on occasion: the *Hurtige Hane*[15] claimed she had put in for the Texel, where she was detained, for water, yet she had passed close to Yarmouth only a few days previously; 'an idle pretence,' said Scott, since there was 'no absolute and unavoidable necessity'.

More original was the plea of the master of the *Shepherdess*.[16] He had been intercepted on course for Le Havre and claimed that he had had no clear idea where he was going, as he was drunk at the time. Indeed, he had spent most of the voyage in a state of intoxication. Few judges, then or now, could resist such an opportunity, and Scott was no exception: '. . . if such an excuse could be admitted there would be eternal carousings in every instance of violation of blockade. The master cannot, on any principle of law, be permitted to stultify himself . . . The owners of the vessel have appointed him their agent, and they must in law be bound by his imprudence.'

But in 1804, when this judgment was given, there was not too much time for frivolity, in court or elsewhere. The cessation of hostilities on 12 October 1801, followed by the conclusion of the Treaty of Amiens on

25 March 1802, had been regarded by both sides as little more than a truce.[17] It was no surprise to either side when, with Britain's failure to evacuate Malta building up as a *casus belli*,[18] war was resumed in May 1803. It was, even more than before, a war of national survival. Napoleon was now undisputed master of France, seeing Britain as the chief adversary to his plans to unite Europe under a dominant France. He was prepared to invade Britain itself in order to achieve her subjugation.

The war started well for Britain – who declared some time before Napoleon had expected – with a swoop on French and Dutch commerce, following the customary proclamation of General Reprisals against the French and Batavian republics.[19] This had the dual effect of causing economic damage to the enemy and depriving him of prime seamen, who would take time after capture to wend their way back to the continent – if they ever did, for they might enter British naval service one way or another rather than do so. Prizes, and detentions under embargo in British ports, were numerous; the *Naval Chronicle* reported with glee on 14 June: 'The Catwater [at Plymouth] is quite a wood of prizes and detained Batavians . . . 105 sail of all descriptions . . . the computed value cannot be less than a million and a half sterling'.[20]

It did not last long. By 4 September the *Lord Nelson* Letter of Marque 'did not see anything she could make a prize of, as neutrals since the war are too well covered with papers of all sorts for all nations, to be meddled with'.[21] This is borne out by the logs of naval ships on patrol off Ushant; the prize-taking tailed off as early as mid-June, to be replaced by a less triumphant catalogue of one or two boardings a day of neutrals, nearly all allowed to proceed on their way after examination of papers.[22]

In any case, matters of more immediate national security soon occupied the Navy. As early as the summer of 1803 the construction and fitting out of gunboats was detected along the north coast of France.[23] By early 1804 the so-called Boulogne Flotilla was a reality, with thousands of flat-bottomed barges, designed for the transport of troops, building and a complement of escorting gunboats. The Royal Navy was active in harrying these forces, so far as it could, but often they did their training and manoeuvring under the cover of shore batteries.

Many modern historians do not rate highly the chances of Napoleon's success with such an invasion force. Contemporary reports and accounts, however, show public alarm to have been very high. In March 1804 Pitt, the Prime Minister, advocated addition of many small gun vessels to the fleet: 'the invasion flotilla can only be successfully resisted by vessels of a similar description'. But Captain Sir Edward Pellew swayed the House of Commons with a speech in which he cited the 'triple bulwark' of battle fleet, powerful cruising and patrolling forces, and resistance inshore and on the British beaches. Pitt's initiative was defeated and Lord St Vincent remained in office as First Lord of the Admiralty for the time being.[24]

In view of all this activity and alarm, it is surprising that the instrument of blockade was not employed until 9 August 1804.[25] Le Havre and the Seine ports had indeed been under blockade since September 1803, but now this was extended to every port of any size from there right up to Ostend – in fact, all the invasion ports. This was much more a strategic than a commercial blockade and it probably had the effect of keeping genuinely neutral shipping well away from the French coast, though given the constantly belligerent nature of activity in that area one would expect they would need no further incentive to do so.

There were few opportunities, then, for commercial prize-taking along this coast during this anxious time. Control was, however, extremely tight and boardings frequent; the logs of HMS *Speedy* throughout the summer of 1805 record a scene of constant activity by cruisers in the Channel as well as forays with more warlike intent towards the French coast.[26]

As is well known, and outside the scope of this book, the wider naval campaign of 1805 – which itself followed strategic blockades of Brest and Toulon from 1803 onwards – culminating in Nelson's greatest victory at the Battle of Trafalgar, eliminated any further threat of invasion. In fact Napoleon had already accepted that the chances of success were too low to take the risk and had dispersed the army encamped round Boulogne some weeks before; the Army of England became the Grand Army on 29 August 1805, seven weeks before Trafalgar.[27] Nevertheless, that battle established for the rest of the war the dominance of Britain at sea and on that dominance ultimately rested the whole system of prize warfare.

The concept of blockade was due to change as the character of the struggle against what was now the French Empire changed. Before turning to this, however, it is worth considering one last outpost of the old, classical blockade.

In the summer of 1805 Captain Sir Home Popham was given the command of six, mainly sixty-four-gun, line of battle ships and with an army contingent set out with instructions to retake the Dutch colony at the Cape of Good Hope. This was achieved by the end of January 1806 and Popham's imaginative mind turned to what might be done next with the forces at his disposal. Lines of communication were so long that suggestions to and instructions from London would take well over half a year to become final.[28] Popham (who had elevated himself to the rank of commodore) therefore decided to take his own initiative, though there is evidence that he had discussed it with British politicians before he left Britain.[29] It was an ambitious scheme to insert British forces in the Spanish colonies of South America in the River Plate area, with the object of ousting the Spanish authorities and establishing a régime of the existing settlers under the aegis and protection of Britain.[30] Popham based his plan on the perceived weakness of Spanish forces in the area and willingness of the settlers to go along.

The force, consisting of most of the ships under Popham's command and about 1,500 troops, sailed from the Cape in April 1806 and established itself in the Plate Estuary in mid-June. Subsequent operations ashore began successfully, suffered reverses due mainly to the unwillingness of the settlers to come under British 'protection' and, after belated reinforcement and several changes of command both in the army and navy, ended in ignominious withdrawal in September 1807.

Popham at his subsequent court martial was adamant that personal gain had had no part in his objectives: 'I have had the mortification to hear it said, since my return, that sordid, instead of honourable, motives operated to induce me to undertake this expedition'.[31] He went on to cite instances where captured property, to the value of several million dollars, had been restored to its settler owners. However, some of his correspondence before and during the operation was not so high-minded. He wrote to Baird, the General at the Cape, on 6 July 1806: '. . . independent of all other duties I have taken the superintendance of the prize commission, and if we can get our property fairly out of here, I think you will be fifty thousand pounds richer than the last time you shook me by the hand . . .'.[32] It is a fair bet that if Baird was going to be richer by that amount, Popham stood to gain at least as much.

One of the legal instruments he used was blockade. This was notified to the authorities at Monte Video on 23 September 1806. No notification could be given to neutral governments, but the Governor of Monte Video had told the masters of neutral ships in port and asked them to sign a paper acknowledging the notification. Many of the American masters refused. Numerous captures were subsequently made, including that of the American schooner *Rolla* by the *Medusa* on 20 November.[33]

This case came to the Admiralty Court,[34] no doubt as a test case for the many other captures made about that time in the Plate. It was argued for the claimants that the blockade was unauthorized, vicious and ineffectively enforced. Scott, however, held that the blockade, however instituted, had subsequently been recognized by the British government: it had 'retained the footing'. Though Popham had acted without authority, a commander had 'a portion of sovereign authority', and this must extend, on a distant station, to 'the commerce of the enemy'. The blockade had been effective to the extent that only a few ships had been allowed to pass, and that with good reason. Thus all the criteria had been fulfilled and the *Rolla* was condemned.

Scott in his judgment specifically excluded any criticism of Popham which had appeared at his court martial, which took place a good deal earlier. That, he said, was a matter for the naval authorities. They had severely reprimanded Popham for leaving his assigned station at the Cape without permission, but this was not within the province of the Admiralty

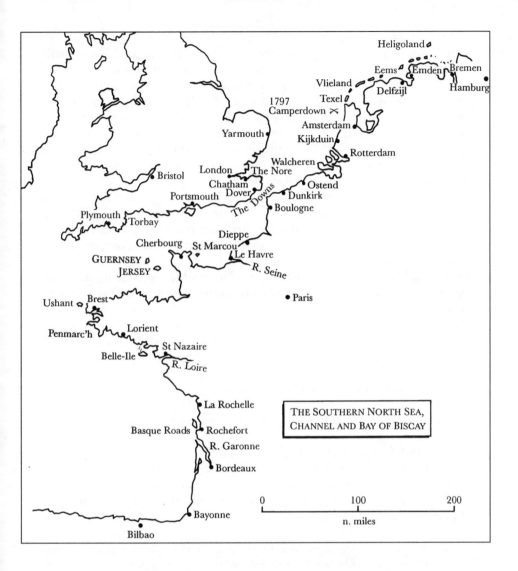

THE SOUTHERN NORTH SEA, CHANNEL AND BAY OF BISCAY

Court. Presumably Popham's authority to command His Majesty's forces had not been prejudiced by his actions, so any suggestion that the blockade was *ultra vires* on that account could not be sustained.

The Rolla might well be called the last classical blockade case; though appeals from the Plate affair rumbled on,[35] Scott's judgment was not overturned. But Blockade was never thereafter that simple as a term of art in the law of war. The reason lies in the increasingly total nature of the economic side of the war.

As Napoleon's Empire reached its height, his irritation with Britain's control over its sea communications grew. Towards the middle of 1806, after his victories at Ulm and Austerlitz, with the German states compliant and peace negotiations even with Britain and Russia still holding some promise, he must have been mightily annoyed by a British proclamation of 16 May 1806[36] imposing a blockade from the Elbe to Brest – a coastline of well over a thousand miles – 'taking into account the new and extraordinary means resorted to by the enemy for the purpose of distressing the commerce of His Majesty's subjects'. The proclamation added that neutrals not carrying enemy goods or contraband of war might trade, except to ports between Ostend and the Seine which were still strictly blockaded.

It is clear from its preamble that the British government regarded this measure as a retorsion against the increasingly severe administrative restrictions imposed by Napoleon – either directly or through influence – on British trade with continental states including those that could still assert some claim to independence. In modern language, it was a relatively modest escalation of the economic struggle. But it evoked a furious response from French ministers. One of these reads:

> *La déclaration de 1806 anéantit d'un seul mot les droits de tous les états maritimes, en mettant en interdit de vastes côtes et des empires entiers;-*
>
> *Par cette déclaration toute navigation fut interdit aux neutres;*
>
> *De ce moment l'Angleterre ne reconnut plus de neutres sur les mers.*

(The declaration of 1806 sought to nullify at a stroke the rights of all maritime states, by putting into interdiction vast stretches of coastline and entire empires; by this declaration all navigation was denied to neutrals; from this moment Britain no longer recognised neutrality at sea.)[37]

This was a shrill reaction and was not justified by the language of the proclamation itself. Clearly neutrals were still recognized, and swift subsequent relaxations, for the Baltic trade for instance, bore this out.[38] But it was, indeed, a new departure, the first time such a two-tier blockade had been openly proclaimed. It clearly had touched a raw nerve; it must have dealt a blow to whatever hopes Napoleon had left for a patched-up peace with Britain; and it gave the French administration the chance to accuse Britain of an unforgivable international misdemeanour which could only lead to further escalation of the conflict. Napoleon being the man he was, this would follow, and did, in the Berlin Decree of December 1806. But that is for another chapter.

NOTES

1. ADM 2/1079.
2. 1 C. Rob, p. 80 [1798].
3. ADM 1/3894.
4. See Chapter 8.
5. 1 C. Rob., p. 146 [1799].
6. 1 C. Rob., p. 170 [1799].
7. *The Columbia*, 1 C. Rob., p. 154 [1799].
8. C. John Colombos, *International Law of the Sea*, 6th edn (Longman, 1967), p. 725.
9. ADM 50/36.
10. C.C. Lloyd (ed.), *The Keith Papers*, vol. II (Navy Records Society, 1950), p. 394, for Keith's Indian Ocean takings in the 1790s.
11. 3 C. Rob., p. 147 [1800].
12. 3 C. Rob., p. 147 [1800] at 157–8, quoted in Lynne Townley, 'Sir William Scott, Lord Stowell and the Development of the Prize Law in the High Court of Admiralty 1798–1828' (unpublished thesis, University of Birmingham, 1995), p. 342.
13. Townley, 'Sir William Scott, Lord Stowell and the Development of the Prize Law', p. 341.
14. 2 C. Rob., p. 110 [1799].
15. 2 C. Rob., p. 124 [1799].
16. 5 C. Rob., p. 262 [1804].
17. William James, *The Naval History of Great Britain*, vol. III (Bentley, 1847), p. 162; David French, *The British Way in Warfare* (Unwin Hyman, 1990), p. 106.
18. John B. Hattendorf, in J.R. Hill (ed.), *The Oxford Illustrated History of the Royal Navy* (Oxford University Press, 1995), p. 114.
19. IX NC, pp. 403–7.
20. X NC, p. 82.
21. X NC, p. 258.
22. ADM 51/1461, 51/1665.
23. James, *The Naval History of Great Britain*, vol. III, p. 178.
24. XI NC, pp. 316–31.
25. 5 C. Rob., p. xi.
26. D.B. Ellison, *Pressganged: The Letters of George Price of Southwark* (Ellison's Editions, 1994), pp. 28–48.
27. J. Holland Rose, *The Life of Napoleon I*, vol. II (Bell, 1920), p. 18.
28. John D. Grainger (ed.), *The Royal Navy in the River Plate, 1806–1807* (Scolar Press for the Navy Records Society, 1996), p. ix.
29. Ibid., pp. 4 and 19.
30. See Hugh Popham, *A Damned Cunning Fellow* (Old Folly Press, 1991), pp. 144–65, for another account of the campaign.
31. XVII NC, p. 239.

32. Grainger, *The Royal Navy in the River Plate, 1806–1807*, p. 36.

33. ADM 51/1595.

34. 6 C. Rob., p. 364 [1803].

35. HCA 30/466, Appeal Court Notes, *The Prince* (3 February 1810).

36. *Notifications, Orders and Instructions relating to Prize Subjects during the Present War* (Strahan, for Butterworth and White, 1810), p. 19; *London Gazette*, 1806, p. 618.

37. Biederman, *Manuel Diplomatique sur le dernier état de la Controverse concernant les droits des neutres sur la mer* (Brockhaus, Leipsic, 1814), p. 77. The authorship of this exposition of, and argument against, the French position is uncertain; the name 'Biederman' appears only on the spine of the book. However, the texts quoted are authentic.

38. *Notifications, Orders and Instructions*, p. 20, instruction of 21 May 1806.

CHAPTER FIVE

Orders in Council

The British Proclamation of 16 May 1806,[1] declaring what amounted to a two-tier blockade, strictly enforced between Ostend and the Seine and less rigorously outside those limits between the Elbe and Brest, helped to convince Napoleon that Britain would pursue a war *à outrance*, with maritime trade as one of its chief and chosen areas of conflict.

He took his time, however, to make a riposte. He had still some glimmer of hope in the summer of 1806 for a negotiated peace that would be to his advantage,[2] and there were many other things on his mind. It was not until 21 November 1806 that he issued the Berlin Decree, which instituted in the law of the Empire what has come to be known as the Continental System.

The objective was essentially a mercantilist one: to ruin Britain by denying to her all trade with the continent of Europe, without which her economy could not survive. Since Napoleon now controlled the greater part of Europe and nearly all its harbours either directly or through the influence of arms from landward, this was in theory a reasonable aim. It did not take into account the power of the market, exercised through a multitude of individual traders; nor the subtlety of commercial management by the British government, exercised with the essential tool of sea control. But that was to take years to work through, and is the central story of this chapter.

The Berlin Decree[3] was relatively brief, as these things go. There was a recital of reasons for the decree: the first four were Britain's failure to honour international law, making prisoner the crews of merchant ships, taking neutrals as prizes, and blockading purely commercial ports without reason. From the fourth of these followed the charge that Britain sought through war to promote her own trade to the detriment of continental economies; it followed that anyone carrying on trade with Britain was her accomplice; and Britain's barbarous conduct must be met with condign measures justified by natural law.

The operative articles then followed: (1) the British Isles were put under blockade; (2) all commerce and correspondence with Britain were forbidden; (3) all British subjects in states under the control of the Empire or its allies would be made prisoners of war; (4) all property belonging to British subjects was declared to be good prize; (5) all British, and British colonial, produce was declared to be good prize;

(6) half the proceeds of such prize was to go to compensate those who had suffered losses through the activities of British cruisers; (7) any vessel which visited a British port was henceforth barred from ports under Empire control; (8) any such vessel using false papers would be subject to condemnation as if it was British. Three final articles set out the judicial and administrative arrangements, with a further knock at British barbarism.

The British response was relatively swift. An Order in Council dated 7 January 1807[4] indicated in its preamble that it was a direct retorsion against the Berlin Decree. Its main operative paragraph read:

> No vessel shall be permitted to trade from one port to another, both which ports shall belong to or be in the possession of France or her allies, or shall be so far under their controul as that British vessels shall not trade thereat; and the commanders of HM Ships of war and privateers shall be, and are hereby instructed to warn every neutral vessel coming from such port, to discontinue her voyage, and not to proceed to any such port; and any vessel after being forewarned, or any vessel coming from such port, after a reasonable time shall have been afforded for receiving information of His Majesty's Order, which shall be found proceeding to another such port, shall be captured and brought in and, together with her cargo, shall be condemned as lawful prize.

This was backed up three days later by a general order to Commanders in Chief briefly saying that the trade of neutrals between one French-controlled port and another was prohibited and that 'orders in form will be sent to you as soon as they can be got ready'.[5] The usually efficient Admiralty machine had been overloaded.

It is likely that it remained in that state for several months. A succession of orders and counter-orders issued from the Council, concerned mostly with the North German ports and the loosening or tightening of regulations for trade from and to them.[6] This no doubt had some connection with the issue of another decree from Napoleon, this time from Warsaw on 27 January 1807, which ordered the seizure of all English goods and colonial produce in the Hanse towns.[7]

These complications continued throughout the year, as alliances were formed and collapsed, as neutrality was judged to be genuine or opportunist, and as the British government juggled with the various interests – commercial pressures, the need for strategic materials, nursing potential friends, deterring potential enemies. Orders in Council continued thick and fast. Denmark, as before in 1800-1, was a particularly thorny problem, exacerbated by the fact that Sweden was this time allied to Britain. As difficulties with Denmark came to a head in the summer of 1807, orders were given for Danish ships to be brought in, but their crews were to be treated 'with all possible civility and attention and not by any means as prisoners of war'.[8] Gambier's expedition to Copenhagen in September of that year, burning quite a large part of the city and seizing the whole Danish fleet to be held 'on temporary deposit', was an extreme example of these attempts to use an iron hand in a velvet glove.[9] It was followed by partial relaxations for the Danish trade including provision for the issue of licences; but general reprisals against Denmark were imposed on 11 November 1807.[10]

How the cruisers, charged with enforcing the shifting regulations in these turbulent years, managed to cope is a matter largely for conjecture. Little appears from the ships' logs; they recorded facts, not opinions or preoccupations. Some indication may perhaps be read from an exchange between Sir John Nicholl, the King's Advocate, and the Admiralty at about this time. On 18 March 1806 he complained that 'it frequently happens that the master or captain of a prize is not sent into port with his vessel in order to undergo his examination for the purpose of proceeding to adjudication', pointing out the inconvenience caused. He suggested it would be 'advisable to send circular Directions to the Commanders of His Majesty's cruizers, enjoining them in all cases if possible to send in the Master . . .'.[11]

The suggestion was taken up, but over a year later: on 7 April 1807, a circular reminded cruising captains that they must send in the 'captain or master' of a prize to answer the Interrogatories.[12] The system was showing strain. No doubt this was only a minor factor in the considerations that induced the government to take further measures; they had weightier matters to think about than the difficulties of frigates or gun-brigs in bringing in prizes. But change was on the way.

It came in the form of a further Order in Council, dated 11 November 1807.[13] The preamble admitted that the previous Order had not 'answered the desired purpose'. The Order itself began by stating that all ports controlled by France or her allies were to be 'subject to the same restriction *as if* [my italics] the same were actually blockaded by His Majesty's naval forces in the most strict and rigorous manner'.

There followed ten amplifying and modifying instructions. The first of these was clear enough: 'All trade in articles which are the produce or manufacture of the said countries or colonies [France and her allies] shall be deemed and considered to be unlawful . . . every vessel trading to and from . . . shall be captured and condemned as prize . . .'.

But sophistication followed. Several sections of the Order exempted ships and cargoes of all states not specified as French or allied to France, but only on certain conditions of port of departure and destination: briefly, that neither should be in the area under actual or notional blockade. There then followed two articles that set the pattern for the way the system was to operate in practice: commanders of warships, privateers and commissioned ships were to warn all vessels that had begun their voyages before the Order was issued to proceed to a British-controlled port; and any vessel that failed to comply with that instruction was to be considered lawful prize.

The requirement to go to a British-controlled port founded the Licence system which was the administrative underpinning of the November 1807 Order in Council. Licences had been used in previous wars, and in this one had already been used to control trade in certain commodities,[14] or of certain countries.[15] Now the practice, operated by the British Customs and Excise service, was to become general.

Tables appended to the Order showed the 'exceptions of trade not prohibited'. These were detailed but are by no means clear to the modern reader unversed in the complexities of the commercial and manufacturing patterns of the time.[16] They appear – and all subsequent evidence bears this out – to be designed to give Britain the ability to import desirable goods from the continent and to export those British products continental traders might wish to import, whether their ruler decreed it or not.

This opaque language would not make the system any easier in operation for British ships at sea. A positive deluge of further orders and instructions descended on them in the second half of November 1807. The first, on 18 November, pointed out that nothing in the 11 November Order prevented any vessel, not under other restriction, bringing in to Britain cargo which was not of enemy origin. There was particular sensitivity in this Instruction to American interests.[17] On 26 November an Additional Instruction to Cruizers[18] clarified a further point but then promptly modified it: neutrals clearing out from British ports and sailing direct to British ports were not to be molested, to whomsoever the goods *appeared* to belong; but if suspicion arose as to their destination, they were to be sent in.

There then followed Orders A, B and C, which must have struck terror into the heart of many a frigate and gun-brig captain. They occupy some five pages of close type in one semi-official publication,[19] and can scarcely have been less in the printed form in which instructions were now being issued to the fleet. But on analysis, they were not unhelpful, and much clearer than the Tables which accompanied the 11 November Order.

Order A was relatively simple; it gave the dates on which the 11 November Order was to take effect. These were graduated according to average sailing times which were of course well known; the latest was for China, on 1 June 1808. A further twenty days' grace was allowed if loading had begun before the cut-off date.

Order B in essence laid down the Licence system. East India Company goods, British and prize goods might be sent to French West India colonies and re-export of foreign goods was permissible by licence; export, with some restrictions, was permitted to 'ports not actually blockaded' (the two-tier system again); re-export was similarly permitted but only by licence, for which landing at a British port was necessary. There was the rub: as it subsequently turned out, a tax was chargeable.

Order C was concerned mainly with the position of Gibraltar and Malta as entrepôts for the Mediterranean trade. It was clearly to Britain's advantage that the maximum latitude should be allowed here and powers of licensing were liberally delegated to the governors of those places. Moreover, these licences were to apply only to manufactured articles; raw materials might go without licence to and from 'places not in actual blockade'. Cruisers were specifically enjoined to respect licences and allow their holders to pass and repass.

The Admiralty was clearly worried that too great a burden of decision had been placed upon cruising captains and the flag officers commanding them. Reports coming back from sea no doubt reflected the difficulties of working the system. On 3 February 1808 a printed circular was issued signed by John Barrow, the Second Secretary of the Navy; it was meant to be helpful.[20]

It explained that the 11 November Order in Council established 'a principle of capture to a great degree new . . . In visiting and searching neutral vessels . . . the Property, at least in the cargo, is in many cases immaterial, the *Destination* [Barrow's italics] having now become the principal ground of Prize'. All ports of the enemy and all ports from which British ships and commerce were excluded were now 'under the restrictions of blockade'.

'If the matter rested here, your duty would be plain and simple; but it has been thought necessary to admit to these restrictions some *Exceptions*.' Six were then detailed. Four applied to neutrals. It was permissible for a neutral to go to an enemy colony and then back to his own country; similarly from a British West Indies free port and back; from Britain, Malta or Gibraltar to a port 'not actually blockaded' (the ports 'actually blockaded' were detailed in a Note, and covered very large tracts of the Dutch, French, Spanish, Italian and Turkish coasts); and from British or allied ports to restricted ports, but not back again. Then came two 'exceptions' of more general application. Goods laden in Britain and cleared out were protected; and the produce and manufacture of hostile countries were not affected when in a British ship.

Licences 'should protect the vessel from interruption, unless, on examining the licence, the vessel appears to be acting in manifest violation of it'. Finally, the letter sought to sum up: 'The great cause of capture is the trading at ports where British ships are not admitted; and the great exemption from capture is the going from or coming to a British or Ally's port.' Cruisers were instructed to act with 'great vigilance' and 'great caution', particularly in the case of ships coming from a restricted port; if they were truly destined for Britain, 'the clearances and papers must necessarily all be false and colorable, in order to elude seizure in the ports of the enemy'. The Master should be consulted and boarding officers' reports recorded and closely scrutinized. If the ship was sent in, it would be best to send her in to the 'port of alleged destination', and 'It will be much for your advantage . . . to send to your agent by the Prize Master a short statement of your reasons for detention'.

Whether Barrow's letter was of great help to cruising captains is somewhat doubtful. Its statement of principle – and very frank admission of government's condonation of 'false and colorable' papers – may have saved some from misinterpretation of the essence of the Order, but it may have gone too far away from the simple test of 'licence or no licence'. Of course, the licence system took some time to become fully established and while it was doing so perhaps the details of Barrow's circular were helpful. Later in 1808 and 1809 several further circulars[21] enjoined extreme caution in detaining ships trading under licence.

Given this radical change in the business of blockade, it is little wonder that the Admiralty Court was in 1808 and 1809 awash with licence cases.[22] Scott soon laid down a principle that in general he followed throughout: in *The Goede Hoop*[23] he said: 'Where the holder of a licence has acted *bona fide* the Court will construe such licence liberally, and where a voyage has not been completed within the time specified in a licence, the Court will not condemn the vessel if the non-completion has been caused by circumstances over which the Master has no control'.

In the same case, Scott set out the policy reasons for the licence system.

It is notorious, that the enemy has in this war directed his attacks more immediately against the commerce of this country than in former wars; and a circumstance of still greater weight is, that he has possessed himself of all those places that in former wars remained in a state of neutrality . . . to say you are to have no trade with the enemy is to say you shall not trade at all . . . The question then comes to this, how is the foreign commerce of this country to be maintained? It must be either by the relaxing of the ancient principle entirely, and permitting an unlimited intercourse with the ports of the enemy . . . or it must be by giving a greater extension to the grants of licences.

That was the policy justification, but what about the law? The Orders in Council had already come under fire from no less a person than Lord Erskine, a pre-eminent Law Lord of the day and one who, though not a member of Doctors' Commons, had made a name in maritime cases on the King's Bench and given Opinions on prize matters.[24] Erskine made a very severe speech in the House of Lords on 8 March 1808[25] in which he 'arraigned' the Orders in Council as a violation of the law of nations and the law of the land. His argument is too lengthy to be examined in detail here, but its essence was that Britain, more especially in her role as the guardian of the world against tyranny, must 'declare the right of neutral nations to the commerce secured to them by the general law of the civilised world' and must not pass legislation or regulations that undermined that principle.

Erskine's proposed resolutions did not pass, but his speech must have had considerable influence. It is therefore surprising that the legal justification for the Orders does not appear to have been challenged in the Prize Court until over a year later. Then, in *The Fox*,[26] it was submitted that the Orders were contrary to the law of nations. Scott was frank in his judgment: the Orders in Council were 'doubtless a great and signal departure from the ordinary administration of justice in the ordinary state of the exercise of public hostility, but was justified by that extraordinary deviation from the common exercise of hostility in the conduct of the enemy'. In fact, a departure from law was justified on exceptional policy grounds and the law passed by the British government was to be presumed valid in consequence.

Meanwhile the Empire had not been idle. It struck back against the 1807 Order in Council with the Milan Decree of 17 December 1807.[27] This pointed out that by its latest Order Britain required neutrals not only to submit to visit but to go to British ports and be taxed before proceeding; alleged that this amounted to denationalizing of ships that submitted; and revived a long-held French contention that '*le pavillon couvre la marchandise*' – 'free ships free goods'. In consequence it declared that ships submitting to British visit, or going to British ports, or paying British dues, had lost their nationality and become British property and therefore liable to seizure as good prize. Moreover, the British Isles were declared in a state of blockade and all ships proceeding to and from them, and to and from places under British control, were similarly liable to seizure.

When analysed, the Milan Decree does not go very much further than the Berlin Decree; in fact, there was not much further to go. The 'denationalizing' clause was meant to be a final deterrent to those tempted to trade with Britain or acquiesce in her measures; but the merchants knew where the power lay at sea; the French Navy was hardly in evidence and though French privateers were active in the Channel, and some Dutch and Danes in the North Sea, and these caused concern,[28] the trade was lucrative enough to justify both the risk and the administrative tedium of acquiring licences.

There was one further significant change to the Orders in Council, which occurred in April 1809. By then, cracks had begun to widen in the Continental System and the Treaty of Tilsit was seen as an increasingly shaky basis for Napoleon's domination of northern Europe. A Baltic expedition under Saumarez was afoot.[29] Moreover, the acquisition of Heligoland in 1807 was proving valuable in providing a forward base from which licensed vessels could be despatched, and the invasion of Walcheren gave the prospect of a further channel for British goods to reach Europe. Finally, Spain was in general insurrection against France and the Aegean was coming increasingly under British sway.

The Order of 26 April 1809[30] formally revoked and annulled the 11 November 1807 Order, 'except as hereinafter expressed'. It went on to specify the exceptions, which were to apply 'as if' the areas named were actually blockaded: the coast of Holland from the Eems southward (in effect, the whole), all of France, and northern Italy 'from the Ports of Orbitello and Pesaro inclusive'. 'Every vessel trading from and to the said countries or [their] Colonies, Plantations or Settlements, together with all goods or merchandise on board, shall be condemned as prize to the captors.'

While this Order marked a significant shift in the balance of mercantile pressures on the Empire, it did not change too much the nature of operations at sea. Ships of the Royal Navy continued to be employed in large numbers on the coasts of the continent. Some idea of the pattern is to be found in the Order Book of Vice Admiral Sir Edward Pellew when Commander in Chief in the Downs in 1810.[31] From 3 July to 9 November there are sixty-three recorded orders covering forty-two different ships, ranging from ships of the line to despatch vessels.

The instructions cover movements for normal rotation of patrolling ships, replacements for ships damaged either by accident or weather, repair arrangements, replenishment at advanced base ports such as Yarmouth, Sheerness or the Downs, convoys to and from the operational rendezvous off Heligoland, and a constant watch on the Texel where the Dutch battlefleet, with some French reinforcement, lay. In one case specific intelligence is included of a shipment destined for the enemy, which is to be intercepted if possible; all other instructions to cruisers are to the time-honoured formula 'for the protection of the trade and the annoyance of the enemy', or, sometimes, 'enemy privateers'.

The logs of some of the ships involved show what these commands meant in practice. *Britomart*[32] in July and August 1810 recorded 'chace' or boarding on at least ten occasions. The great majority turned out to be ships with valid licences, but one capture was made by the *Britomart*'s boats, the *Intrepid* privateer lugger on 25 July. No one profited much by that, the net amount for distribution being £173 12s 0d paid in April 1812.[33]

The *Désirée* had similar experiences. She took up a patrol station off Kijkduin on the Dutch coast on 18 July. She was particularly busy from 22 to 26 July: seven boardings were recorded and one capture made, a Dutch galliot to be 'sent in for examination'. After this capture, four of the *Désirée*'s seamen were punished with three dozen lashes each 'for plundering the detained galliot'. Three dozen was a severe punishment at that stage of the war,[34] and Captain Farquhar of the *Désirée* was not notably a flogging captain; it is some indication of the way in which the integrity of prizes and their cargoes was safeguarded. The ship's company would have had little sympathy with the pilferers; the more that was plundered, the less there was for them to share.

Désirée's cruise went on through August, much of it in weather that rendered the log, two centuries later, almost illegible. Chase and boarding, inspection of licences, reconnoitring the Texel to ensure there was no naval movement, split topsails: the slogging rhythm and routine are apparent. On 9 September however there was a notable success: a Dutch dogger, *De Jonge Hendrick*, laden with salt for Rotterdam, was captured. It was some reward for their labours – though, as it turned out eight months later, not much; an able seaman's share was 12s 5d.[35] And pride, such as it was, came before a fall; on 11 September the *Désirée* grounded off the Texel and took most of the day, jettisoning some stores and helped by the *Bold*, to get off. She remained on station, pumping ship frequently, and took an opportunity on 14 September to send in the majority of the dogger's crew to Harlingen on board a licensed schuyt from London.

These logs, Pellew's orders, and many other records,[36] give some indication of the scale and nature of the operations connected with the Orders in Council. So far as the flag officers and ships were concerned, they had been given a job to do and were doing it to the best of their ability, with a good notion of what constituted a valid licence and a lawful passage and what did not. The finer points of controversy over the law concerned them only in so far as they might not see the proceeds of a doubtful prize. It was hard and often unrewarding work, but it was there to be done.

But the documents also point to the curiosity of a system that openly, though selectively, condoned trading with the enemy. Scott's rationale has already been noted; Professor Lloyd has gone further and written that the Orders in Council were 'soon revoked in practice'; ostensibly they banned all direct trade but 'the reality was far different'.[37] It amounted to 'the deliberate encouragement of smuggling'; and observing the number of licences issued, about 20,000 annually up to and including 1811, it is hard to gainsay this.

The French reaction was in practice nonplussed, but in public supremely confident. A Report by the Ministry of Foreign Affairs and communicated to the French Senate on 10 March 1812[38] sought first to justify the French position at law, basing it on the provisions of the 1713 Treaty of Utrecht and asserting in particular 'free ships free goods', a narrow definition of contraband and a severe criterion for blockade. It then described the course of the legal escalation from May 1806, naturally presenting the French measures as response. Finally, it sought to assess the effects of the Berlin and Milan decrees.

At this point the Report shows all too clearly the defects and dangers of totalitarian rule. Its fawning language is one thing, its desire to tell the Emperor what he wanted to hear is another. The wholesale issue of licences by Britain is presented as an admission of defeat, an abrogation of her Navigation Acts on which her mercantile power was founded; her factories are said to be deserted, poverty and unemployment everywhere. The Report urges that the Decrees remain in full vigour, backed by force, until Britain should return to the principles of the law of nations as expressed in the Treaty of Utrecht.

This was far from the true picture. There was dearth in Britain in 1812 but it was due to a variety of causes and the French measures were not principal among them.[39] There was dearth in the Empire too, not so much in France as in the satrapies,[40] and not mentioned in the Report. On the peripheries of the Empire French control simply could not give effect to the Decrees and states nominally neutral were even less amenable to the Continental System. Napoleon's attack on Russia – the final decision for which may have been influenced by papers such as the one discussed above – had roots that stretched back at least to 1810, and one of the strongest of those roots was Russia's ambiguous attitude to trade in the Baltic.[41]

In one other area the Orders in Council worked much more to French advantage. The United States of America had remained neutral throughout the wars up to 1812; their preferences had swayed first one way, then another, as one side or the other sought to impose on their trade restrictions that they regarded as too onerous. The institution of licences, with the attendant charges levied by British authorities issuing them, moved the Americans towards the French position though they saw serious difficulties with the Continental System too.[42] A half-hearted British Proclamation of 24 May 1809,[43] giving only partial backing to some careful negotiations by the British Minister in Washington and easing only temporarily the restrictions on American ships, did little to arrest the slide.

It was probably one other factor that swung the balance decisively. Britain had persisted throughout the war in asserting the right to press seamen from American ships; the *Désirée*'s log, previously cited, shows one such impressment at sea on 22 July 1810[44] and this is a single example of a widespread practice. Matters came a head on 16 May 1811 in a set-to between HMS *Little Belt,* sixteen guns, and USS *President* of fifty-two guns, which started with an attempted impressment by HMS *Guerrier.*[45] Though there were expressions of regret immediately after the action, public opinion was inflamed and the matter dragged on, each side accusing the other of firing first.

Thus, when President Madison made his statement to Congress on 1 June 1812 which led to the 'unnecessary war' with Britain, the first of his complaints was against unjust impressment. It was a slight on American honour and a sensitive issue. His second complaint was against the Orders in Council and their operation: British cruisers 'hover[ed] over and harass[ed] our entering and departing commerce'; Britain sought to create a monopoly for her own commerce and navigation; British Prize Courts were 'no longer organs of public law, but the instruments of arbitrary edicts'.[46]

In fact the British government did on 19 June 1812 repeal the Orders in Council, mainly to appease the United States but ostensibly because it had received sufficient assurance of the revocation of the Berlin and Milan Decrees – a matter which had been shrouded for months in conditional clauses and consequent allegations of bad faith on both sides. But the British action was too late to affect the issue between Britain and America: war was declared on 18 June.

A general embargo on American shipping was declared on 31 July.[47] Britain at once began to exercise effective control over American East Coast ports;[48] much havoc was wreaked on American privateers as well as merchant traffic.[49] The 'pickings', as they were openly called by at least one agent, may have amounted over the two and a half years of war to half a million pounds;[50] the damage to the American economy was significant.

By one of those curious anomalies that abound in the business of economic warfare, an exception was made of American ships taking grain to Portugal to supply Wellington's army for the Peninsular War. It was important for Britain that this trade should continue; Britain was suffering food shortages in 1810–12.[51] The American ships operated under licence as they would have done under the Orders in Council system.

Much of the history of the American War emphasizes the nasty shock to British naval confidence in its own prowess, indeed invincibility – quite rightly, for the trauma is prominent in contemporary writing, notably the *Naval Chronicle.* The defeat of several British frigates in single-ship actions with American ships of marginally superior force was a blow to pride countered only by the *Shannon*'s successful action against the *Chesapeake* on 1 June 1813. Philip Broke, captain of the *Shannon,* was an exceptionally dedicated officer who, like Nelson before him, sometimes relinquished the chance of a prize to better his odds for meeting or fighting the enemy. He 'would not spare hands to navigate his prizes into port; and he therefore burnt them, to his own severe loss'.[52] It is said that his ship's company agreed this was a proper course of action.

In fact it was a course followed by several other units of the force off the North American coast. In the long list of American ships taken between 30 March and 22 July 1813,[53] by many ships other than the *Shannon*, well over a dozen are recorded as having been burnt. Mostly, these were small vessels in ballast; if laden, their cargoes were generally removed first.

One, however, is of particular interest and may form a useful pendant to this chapter's discussion of operations. The American merchant vessel *Actaeon*, of 336 tons and fourteen men, in ballast from Cádiz bound for Boston, was taken by the *Hogue* (sixty guns, Captain Thomas Bladen Capel, senior officer of the forces on the north-east American seaboard) on 12 May 1813, and burnt that evening.[54] But almost exactly two years later the case came before the Admiralty Court;[55] for the *Actaeon* had sailed under licence issued by the British Minister at Cádiz, and the owners claimed damages against Captain Capel.

The King's Advocate, for Capel, argued that 'costs and damages were not to be awarded against captors, except there was full proof they were guilty of wilful misconduct', and that some of the circumstances of the issue of the licence were suspicious. But Scott would have none of it: 'if a party is unjustly deprived of his property . . . he is entitled to restitution with costs and damages'. Of course, if he had 'by his own conduct in some degree contributed to the loss', he would get less; but there was no evidence of such conduct by the American owners or master in this case. As for Capel, if the government thought his conduct acceptable he would no doubt be indemnified by them 'upon a proper representation being made'. So Capel was out to the tune of £4,000.

There is one final twist to the tale. In the *Hogue*'s log for 12 May 1813[56] the boarding, capture and setting on fire of the *Actaeon* are recorded. But earlier that day occurs the entry 'Punished – Dempsey, Able Seaman, with 60 lashes for contempt to Captain Capel'. Five dozen was very severe, even for such an offence. What had been said? Had it anything to do with prizes? (Several, captured by other ships, were in company.) It will never be known; but half a dozen stories could be written round Captain Capel's (and Able Seaman Dempsey's) unfortunate day.

As this case shows, the licence system lived on in spite of the repeal of the Orders in Council. Whether the one legally enabled the other is not for a layman to judge. Nor is it easy to explain how the licence system worked; as well might one ask how the human mind functions; both are examples of intricately networked systems. It is not even clear just who was authorized to issue licences; the Orders and Proclamations are silent on the matter, and the only proforma for a licence that can be found in the *London Gazette* is on a specialized topic, imports into Newfoundland.[57] It appears that Ministers and Consular authorities abroad, and Customs and Excise authorities in Britain and the colonies, were the main issuing authorities, but sometimes higher-placed bodies may have stepped in; there is a reference in one of Scott's cases[58] to the 'Council Board', apparently an instrument of the Privy Council itself.

Admirals were reluctant to become involved in that end of the business. Pellew as Commander in Chief in the Mediterranean agreed to work out a policy on licences with the Minister at Palermo;[59] and Thomas Byam Martin, recalling his experiences in the Baltic in 1812, wrote 'by the exertions of my people 124 loaded ships [in Riga] were speedily placed beyond the reach of the enemy, and in order to provide freight for the hemp, naval stores and merchandise for England, I took upon myself the great responsibility to grant licences to ships of all nations, even to Americans . . .'.[60] But in general, naval officers found quite enough difficulty in unravelling the knotty problems of licences encountered at sea without going into the intricacies of their issue as well.

This book will not attempt an analysis of the relative costs and benefits of the Orders in Council and the licence system. They were hotly debated at the time: Henry Brougham, backed by the emerging industrial interests of the north, conducted an influential campaign against the system, while the older shipping and colonial interests were all in favour of it.[61] Discussion has been continued by historians ever since.[62] On one point, however, there can be no controversy: the Orders in Council took up a vast swathe of the warring nations' people, political, legal, administrative, merchant and naval, over several critical years of a war that was to shape history for centuries to come.

NOTES

1. LG (1806), p. 618.
2. J. Holland Rose, *The Life of Napoleon I*, vol. II (Bell, 1920), pp. 104–5.
3. The French text used here is in Biederman, *Droits des Neutres* (Brockhaus, Leipsic, 1814), *Pièces Justificatives*, p. 14.
4. *Notifications, Orders and Instructions relating to Prize Subjects during the Present War* (Strahan, for Butterworth and White, 1810), p. 26.
5. ADM 2/1081.
6. *Notifications*, pp. 28–9.
7. Rose, *The Life of Napoleon I*, vol. II, p. 105.
8. ADM 2/1081, Instruction of 29 August 1807.
9. LG (1807), pp. 1154, 1156, 1231–2, 1298; see also, A.N. Ryan, 'The Copenhagen Operation 1807' in N.A.M. Rodger (ed.), *The Naval Miscellany*, vol. 5 (Navy Records Society, 1984).

10. *Notifications*, pp. 35–42.

11. ADM 1/3898.

12. ADM 2/1081.

13. *Notifications*, p. 52; LG (1807), p. 1529.

14. Ibid., p. 27, Order of 4 February 1807.

15. Ibid., p. 38, Orders of 10 September 1807.

16. See for but one example J. Dhondt, 'The Cotton Industry at Ghent During the French Regime' in F. Crouzet, W.H. Chaloner and W.M. Stern (eds), *Essays in European Economic History 1789–1914* (Edward Arnold, 1969). Dhondt traces several economic cycles, some of catastrophic scale, in this industry over the years 1806–14, related to many factors as well as the influence of the Continental System and the Orders in Council.

17. *Notifications*, p. 64.

18. Ibid., p. 65.

19. Ibid., p. 66ff.

20. ADM 2/1082.

21. Ibid., circulars of 23 June 1808, 23 August 1809.

22. Lynne Townley, 'Sir William Scott, Lord Stowell and the Development of the Prize Law in the High Court of Admiralty 1798–1828: with particular Reference to the Rights of Belligerents' (unpublished thesis, University of Birmingham, 1995), p. 355. Townley notes that Edwards found it necessary to bring out a separate volume of Reports on Licence cases.

23. Edw., p. 327 [1809].

24. W.S. Holdsworth, *A History of English Law*, vol. XIII (Methuen, 1952), p. 582. Papers in the possession of Lord Digby contain a learned opinion by 'Mr. Erskine' concerning a dispute on entitlement to prize money between Admirals Robert Digby and Pigott on the North America station in 1782.

25. Townley, 'Sir William Scott, Lord Stowell and the Development of the Prize Law', p. 349n.

26. Edw., p. 311 [1809].

27. Biederman, *Droits des Neutres, Pièces Justificatives*, p. 26.

28. XXIV NC, p. 327; ADM 1/3993, information supplied by Michael Dun.

29. A.N. Ryan, *The Saumarez Papers* (Navy Records Society, 1968), p. 81ff.

30. LG (1809), p. 603.

31. NMM PEL/4.

32. ADM 53/228.

33. HCA 2/357.

34. John D. Byrn (Jr.), *Crime and Punishment in the Royal Navy* (Scolar Press, 1989), p. 176.

35. HCA 2/357.

36. E.g., ADM 1/560, North Sea Reports from Admirals Russell, Gardner and Strachan.

37. Christopher Lloyd, *The Nation and the Navy* (Cresset Press, 1954), pp. 191–2.

38. Biederman, *Droits des Neutres, Pièces Justificatives*, pp. 34–41.

39. Nicholas Tracy, *Attack on Maritime Trade* (Macmillan, 1991), p. 73.

40. Erik Buyst and Joel Mokyr, 'Dutch Manufacturing and Trade during the French Period (1795–1814)' in Erik Aerts and Francois Crouzet, *Economic Effects of the French Revolutionary and Napoleonic Wars* (Leuven University Press, 1990), p. 74.

41. Rose, *The Life of Napoleon I*, vol. II, p. 233.

42. Captured letters reprinted in Edw. Appendix, notes to pp. 228 and 257, illustrate the dilemmas the Americans faced.

43. LG (1809), p. 733.

44. ADM 53/432.

45. XXVI NC, p. 34.

46. XXVIII NC, pp. 132–6.

47. See Chapter 4; and W.L. Clowes, *The Royal Navy: A History from the Earliest Times to 1900*, vol. 6 (Chatham edn, 1997), pp. 1–180, for Vice President Theodore Roosevelt's account of the war.

48. Tracy, *Attack on Maritime Trade*, p. 78.

49. XXVIII NC, p. 257; XXX NC, pp. 240, 250–5.

50. Tony Gutridge, 'George Redmond Hulbert, Prize Agent' (unpublished thesis, Portsmouth Polytechnic, 1981–2), p. 78.

51. David French, *The British Way in Warfare* (Unwin Hyman, 1990), p. 114.

52. XXX NC, p. 42.

53. XXX NC, pp. 250–5.

54. XXX NC, p. 255.

55. 2 Dods., p. 48 [1815].

56. ADM 51/2527.

57. LG (1809), p. 734.

58. *The Vrow Cornelia*, Edw., p. 350 [1810], Edw., *Licence Cases*, p. 23.

59. NMM PEL/20, Pellew to Admiralty, 25 July 1811.

60. Sir R. Vesey Hamilton (ed.), *Journals and Letters of Sir Thomas Byam Martin*, vol. 1 (Navy Records Society, 1903), p. 254.

61. Townley, 'Sir William Scott, Lord Stowell and the Development of the Prize Law', p. 360n.

62. See particularly the work of and under the aegis of F. Crouzet, referred to in note 40 above and in *Britain Ascendant*, trans. M. Thom (Cambridge, 1990), pp. 262–317.

CHAPTER SIX

Fighting the Enemy

And why, pray, did His Majesty's Ships not spend all their time picking up merchant prizes and enriching themselves, with no serious fighting, while ignoring their prime business of capturing, sinking, burning, driving ashore or pursuing into port the war vessels of His Majesty's enemies?

As usual, the answer is not a simple one. It must first be remembered that the late eighteenth century was notable for its consciousness of Honour. The word occurs over and over again in contemporary literature; and one of the principal manifestations of honour was courage, daring and good conduct in battle. Secondly, it was an age of patriotism: this was less apparent before about 1797 than after, when Britain was generally perceived as being engaged in a struggle for survival against an overweening foreign tyranny. Especially in well-led ships, where these rather high-flown concepts percolated by example and osmosis through a whole ship's company, honour and patriotism were powerful drivers in the Navy's view of the duty and service it had to perform.

However, they did need institutional backing, particularly so in view of the attractions of prize money. There was in fact plenty of such backing, which can conveniently be divided into two classes: sticks and carrots.

The first and thickest stick was the Act establishing the Articles of War.[1] The version of the Articles during the wars of 1793–1815 had been in force since 1749, and that had in its turn been introduced to increase the sanctions against any tendency to hang back when engaging the enemy was in prospect – a tendency most shamefully displayed at the Battle of Toulon in 1744.[2]

In consequence, several sections of the 1749 Articles were condign in their discouragement of failure to engage the enemy. Article X prescribed Death, or 'such other punishment as from the nature or degree of the Offence a Court-Martial shall deem him to deserve' for any commander who did not, on encountering 'any ship or ships which it shall be his Duty to engage', make the necessary preparations for fight and 'encourage the inferior officers and men to fight courageously'. Article XI did similarly for anyone who failed to carry out orders in time of action, or did not 'use all possible endeavours to put the same effectually in Execution'. 'Duty to engage' covered encounters with enemy ships of equal, or marginally superior, force; no one expected a frigate to take on a line of battle ship in a one-to-one engagement.

Articles XII and XIII were even more severe about offences which occurred 'through Cowardice, Negligence or Disaffection'. Article XII was about Fleet action and seems to stem directly from Toulon: 'Every person who . . . shall in Time of Action withdraw or keep back . . . or shall not do his utmost to take or destroy every ship which it shall be his Duty to engage, and to assist and relieve all and every of His Majesty's Ships, or those of his Allies . . . shall suffer Death'. Article XIII was of more general application: 'Every Person . . . who . . . shall forbear to pursue the Chace of any Enemy, Pirate, or Rebel, beaten or flying; or shall not relieve or assist a known Friend in View to the utmost of his Power, being convicted of any such Offence by the Sentence of a Court-Martial, shall suffer Death'.

Convoy duty was especially safeguarded in Article XVII. Ships with convoys committed to their charge must

> diligently attend upon that Charge, without Delay . . . and whoever shall be faulty therein, and shall not faithfully perform their Duty, and defend the Ships and Goods in their Convoy, without either diverting to other Parts or Occasions, or refusing or neglecting to fight in their Defence, if they be assailed, or running away cowardly, and submitting the Ships in their Convoy to Peril and Hazard; or shall demand or exact any money or reward from any Merchant or Master for convoying of any Ships or Vessels intrusted to their care, or shall misuse the Masters or Mariners thereof; shall be condemned to make Reparation of the Damage to the Merchants, Owners, and others, as the Court of Admiralty shall adjudge, and also be punished criminally according to the Quality of their Offences, be it by Pains of Death or other Punishment, according as shall be adjudged by the Court Martial.

From 1803, a big stick was applied to merchant ships too: an Act of that year[3] made Convoy compulsory for British registered merchant ships and laid down severe penalties for ships separating from convoy, including automatic annulment of their insurance. There were of course many exceptions to the requirement, including licensing arrangements for independent voyages, waiver of the rules for traffic from one British port to another, dispensations for East Indiamen and exemptions for homeward bound traffic where local commanders could not provide convoying forces. However, there is evidence that the Act did impose needed discipline, and from then until the end of the war the Doctors' Commons files contain numerous letters about complaints from convoy commanders of the conduct of merchant ships under their charge.[4] The complaints were followed up, too; on several occasions officers from the escorting vessels had to be given leave from their ships in order to attend court as witnesses.

To some extent the naval officers reporting these offences must have been covering their backs against counter-charges of mismanaging their convoys under Article XVII of the Articles of War; but their indignation against recalcitrant merchantmen often has the ring of truth.

A second stick to ensure the engagement of His Majesty's Ships in the main business of war was closely related to trade protection. Merchants – even those who railed against the delays caused by convoy – were sensitive to losses from privateers, which continued to occur quite close to British shores even when, in the last decade of the war, the French fleet was bottled up in its bases. The Admiralty, and through them Commanders in Chief and cruisers, were acutely aware of these commercial pressures and in the customary orders for cruising ships privateers were a prime target.

A long apologia,[5] in response to a letter from the Committee of Lloyd's expressing alarm at losses to privateers, was made by the Admiralty Office on 14 March 1809. This gave, for the previous six months, figures for convoyed ships and independents and for captures and recaptures of merchant ships in the Channel. The proportion of losses was, from these figures, 1.5 per cent of sailings. In the same period thirty-three men of war or privateers were captured from the enemy. This document too emphasized the importance of convoy discipline.

The third stick was a matter of opportunity. 'Pleasant days' for prize taking, such as the 1803 swoop in the aftermath of the British Declaration of War or the predation on American trade in 1812–13, were relatively rare. Much more often enemy character, the acid test for legal condemnation, sought to cloak itself in neutrality that was hard to penetrate. The cases covered in Chapter 3 show that it was possible for cruisers to smell rats if they had time and perception, but no one supposed it was easy. Similarly, blockade, complicated as it later was by the licensing system, did not give opportunities for easy pickings. Thomas Lord Cochrane's highly successful operations in the *Imperieuse* in the Mediterranean in 1808 were mostly against French forces ashore;[6] he claimed long afterwards that it was not financially worthwhile to seek prizes afloat and by implication that he had found a better and more certain way of 'annoying the enemy'. Cochrane gave corrupt court practices as his reason for this change, but in fact the Western Mediterranean was not a happy hunting ground at the time.

The fourth stick was the disapproval of senior officers. This may seem surprising in view of the fact that the flag officers under whose direction cruisers operated stood to gain from their prize-taking. And there were flag officers, Bridport being a notable case, who had a reputation for avarice.[7] But others, more influential, set a balanced example and imposed stricter standards.

Of these the two most prominent were St Vincent and Nelson. Neither were strangers to prize money or its attractions and a dispute between them on that very subject made headlines.[8] But when it came to choices between prize-taking and fighting the enemy, everyone in the navy knew that for these officers there was no contest. Nelson relinquished the prospect of easy prizes during the pursuit of the French which ended at Aboukir Bay. St Vincent, having undergone something of a Damascene conversion after his injudicious pursuit of prize money in 1794–5,[9] was constant in his criticism of officers who sought riches rather than success for British arms, and few were spared: 'Captain Lawford [of *The Maria* case] was once a good fellow, but since he has got rich he is . . . dilatory and negligent';[10] 'Sir J. Warren will intrigue for a chief command on the coast of Portugal . . . he wants money';[11] and more generally 'Prize money, or looking forward to retirement, appear to be the governing actions of all the officers' minds'.[12] These extracts from correspondence come late in St Vincent's career, but his train of thought was apparent long before: his journal for the time of his command of the Channel Fleet in 1798–1800[13] is full of orders to cruisers very precisely drafted and in no case is prize mentioned. The most common formulation is 'for the protection of the trade and the annoyance of the enemy', though this is often varied to include a specific mention of enemy privateers.

The obverse of disapprobation for greedy motives and actions was approbation for patriotic and martial ones; here the stick turned into a carrot. The most obvious indication of this comes from the *London Gazette* and, shadowing it, the *Naval Chronicle*. Every action against enemy ships of war, including privateers, and every action against the shore was recorded, often in great detail. The report from the captain of the ship, or senior officer involved directly in the operation, was often printed in full, together with the covering letter by which the flag officer transmitted it to the Admiralty. When casualties were sustained, they were reported, officers invariably by name and ratings usually.

In contrast, merchant prizes were hardly ever reported singly and, for the home station, not even summarized. Occasionally, a highly successful squadron or single-ship cruise would be reported.[14] Despatches from foreign stations sometimes included a six-monthly rundown of prizes taken, occasionally detailing ships by name, with an indication of the cargo, but usually not.[15]

The criterion for a report, including the credit that went with it, was whether armed resistance had been offered. Thus a cutting-out action by a ship's or squadron's boats would usually get a mention because the vessels assailed would have protection from supporting craft, shore batteries or both, and these were certain to open fire even if (as sometimes happened) ineffectually. However frequent such operations became, they could easily go wrong and demanded much courage and hardihood on every occasion. So eager became the ships of the fleet to embark on cutting-out, indeed, that the Admiralty in 1810 enjoined

Gambier – scarcely the most enterprising of Commanders in Chief – to caution commanding officers 'not to employ their boats on enterprises of the nature of those abovementioned when their ships are not in a situation to be brought up to support them'.[16]

It is plain that the way to become known, to gain kudos and probable promotion, was to succeed in action against enemy fighting forces. Captures of merchant ships, however hard earned with sweat, privation and split topsails, would scarcely bring the ship's name to notice, let alone the names of individuals. The bloodless capture of a privateer, though it would get the ship's name known and be approved by their Lordships particularly if the privateer was fit for naval service (it is interesting how many of the reports of capture are accompanied by comments such as 'a new vessel, sails extremely well'), would not usually be accompanied by any commendation of an individual. If resistance was offered by a privateer, that was a different matter; there was an opportunity for officers and men to distinguish themselves and be mentioned in the despatch. Many such actions found their way into the early history books,[17] which depended largely on the *Gazette* as a source. Immediate recognition might attend those mentioned.

A more certain way to promotion, however, was a successful action against the full-fledged warships of the enemy. Here a full account of the proceedings was certain to appear in the *Gazette* and anyone who had distinguished himself could expect a mention. In ship actions the First Lieutenant as second-in-command would be exceptionally well placed, with the possibility of immediate promotion to Commander, particularly on a foreign station. Junior officers would have a better chance of distinction if the ship's boats were involved.

There was a more grisly aspect to all this. Action against the enemy generally meant casualties; and casualties meant vacancies; and vacancies meant at least temporary promotion for some. In fact the recorded casualties for most of the actions being discussed here were surprisingly light, seldom amounting to more than 2 or 3 per cent of the forces involved. But they generally bore more heavily on the officers than the ratings and it was not for nothing that the mordant Thursday toast in the Wardroom was (and still traditionally is) 'A Bloody War or a Sickly Season'.

Honour and glory, then, were the way to promotion and hence to eventual profit. But there was a more direct financial incentive in fighting the enemy – particularly if he could be captured. If fit for service, the captured ship was bought in to the navy. No evidence can be found of any penny-pinching in such transactions; George Rose, the Treasurer of the Navy from 1807 to the end of the war, was notably sensitive to and a crusader for fairness in prize matters,[18] and he would have made sure full market prices were paid. Moreover, the ordnance and naval stores were all bought in and could fetch tidy sums; even an unserviceable musket was valued at 7s while serviceable ones were worth nearly three times that.[19]

There was further encouragement, however. A long and most detailed section of each Prize Act[20] provided for a Bounty of 'Five pounds for every man who was living on board any [ship of war or privateer] taken, sunk, burnt or otherwise destroyed at the Beginning of the Attack or Engagement.' The number of such men was to be proved by the oath of three or more of the officers or men of the enemy ship: but if fewer than three survivors were available, even the evidence of one would do, provided it was given on oath to competent British authorities whose functions in dealing with it were meticulously detailed.

The Bounty was universally known as 'Head Money' and that is how it will be termed in this book. The scales for its distribution were exactly the same as for all other prize money.[21] Plainly, no one, not even a captain or flag officer, was going to make a fortune out of head money for a single-ship action; even a captured line of battle ship with a crew of 800 would make only £4,000. Nevertheless, it was a greatly prized privilege, as is shown by the meticulous detailing in the *Gazette* reports of the number of crew in every privateer or warship engaged or taken. In many cases, where enemy vessels had been destroyed rather than captured, it would be the only recompense for a hard fight, so it had immense symbolic importance as well as some financial attraction.

It is somewhat surprising that few head money cases appear in the Admiralty Court Reports for these wars. It is unlikely that any case of interest in law would have gone unrecorded; all the reporters, Robinson, Edwards and Dodson, were legally perceptive in their selection. The inference must be that wherever a case for head money could possibly be made, it was granted without demur. A brief note of an appeal case[22] bears this out: the *Imperial*, said to be of 136 guns though by some other accounts of 130, was driven ashore at the Battle of Santo Domingo in 1806 and the number of her crew and even, in legal terms, her character as a warship could not at first be established. But eventually a single illiterate survivor was found and his testimony was considered sufficient.

Of course there would be many occasions when even this minimal evidence would not be available. To return briefly to the story of the *Brilliant* with which this book began, the crew of the Dutch privateer driven on shore in 1797 all ran away, so that although her name was known and character as a privateer beyond doubt, no head money could be paid.

The head money cases which are fully reported from the High Court of Admiralty are generally concerned with entitlement as between ships concerned in the action. The two principal cases dragged on for years, with considerable acrimony, before coming to court.

Scott was not slow to deplore the delay in bringing such suits. In *The Gloire*,[23] a case which came before him in 1810 after many years' wrangling, he said that even had the matter been settled by arbitration, the parties 'must finally have come to this court for a decree, otherwise the head money would not have been paid'. On the general principle, he was quite clear: 'Head Money . . . is the peculiar and appropriate reward of immediate personal exertion . . . it has always been considered in a more rigid manner by the Courts than those which arise out of the general interests of prize'. Ships which were 'not engaged in fight, [not] actual captors, [but] merely in sight and in chase', had claims which were 'quite unsustainable'. For 'a general engagement, in which case there can be no selection of combatants . . . all are equally admitted to partake'; but in a 'general and remote chase', the 'mere endeavour to come up with and close with the enemy' would not sustain a claim.

Similar delays affected the second case, *The Ville de Varsovie*.[24] It arose out of the attack on the French fleet in the Basque Roads in 1809 and did not come to court until June 1818. Captain Thomas, Lord Cochrane, claimed by counter-monition that he and the crews of the ships under his immediate command should alone receive head money and that the main fleet commanded by Admiral Lord Gambier should not benefit from the action since it had not taken an active part.

Cochrane's case was founded upon the facts.[25] He had persuaded the Admiralty to approve his scheme, which involved several explosion vessels and fireships with which he in the *Impérieuse* frigate would approach the boom across the mouth of the Charente river, blow it up and so terrorize the French fleet lying in the river that they would be prey to a subsequent attack by the British blockading fleet. Gambier had with some reluctance given Cochrane the go-ahead. In the event only one of the explosions went off and the fireships did not reach their targets, but the effect on the French fleet was as planned: several cut their cables and drifted ashore, where, as Cochrane with increasing impatience signalled to Gambier, they could in his judgement easily have been taken. Gambier's response was half-hearted, governed perhaps by preoccupations about wind and tide in those inshore waters. No ships were captured, but several were regarded as 'driven on shore' and therefore qualifying for head money, including the line of battle ship *Ville de Varsovie*.

Scott's judgment first expanded on what he had said earlier in *La Gloire*: 'the distribution of head money, the bounty of the state itself and not the fruit of fortunate acquisition . . . is . . . a reward for real and active service and personal exertion'; title was insufficient 'if the endeavour does not bring them within the capacity of actual sharing of that peril'. But he then set out on further exposition, beginning with the case of the *Rippon* (unreported); her coming on to the scene and precipitating the surrender of the *Weser*, which was engaging two lesser ships, had entitled the *Rippon* to head money even though she had not fired a shot.

Scott went on to analyse the concept of 'united force' and 'association for one common purpose' which he regarded as tests for entitlement. The Battle of the Nile was a clear case of such association and the *Culloden*, though aground throughout the action, had been entitled to the common distribution. Had there then, in the Basque Roads affair, been any severance or dissociation at any time that could break the concept of common purpose? Scott could find none; the Roads were blockaded, and 'there is no occupation which so completely unites and, as it were, identifies the vessels engaged in it, as that of blockade'. Control and superintendence throughout rested with Lord Gambier. Cochrane claimed that Gambier had not given him all the help that ought to have been afforded, but another court (a reference to Gambier's Court Martial in 1810)[26] had decided otherwise. French witnesses had attributed the disaster to their fleet, including the *Ville de Varsovie*, to 'the fleet under Lord Gambier'. Cochrane's claim was rejected.

It is impossible entirely to exclude personalities from this case. Cochrane was a man who generated controversy wherever he went, and his sense of injustice over the Basque Roads affair was – like many of his other grievances – passionately felt and expressed. It could be argued that he had brought the case at least as much to blacken reputations as to get justice; it could not have been for the money, which was minimal by his standards. As will be seen from later chapters, he had been a thorn in the side of the Prize Courts for years and Scott had no reason to be sympathetic to him.

Was then Scott's judgment in any way coloured by these factors – or even by the fact that Scott was a Tory while Cochrane was a Radical? Certainly the judgment reads in parts more like advocacy than impartial analysis. Moreover, it is hard to reconcile some parts of *The Ville de Varsovie* with the earlier *Gloire* judgement, where on the face of it more stringent tests for entitlement to head money had been applied. Read on its own, *The Ville de Varsovie* judgment is scarcely assailable, but *The Gloire* raises doubts about it. By 1818, Scott was a tired man; he had held his important office for twenty years during the most intense maritime war in history up to that time. There may have been more than a trace of impatience in a case which he clearly thought ought never to have been brought. But a great jurist still shines through.

Probably the best illustration of the way an officer's career could lead through fame to fortune is the war record of Edward Pellew, later Lord Exmouth. As a midshipman, he distinguished himself in the debacle of Saratoga and was promoted to lieutenant in 1778 and commander in 1780. He made one or two captures late in the War of American Independence but was reported to be 'rich only in reputation' when that war ended in 1783.[27] In 1793 he was quickly in action as captain of

Nymphe; her captures of the *Sans Culotte* privateer and *Cléopatre* frigate were two of the earliest successes of the war. In passing, a share of head money for the *Cléopatre* was claimed by the *Venus* which had been in company, but arbitration decided otherwise.[28]

Pellew's dazzling career continued throughout the remaining years of the century. He commanded ships of steadily increasing force; *Nymphe* of 36 guns was followed by *Arethusa* of 44 and *Indefatigable*, also of 44 guns but cut down from a 64 and therefore of heavier metal and tougher scantlings. Every year brought distinction: in 1794 as a part of Sir John Borlase Warren's squadron in the capture of the *Pomone* (64); in 1795 amongst a convoy sheltering under Penmarc'h; in 1796 against a tough opponent, *La Virginie*, which although of only 40 guns gave him a hard fight; and in 1797 perhaps his finest hour of action when with *Amazon*, another frigate, he drove the line of battle ship *Droits de l'Homme* (74) ashore in a fearful storm on the Brittany coast. The *Amazon* also was lost and only by quick reactions and consummate seamanship did *Indefatigable* weather the rocks. Head money for the *Droits de l'Homme* was clearly awardable if evidence of crew numbers could be found; Pellew is said to have written to the French captain Lacrosse, who had survived where so many had perished, and received the courteous answer that including troops there had been 1,600 on board.[29] It was a courtesy that would have been far less likely ten years later.

But Pellew's 'pleasant days' – there were numerous cheaply won prizes as well as hard-fought naval opponents – came to an end when the Admiralty limited the period in command of frigates and in 1799 he went on to line of battle ships, first the *Impetueux* (74) and then the *Tonnant* (80). The French names indicate ships taken from the enemy at an earlier date; it has been calculated that in all, some 450 captured warships were added to the Royal Navy in the period from 1793 to 1815.[30] In ships of the line Pellew had less scope for action and much graver crew problems; perhaps the one followed the other. In any case, he took a very strong line with incipient mutineers.[31]

His flag as a rear admiral duly arrived in 1804 and he was appointed to the East Indies station, taking out a convoy of Indiamen under the escort of his flagship *Culloden*.[32] The voyage to Penang took five months; it is worth recalling such timescales when considering the way in which war was commanded and conducted at that time.

As a Commander in Chief in those circumstances, Pellew was bound to have great freedom of action. But he was not entirely trusted, particularly by Pitt, the Prime Minister, who had not forgiven him for speaking out in the House of Commons[33] against Pitt's plan for anti-invasion gunboats. In consequence, the Admiralty split the India Command and appointed Sir Thomas Troubridge, slightly junior to Pellew, to the eastern half. This was the most lucrative part, including as it did the rich Dutch colonies in the East Indies, ready for picking off one by one.

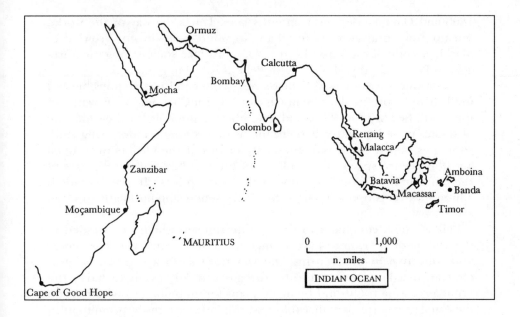

A bitter dispute broke out between the two admirals. Both claimed that potential prize money had little or nothing to do with it; Pellew wrote from *Culloden* in 1805, 'I never cared much about riches and we have enough to make me comfortable'.[34] But his letters are full of resentment about it: 'he [Troubridge] has however . . . as many eggs as give him £50,000 already paid hard cash . . . but with this he is not satisfied . . . so that I am literally left to starve'.[35] (Since in the next breath he speaks of 'mustering £2,000 a year as we are', Pellew's use of 'literally' may be thought some small exaggeration.)

The dispute ended tragically. After an Inquiry, Troubridge was recalled to the Cape. In high dudgeon, he went in his flagship the *Blenheim,* a notoriously unseaworthy vessel that had grounded and been badly damaged on service the previous year. She was last seen on 1 February 1807 in a storm in the south-west Indian Ocean;[36] it was presumed that she and her consort *Java* were lost with all hands.

Meanwhile, Pellew continued his work in the Indian Ocean. It was immensely active as well as lucrative. He insisted on convoys for the Indiamen; he picked off Dutch colonies one by one with very few casualties and great booty. It was a highly successful command, but it had its unsavoury side. Pellew promoted both his sons, Fleetwood and Pownoll, to command at a very early age indeed and gave Fleetwood in particular quite unjustified opportunities to enrich himself which might well have gone to more senior captains. Nepotism had not been unknown to Troubridge either; his son Edward was made Lieutenant in February

1806 and Commander seven months later. It was the way of the world, but no more praiseworthy for that. No wonder St Vincent growled to Markham, one of the Naval Lords, 'You must take some strong measures against Pellew . . . the whole race of Pellews is bad in grain . . .'.[37]

Strong measures or not, Pellew's next command was responsible but unlikely to be profitable. The north-east English Channel, the Downs and the North Sea in 1808–9 boasted a number of admirals;[38] Pellew was one of them. As we have already seen, the work was tough, unforgiving stuff, coping as best it could with the complexities of the Orders in Council and the licence system, the foulness of the weather and the vagaries of the authorities, from customs officers to pilots. It was as much administrative as operational, as the more senior appointments so often are.

Pellew's next command in the Mediterranean, which he assumed in the middle of 1811, must have seemed much more attractive. His energy and initiative in prosecuting the war were soon apparent. He was constantly asking the Admiralty for more small vessels to harry the French coasting trade, and he made plans for amphibious operations on the Catalan coast; it is noticeable that the latter are more prominent in his correspondence than the former.[39] Operations in the Adriatic were highly successful, the highlight being the engagement off Lissa between a force of British frigates under Hoste and a French/Venetian squadron of somewhat superior force, resulting in a comprehensive victory for the British.

Fame therefore there was in plenty, but by Pellew's standards little fortune. One of his biographers says that the carriage of bullion in ships under his command, yielding freight money, was more lucrative than his income from prizes. He wrote to Admiral Keats in September 1813: 'Your prize concerns here I believe go badly – what with bad Agents, bad Courts, bad fortune, bad plagues and a bad look out, I fear we are all in a bad way. The total of my whack up to 1 February stands at £10,200 and at Malta we are breaking and the Court at a stand still.'[40]

Pellew's outstanding career culminated in 1816, after the fall of Napoleon, with the bombardment and submission of Algiers and the suppression, for the time being, of the Barbary pirates. He finished the war an extremely rich man; his prize money is estimated to have amounted to over £300,000, equivalent in 1990s terms to £60 million. He was an archetype; others could dream of similar success though very few would get anywhere near it. But the salient point, in the context of this chapter, is that fortune followed fame and fame was founded upon unquestioned professional competence, courage and skill in action against the enemy and firm and inspiring leadership.

Some officers displayed all these qualities but were in no way so fortunate. To end this chapter on a less triumphant note, consider the career of the worthy Captain George Duff.[41]. A lieutenant in 1779 and a commander in 1790, he was made post in February 1793 and almost at once sent to command a ninety-gun line of battle ship. Subsequent frigate commands were not blessed with good fortune and he was all too soon back in command of ships of the line. In consequence, he missed any real chance of acquiring substantial prize money, for ships of the line did not go chasing after merchant vessels or privateers, remaining generally with the main fleet or detached squadrons of significant force ready to meet similar units of the enemy.

Duff was an outstanding officer, a man with vast professional experience and expertise but above all with a real talent for commanding a big ship and a large and diverse ship's company. In 1805 he was in command of the *Mars* in Nelson's fleet; Nelson deputed him to command a detached squadron of some five of the line for a close watch on Cádiz, possibly to lure the Combined Fleet out, certainly to give warning of their preparations over and above that provided by Blackwood's frigates. The planned use of the squadron in battle never came to fruition because Nelson's numbers were not great enough, but it shows how highly he thought of Duff.

Duff's letters to his wife at the time show not only his devotion to her – he wrote something every day, sending off the letters as serials when opportunity offered – but a sense of impending action. He said in one that he had made what provision he could for her but 'our small funds' were much less than he could have hoped. Then a few days later came a letter beginning 'I have taken a Prize today!' It was a cask of wine that was seen floating down the side of the *Mars* and had been brought to his cabin. He added with some glee that the wine inside seemed drinkable.

At Trafalgar the *Mars* was third in the leeward line to Collingwood's flagship *Royal Sovereign* and was early in hot action with the *Pluton* and *Fougueux*. Duff was killed on his own quarterdeck. Some of the letters written about him after the battle by members of his own ship's company parallel in affection the better-known ones about Nelson.

His widow would not have been left penniless. She would have received some £2,389, which was the captains' share of the money specially awarded by government for the action, as well as £973 representing further pooled money from the prizes, amounting in all to £3,362,[42] combined with any money Duff had put together during his life. But considering that her husband had been due for a Rear Admiral's flag at any moment, with a consequent appointment where he could scarcely have failed to make a reasonable amount from the proportion of money due to him from prize proceeds under his command, the loss of her man was dreadfully compounded. It was a capricious war in a hard world.

NOTES

1. 22 Geo. II c.33.
2. N.A.M. Rodger, *Articles of War* (Kenneth Mason, 1982), p. 9.
3. 43 Geo. III c.56.
4. ADM 1/3898, 16 June 1807; ADM 1/3899, 30 Jan 1809, etc.
5. ADM 1/3993.
6. XX NC, p. 326.
7. C. Northcote Parkinson, *Edward Pellew, Viscount Exmouth* (Methuen, 1933), p. 196.
8. V NC, p. 254; Michael Lewis, *A Social History of the Navy 1793–1815* (George Allen and Unwin, 1960), p. 321.
9. See Chapter 2.
10. Sir Clements Markham (ed.), *Selections from the Correspondence of Sir John Markham* (Navy Records Society, 1904), p. 37.
11. Ibid., p. 50.
12. Admiral Sir William James, *Old Oak* (Longman, Green, 1950), p. 199.
13. ADM 50/93.
14. See, e.g., XVIII NC, p. 152; XXIV NC, pp. 254–5.
15. XXX NC, pp. 240ff. and 250–5 are more detailed than most.
16. RNM 302/77 (25): Barrow to Gambier, 8 October 1810.
17. William James, *The Naval History of Britain*, vol. III (Bentley, 1847), p. 205 for but one example. Numerous others occur in even earlier work such as that of Edward Pelham Brenton, where the careers of individual officers might still be thought susceptible to influence by such advocacy.
18. ADM 1/3657.
19. PRO WO 52/130, bills 7225 and 7226.
20. 45 Geo. III c.72 s.5. This Act superseded the 1793 and 1803 Acts which contained almost identical provisions.
21. Ibid., s.6.
22. HCA 42/438.
23. Edw., p. 280.
24. 2 Dods., pp. 301–21 [1818].
25. XXII NC, pp. 16–17.
26. XXII NC, p. 215.
27. Edward Osler, *The Life of Admiral Viscount Exmouth* (Smith, Elder, 1835), p. 70.
28. Parkinson, *Edward Pellew*, p. 94.
29. Osler, *The Life of Admiral Viscount Exmouth*, p. 162.
30. Daniel A. Baugh, in J.R. Hill (ed.), *The Oxford Illustrated History of the Royal Navy* (OUP, 1995), p. 125.
31. Parkinson, *Edward Pellew*, p. 195; Osler, *The Life of Admiral Viscount Exmouth*, pp. 185–7.
32. NMM PEL/31.

33. *Supra*, p. 38.
34. Parkinson, *Edward Pellew*, p. 327.
35. Ibid., p. 367.
36. John D. Grainger, *The Royal Navy in the River Plate, 1806–1807* (Scolar Press for the Navy Records Society, 1996), p. 273.
37. Markham, *Selections*, p. 53.
38. ADM 1/560.
39. NMM PEL/20.
40. Parkinson, *Edward Pellew*, p. 405.
41. XX NC, p. 265.
42. RNM 1983/1062. See also, D. Howarth, *Trafalgar: the Nelson Touch* (Windrush, 1996), p. 146.

CHAPTER SEVEN

Joint Capture

Capture of a single ship by a single ship was the simple, classical prize situation, and analysis[1] suggests that 80 per cent of captures were of this kind. That left a sizeable rump of situations in which either several ships were captured by one, or one ship was captured by the efforts of several, or a combination of both.

When several ships were captured by one, either on the same day or within a short space of time, there were provisions in the Prize Act[2] for as many as six to be adjudicated in the same hearing. Strictly, this applied only to enemy privateers under 70 tons each, but the records suggest that grouping of this kind was applied in effect to merchant captures as well.

That was the simplest of the multiple situations. Curiously, the next in order of simplicity was the most obvious several-against-several action, the major battle. Here the concept of 'common purpose', analysed by Scott in the head-money case of *The Ville de Varsovie*,[3] was of clear application: all who had formed part of the engaged fleet should take equal benefit, according to the laid down scales of distribution, from whatever had accrued in the way of prizes, shattered and battered as many of them might be.

In the case of Trafalgar, the damage to the enemy fleet was singularly heavy, many of the nineteen prizes were lost in a subsequent storm and government recognized the importance of the battle for both its strategic and moral impact. It granted a fund of £300,000 to be divided among the victors, as well as any money that accrued from the prizes. A captain, whether of a line of battle ship in the thick of it or of a frigate repeating signals, received a share totalling £3,362; an able seaman's was some £6 10s.[4] Other major battles were treated in a more normal fashion, the value of the prizes with their stores and ordnance generally being considered sufficient recompense; it was lumped together and distribution made on an equal basis to all ships involved.

But questions inevitably arose around the fringes. One of the first cases to come before Sir William Scott was *The Vrijheid*.[5] *Vrijheid* was the Dutch flagship at Admiral Duncan's victory of Camperdown on 11 October 1797 and the case revolved around that battle. The frigate *Vestal* claimed a share in the prize money on the ground that she had been instrumental to the action and had participated in the common purpose, though not actually present at the battle. She had been ordered by Duncan to cruise off the Texel and reconnoitre the Dutch fleet and subsequently, on 8 October, to proceed to England with despatches. She rejoined on 13 October, having done her best throughout to maintain contact with Duncan and return as quickly as possible.

The case came before Scott on 19 June 1799 and he clearly wished to make it a leading one. He went back to the wording of the Act of Parliament and Proclamation then in force, then proceeded to set out the principles by which entitlement was to be tested. The tests were less stringent than they were for head money. In the case of prize money, 'a constructive assistance' was all that was necessary; being in sight of the prize at the point of capture, provided it was not simply fortuitous, was sufficient to entitle.

The difficulty in the case of the *Vestal* was that she was not in sight of the actual battle. Was then her participation in 'the common enterprise' enough to entitle her? She had formed part of Duncan's fleet, she had acted as one of his scouts, she was running despatches for him; but at the critical time she had been detached. 'The difficulty', said Scott, 'is to say where the joint exercise actually begins.' His analysis of the orders to the *Vestal* took him no further, for battle and her possible part in it was not mentioned in them. He turned to the question of 'Chase', which had been ordered by Duncan at an early stage of the action: 'Was the *Vestal* in sight at the commencement of the chase before she separated?' It seemed most unlikely. Scott concluded, with what appeared to be genuine regret, that the *Vestal*'s claim must be rejected.

He did not show similar regret when rejecting the claim of a privateer to participate in the capture of the *Santa Brigada*.[6] This ship (the proper spelling is *Santa Brigida*, but the case is known by the misspelt name) was one of a pair of very richly laden Spanish ships of war whose capture by *Triton*, *Alcmene*, *Naiad* and *Ethalion* on 17 October 1799 is mentioned at several other points in this book.[7] The privateer was in sight of the capture and claimed that she had 'put herself in motion in such a manner as might have been effectual in cutting off retreat'. There was also an assertion that she had diverted the attention of four Spanish frigates which otherwise might have come to the succour of *Santa Brigida*.

Scott was unimpressed. The diversion, if it had occurred at all, was fortuitous; the heading-off, if it had been intended, was not material to the outcome. 'Being in sight only will not be sufficient . . . if, by the mere act of hanging on to His Majesty's Ships to pick up the crumbs of the captors', small privateers should seek to benefit.

The reverse situation, where a privateer capture was alleged to have been influenced by a King's ship, came up in two reported cases. In the first, *The San José*,[8] the ship of that name was captured by the privateer *Mayflower* on 3 March 1805. The *Euryalus*, Captain Henry Blackwood of the *Eenrom* story, claimed a share as having been in sight at the time of the capture. The *Mayflower* alleged that this was not so, but Blackwood produced in evidence a paper signed by the master of the *Mayflower* stating that *Euryalus* 'was in chase of and in sight of [the *San José*], whom we took possession of about half past nine o'clock am and that the said ship's boat, with the First Lieutenant, boarded me at 11 o'clock'. The master was taken on board *Euryalus* to sign this paper.

In court it was alleged that he had signed it under duress. Captain Blackwood, he claimed, 'abused him in very violent language, and swore, that he would distress him and have 20 more of his men pressed . . .' But on returning to his ship, he had not confided in anyone what had gone on.

Scott took this last point as a relevant piece of evidence. He was moreover unwilling to believe that Blackwood could be guilty of 'so foul a conspiracy'. The clinching evidence, however, was in his view the timing of the events. The time between the taking of the prize and the arrival of the *Euryalus*'s boat at the *Mayflower*, one and a half hours, suggested strongly that in the prevailing conditions of wind and weather the frigate must have been in sight at the time of capture. The *Mayflower*'s case for sole right of capture was rejected and *Euryalus* got her share.

It was a curious case, nevertheless. It seems unlikely that the master of the *Mayflower* would have spun a complete yarn in court. There are other references to Blackwood scattered through the archives of these wars that mark him as a tough, even hard, man as well as a highly professional officer. Mrs Jordan, the mistress of William, Duke of Clarence (later King William IV), referred to him in 1810, albeit by hearsay, as 'the most severe not to say *tyrannical* officer in the Service; he certainly flogs his midshipmen . . .', which was of concern to her as her son Henry Fitzclarence was on board the *Warspite*, Blackwood's ship.[9] But in the case of the *San José*, as in so many other of Scott's cases, commonsense and sea knowledge probably arrived at a right conclusion.

Less overlaid with personal acrimony, but probably more important for principle, was the case of *La Flore*.[10] The ship was captured by the privateer *Trimmer*, with a King's ship (not named) in sight but taking no part in the capture. Scott distinguished between the influence of a privateer and a King's ship in such circumstances: the latter were 'under a constant obligation to attack the enemy wherever seen' and therefore must be *presumed* to take part in a capture when in sight. For privateers, 'the same obligation does not exist'. The same principle was applied in the case of *l'Amitié*;[11] HMS *Gannet* was adjudged sole captor, two privateers in sight having shown no inclination to take an active part in the capture: to claim successfully, said Scott, they must show *animus capiendi* by overt act. Even such an act was deemed insufficient in the case of *The Odin*[12] where the boat of an East Indiaman Letter of Marque *Royal Admiral*, faint but pursuing, was in sight of a capture by the boats of

HMS *Trusty*. Scott maintained that it was more difficult to prove 'constructive assistance' by a boat than by a ship.

It may seem from these cases that Scott was inclined to side with King's ships to the detriment of privateers. He certainly could be severe with the latter when they stepped out of line. But his judgments are always well reasoned, and though they may have penalized the occasional doughty privateer who was doing his best to assist in capture, they surely must have dissuaded potential jackals of the sea, hanging on the flanks of cruisers to pick up scraps.

The Navy's view of privateers was not far removed from Scott's. They were considered useful adjuncts so long as they were legitimate under the terms of the Prize Act (which devoted six long Sections to their status and administration)[13] and conducted themselves in accordance with the rules and customs prevailing. But there was a certain air of patronage. 'Lines Written on Board a Privateer at Sea to a Lady in Dorsetshire' in the *Naval Chronicle*[14] are indicative:

In quest of Fortune on the faithless Main
Where Life's whole Comfort is the hope of Gain . . .

The poem goes on to describe the awful people with whom the privateer has to share his quarters and his life. It is very doubtful if it was written by anyone other than a naval officer.

There was one occasion when the Admiralty Court had to rule on the distribution of prize money within a privateer's crew. This generally was left to the owners and crews themselves, much to the relief no doubt of the authorities, but in this case, *The Frederick and Mary Ann*,[15] a point of law arose that could not be set aside: the prize master had acquired certain assets in the prize which he claimed as his sole property. Scott ruled against this: 'Prize interests acquired by a prize master on board a captured ship shall inure to the whole ship's company.' He added that privateering shares, while traditionally decided by agreement, must be 'ruled by equity and reason'.

Where reported cases of disputed joint capture concerned King's ships only, the questions that arose were different and revolved around proximity rather than action or intention. In *The Forsigheid*[16] a squadron had been in chase of the vessel and ordered to remain in sight of it, but at the moment of capture the weather was hazy and no other ship of the squadron could be seen from the capturing ship, the *Director*. Scott ruled that a capture in this sort of weather was not unlike a capture at night, when consorts were in company but not necessarily visible. The squadron was entitled to share. A similar but much later case, *The Union*,[17] was decided in the same way, though in this case the chase finished in the dark.

The same liberal interpretation of 'in sight' was applied in the case of *The Sparkler*.[18] This British ship was recaptured by the *Nimrod* and a share was claimed by the *Armide*, which had been in sight and asserted she had joined in the chase. Scott ruled in *Armide*'s favour, saying 'a ship in sight is entitled to share in the prize from that circumstance alone, unless the case happens to fall within one of the exceptions to that general rule, such as the circumstance of steering a directly contrary course . . . the law is willing to favour the interests of all who contribute their endeavours to capture the vessels of the enemy'. A twist to this story, which cannot have sweetened relations between the King's ships involved, was that a visiting party to *Nimrod* from *Armide* had been assured that no capture had taken place; the truth was later discovered by accident. Scott accordingly ruled that both parties' expenses should be deducted from *Nimrod*'s share, but relented when *Nimrod*'s captain showed that this would exceed his personal prize money.

Bigger game was sometimes the subject of protracted dispute. The *Guillaume Tell*, very last of the French battleships that had survived the Battle of the Nile, was captured off Malta on 29 March 1800 by *Foudroyant* and *Lion*, the *Penelope* (Blackwood again) having delayed her by adroit manoeuvring and gunfire. A claim for a share was put forward by *Northumberland* and *Culloden*, which had formed part of the squadron but were not in company; indeed, the *Culloden* was at anchor in Marsa Xlokk at the time. Here the concept of 'common purpose' seems to have been stretched to its limit, since it was ruled that all ships should share. The case took ten years to settle.[19]

The most complex type of joint capture of all was anything connected with the shore. Booty acquired during a purely naval operation, even if it was against the shore, was not too difficult to settle if the ships taking part in the 'common purpose' were undisputed. In one reported case, *Genoa and Savona*,[20] all shipping and ordnance taken in those ports in April 1814 was condemned as prize; and the *Pompée*, which happened to be passing, claimed a share. This was too much for the Court, who pointed out that the *Pompée* had barely heard or seen the firing, let alone taken part, and ruled that she was not entitled.

But if the army was involved, then the division of the spoils was bound to be more difficult to establish. The complexities of the combined operations in Corsica in the mid-1790s took years to unravel. The problem was recognized and special provision for it was made in the 1805 Prize Act.[21] All lawful prize connected with any fortress on land taken by a combined operation, including ships and vessels defended by that fortress, was to be distributed in such proportions 'as His Majesty, under his Sign Manual, shall think fit to order and direct'. If no such direction was given, then the respective Commanders in Chief might make agreement in writing for the division. Ships and vessels taken in the course of the voyage to or from the land objective were not to be included; they were a naval prerogative.

It might be expected that even with the intervention of high authority established by statute in this way, disputes would be frequent. However, there is remarkably little in the Admiralty Reports to suggest such cases came frequently to court and in at least two instances – the Island of Gorée and the Ile de France (Mauritius) – the first settlement came within a reasonable space of time.[22]

One matter in the case of Mauritius dragged on and was concluded only in 1818. This was about head money in *The Bellone*.[23] The ship had been captured in Port Louis late in 1810 and the soldiers claimed a share. It was referred to the Court by the Treasury for legal decision. Scott said that informal arrangements reached in other cases were irrelevant: 'the Court is bound to confine its exposition within the very letter of the statute, if that letter speaks an intelligible language'. While accepting that *prize* money was covered in the 1805 Act, and an amending Act of 1815, Scott could find no corresponding provisions as to *head* money. He searched back through the Appeal cases of the eighteenth century and found consistent rulings that, as regarded head money, 'conjunct expeditions were entirely out of the statute'. He said he must apply the existing statutes strictly and ruled that the army was not entitled.

One thread will be seen running through all the cases mentioned above, and that is delay. Years could elapse before a decision was reached on what were often quite trivial sums. Compelling statistical evidence will be brought in Chapter 21 to show how joint-capture cases generated delays half as long again as single-ship captures.

It is not easy to unravel the motives of those who persisted in going to court in such circumstances. It could have been principle, and indeed many matters of principle were decided as has been shown. It was more likely to be money and the pressures captains felt to do the best they could for the finances of themselves and their companies. They might have been egged on by their agents in some cases, with inflated ideas of the amounts at stake. But the impression remains of otherwise reasonable men falling out on the 'dissension of a doit', and it can only be that some cases were brought owing to a sense of injustice that simply could not be satisfied except by going to law.

Naturally, there were many more sensible ways of going about questions of joint capture. Particularly on foreign stations, ships that frequently worked together could enter into profit-sharing agreements. In 1796 the Jamaica and Santo Domingo squadron under Rear Admiral William Parker agreed that 'all prizes and property taken . . . and adjudicated as prize to the Navy . . . shall be divided equally amongst such Captains as shall subscribe to this paper, giving leave also to the officers and company of the several ships to join in this agreement', and that liability should be shared if any property taken was found not to be lawful prize.[24] And in 1797 that colourful character Bartholomew James, then a commander in temporary command of the privateer *Fair Penitent* in the Western Mediterranean and Atlantic approaches, agreed to share with *Lively* and *Minerve*; by his account all three did well out of it.[25]

But plans for sharing could be frustrated. In December 1812 Captain Waldegrave of the *Volontaire*, in the Western Mediterranean, came to a provisional agreement with his fellow captains in the *Undaunted* and *Eclair* that they should share prize money while they were on the same, extended, patrol station. Waldegrave put the proposal to his officers and ship's company, but 'the sailors refused to have anything to do with the *Undaunted* or *Eclair* – so that what we take, except they should be in sight, is entirely our own'.[26] There would have been valid arguments on both sides in such a case; without a sharing agreement truly independent captures would be more easily settled, but anything marginal would lead to lengthy and costly dispute. The balance would depend on the way the arrangements for the patrol worked out. It was never put to the test, for there were no subsequent captures on that cruise.

In home waters, sharing was not easy. The throughput of ships on cruising stations was so great that though for a few weeks two or three ships might be working closely together, they would inevitably become separated and sharing arrangements would cause more problems than they would solve. The better course then was for a ship with a flimsy claim to share in a prize simply to keep quiet about it and hope that next time she would be the lucky one.

A final word should be reserved for the flag officers. Here there were two separate causes that could lead to dispute. The first, and simpler, was the question of ships operating directly under Admiralty orders. This did not often happen; it was reserved for vessels on secret or special service. In such circumstances no flag officer was entitled to any prizes the ship might pick up and the captain got a proportionately larger share. A leading case stemming from a series of captures by the *Unicorn* in 1796 was decided in August 1803.[27] Admiral Kingsmill claimed his eighth but since the ship was under Admiralty orders, the claim was denied.

Thomas, Lord Cochrane's exceptionally lucrative cruise in the *Pallas* in spring 1805 was, according to his account written nearly fifty years later, originally under Admiralty orders, but Admiral Young, the Commander in Chief Plymouth, 'wrote himself into them' in order to get half Cochrane's share.[28] It is impossible to test fully the veracity of this claim and the figure of a half squares with no known scale of distribution, but the fact that it was mentioned indicates the sensitivity of the issue.

The question of subordinate flag officers on a station was exhaustively dealt with in the various proclamations dealing with prize distribution. If there were two flag officers, the money was split 2:1 between the senior and junior; if three, the ratio was 2:1:1. Commodores ranked with junior flag officers for this purpose and so did the Captain of the Fleet, the senior captain in the Fleet for the time being. Thus, when John Scott, Nelson's Secretary, was appointed his prize agent in 1803, he set out the general rule that Nelson should receive one half of the 'flag eighth' (always called, in Scott's correspondence, 'flag eight') and Bickerton, the second in command, and the Captain of the Fleet the other half equally divided; but for a prize taken while Nelson was on passage out to the Mediterranean, Nelson was to have two-thirds and the Captain of the Fleet one-third.[29]

The other, more common, area of dispute between flag officers was: who was in charge at the time of capture? Where and when the capture took place were clearly the most important factors, but even if these were accurate there often remained aspects of doubt. The areas of command were not always carefully delineated, the dates of supersession of flag officers not always well defined, and if the capturing ship was joining or leaving a station there was always the question whether she had yet come under the orders of the flag officer to whose area she was going.

An even more fundamental question arose in 1801 when a squadron from the Channel Fleet under Rear Admiral Sir Robert Calder was ordered to the West Indies in pursuit of an enemy squadron.[30]. On arrival at Martinique, Calder wrote to Rear Admiral Duckworth, Commander in Chief Leeward Islands, whose force he joined temporarily on 1 April, that by rulings recently made in home waters Duckworth would be 'entitled to share in everything the squadron under my direction may take . . . and I am entitled to share in everything your squadron may take . . . you are my agent and I will be yours'. Duckworth opposed this as a matter of principle, asserting that Calder's squadron was not in fact under his orders – it was going on to Jamaica almost at once – and therefore sharing would be 'an improper precedent to the injury of the service'. Eventually the dispute, conducted in terms of increasingly chilly politeness, went for an opinion to Sir John Nicholl, the King's Advocate, who ruled that Calder had in fact become a member of Duckworth's squadron until he reached Jamaica and did not again become part of the Channel Fleet until he actually rejoined it.

Such questions could often be sorted out amicably. Nelson, with the advice no doubt of Scott, relinquished several doubtful claims in March 1804.[31] He had previously been a party in a celebrated case against St Vincent which was tried in the Court of King's Bench rather than that of Admiralty, judgment being given on 4 March 1801;[32] it revolved around the *Santa Brigida* (again) and the limits of the respective commands of St Vincent, Nelson and Keith at the time. A curious aspect of this case is that everyone concerned seems to have thought he won. But the admirals in general won too: part of the report of the judgment read, 'It was not necessary, nor had it ever been held, that the Admiral commanding on any station should with his own hand issue the order under which the prizes were taken; but it is sufficient if the orders were issued by any person under his controul or authority.' That must have comforted many flag officers and discomfited as many commanders of cruisers who thought they might by some means have escaped the clutches of the 'flag eight'.

NOTES

1. Sample from HCA 2 files in the PRO: see Appendix 1.
2. 45 Geo. III c.72 s.45.
3. *Supra*, p. 66.
4. David Howarth, *Trafalgar: the Nelson Touch* (Windrush, 1996), p. 146.
5. 2 C. Rob., p. 16 [1799].
6. 3 C. Rob., p. 52 [1800].
7. pp. 16, 176.
8. 6 C. Rob., p. 244 [1806].
9. Hugh Owen, 'The Naval Sons of William IV and Mrs Jordan', 83 The *Mariner's Mirror* (1997), p. 44.
10. 5 C. Rob., p. 268 [1804].
11. 6 C. Rob., p. 261 [1805].
12. 4 C. Rob., p. 318 [1803].
13. 45 Geo. III c. 72 ss.9–15.
14. V NC, p. 161.
15. 6 C. Rob., p. 213 [1805].
16. 3 C. Rob., p. 311 [1801].
17. 1 Dods., p. 346 [1813].
18. 1 Dods., p. 359 [1813].
19. Edw., p. 6 [1808]; HCA 2/350.
20. 2 Dods., p. 444 [1815].
21. 45 Geo. III c. 72 ss.3–4.
22. HCA 2/356 and 2/358.
23. 2 Dods., p. 343 [1814] .
24. NMM DUC/20/1/A.
25. John Knox Laughton and James Y.F. Sulivan (eds), *The Journal of Rear Admiral Bartholomew James, 1752–1828* (Navy Records Society, 1906), p. 343.
26. Letter from Purser Thomas Peckston to his wife, 27 November 1812, p. 9, RNM Ref 1997/65.

27. *The Orion*, 4 C. Rob., p. 362 [1803].

28. Thomas Cochrane, Earl of Dundonald, *Autobiography of a Seaman*, vol. I (Chatham edn, 1995), p. 178.

29. John Scott to Marsh and Creed, 5 October 1803.

30. NMM DUC/20.

31. John Scott to Cutforth, 16 March 1804.

32. V NC, p. 254.

CHAPTER EIGHT

Droits

It was all very well for Sir William Scott to make the legal point, in his letter to Nepean shortly after taking up office, that Droits were essentially the same as prize.[1] His jurisprudence was no doubt correct, but for once his sensitivity to human nature was lacking. For the word Droits, to naval officers familiar with prize law, was a death knell to hopes of high fortune.

In the normal prize situation the capture came under the terms of a Royal Proclamation; the Prize Act was thereby brought into effect; and the Crown's rights were in consequence signed away in favour of the captor. That was straightforward and what every captor hoped would apply. But there were two sets of circumstances where it did not, and both these were distinguished by the use of the word Droits. The terms used were Droits of Admiralty and Droits of the Crown, or *jure coronae*. It does not help researchers that they were frequently used almost interchangeably, even in Doctors' Commons correspondence. In this chapter an attempt will be made to differentiate them in a way that would, it is thought, have been approved by Scott and the senior legal authorities of the time.

The first, Droits of Admiralty, were of great antiquity. In medieval times the Crown's control over maritime affairs was far from absolute and the Lord High Admiral exercised a great measure of independent authority. In consequence the Crown granted away a proportion of prize to the Lord High Admiral to maintain the dignity and power of his office.[2] Under Charles II these Droits of Admiralty were refined by Order in Council. In the future they were to consist solely of the proceeds from enemy ships that, in wartime, had been forced in to British ports through stress of weather, or were wrecked on the coast, or had surrendered within a British port.[3] That was the basis of the law as it stood in 1798.

The Reports on this subject deal, as do all law reports, with the knottier cases. Before coming to them it is as well to point out that the vast majority of Droits of Admiralty matters were settled administratively. Gostling the Admiralty Procurator would write from Doctors' Commons to Nepean or his successors outlining the circumstances of a seizure that came within the Droits of Admiralty rules; typically such a seizure would be by a revenue cutter or harbour authority, though a King's ship would sometimes be involved. The Admiralty would then be invited to make a 'reward' to the seizors. A limited sample of the bills brought in for such cases, and corroborating evidence from the Doctors' Commons files, suggests that the standard reward was two-thirds of the net proceeds,[4] but it could be varied for the degree of merit shown in the capture.

Scott was therefore not called upon to rule too often on Droits of Admiralty which were actually contested in court. One such was *The Rebeckah*,[5] where the capture was made off the islet of St Marcou, then under British control; it lies to the east of the Cotentin Peninsula, in the Baie de la Seine, and forces operating from there were well placed to intercept traffic into and out of both Le Havre and Cherbourg. Scott reviewed the 1665 Order in Council, acknowledging that the Lord High Admiral had the benefit of all captures in 'ports, creeks and roads'. 'But,' he went on, 'I can by no means agree . . . that wherever a ship can find anchorage ground, there is a road or roadstead . . .'. Had St Marcou a road? He considered it rather 'a mere naval station, without inhabitants and without government . . . such a place, so selected and so employed, is hardly to be considered as anything else than as a part or appendage of the naval force'. An interesting sidelight is that the capturing ships, *Arethusa*, *Badger* and *Sandfly*, persisted in the case in spite of advice from Nepean[6] not to pursue the matter. The cargo had perished anyway, but they clearly thought the principle, and the value of the ship herself, worth it.

In somewhat similar circumstances was the *Graff Bernstorff* detained by the *Seine* in St Helen's Roads off the Isle of Wight.[7] In this case,[8] because the vessel had already anchored in a recognized anchorage, the Droit of Admiralty was upheld. The main issue of the case was not droits at all, but the nationality of the owner: another case of a Dutchman masquerading as a Dane, and indeed another in which the ubiquitous Inglehart was involved.

Closely allied to Droits of Admiralty was the legal device of Embargo, the impounding of vessels of a certain nationality either in order to exert pressure short of war on their flag state, or in preparation for war against that state. It was frequently resorted to in the war against Napoleonic France, mainly in retaliation against neutral states which, under the influence of the Emperor, had allegedly discriminated against British trade. Thus an embargo was declared on Prussian ships on 5 April 1806[9] as a reprisal for the exclusion of British ships from Prussian ports and for Prussian seizure of part of Hanover; and on Russian ships on 9 December 1807[10] as a result of the Treaty of Tilsit and Russia's espousal (never more than half-hearted, as it turned out) of the Continental System.

In the second case the embargo was followed by general reprisals against Russian vessels, except those licensed,[11] and the Attorney General was instructed to give jurisdiction to the High Court of Admiralty to 'take cognisance of, and judicially proceed upon, all and all manner of captures . . . according to the course of Admiralty and the law of nations'. Thus in this case, ships detained at sea would become prize in the normal way while ships detained in harbour would be Droits of Admiralty.

But general reprisals did not always follow embargo. Sometimes an embargo would last for years, ending in release of the ships involved because Britain's dispute with their flag state had been resolved without recourse to war. While they remained in limbo in this way, arrangements for their custody and safe keeping in detention rested with the Admiralty Marshal.

This office was held throughout the 1800s by John Crickitt, who emerges from the files as a sad, overworked individual. In January 1801 he wrote 'In obedience to their Lordships' orders I have laid embargoes on a great number of Danish and Swedish ships' (as a result of the Armed Neutrality of 1800). What, he asked, was to be done with their crews? There were 191 ships all told, scattered through the ports of the kingdom.[12] When Russian ships were added later, the number grew to over 300. Crickitt estimated that the expenses of detention were £30–40 per ship. Nepean, the Secretary of the Admiralty, for once seemed at a loss; he asked Gostling, the Admiralty's man at Doctors' Commons, for precedents. Gostling replied that embargo was usually followed by war and condemnation, so that expenses could be defrayed from the proceeds. In this case, however, the ships had been released by the lifting of the embargo without formal war and meeting expenses was 'a matter for his Majesty's Government'.

There matters seem to have hung fire, for in 1805 Crickitt reported his expenses connected with the 1801 embargo.[13] His covering letter said 'I kept 532 ships, with their cargoes and upwards of 4,000 persons on board, in secure custody . . .'. The average charge of £25 per ship covered taking inventory, pilotage, docking, housing sails, pumping out, provision of fresh water and preparing release documents. Crickitt's previous estimate had been a trifle high, but even so his total account was £5,615 for ships detained in London, £10,019 for outports.

Crickitt's letters were written in a monotone of complaint that must have grated with the authorities, and it did not soften in his correspondence about the Prussian embargo of 1806.[14] But when one considers that in addition to his embargo duties he had the task of organizing the escort of prisoners and searches for deserters and had constantly to chase the Board of Admiralty for his travelling expenses too, sympathy can only be with him. His work must have done a great deal to swell the funds accruing from Droits of Admiralty. His death was reported in the *Naval Chronicle* in 1811;[15] eventually his widow received the arrears due to him, amounting to £313 14s 10d.[16]

The other kind of Droit was what Scott had referred to as a Droit *jure coronae*. It was a residual right. Any seized asset which had not been signed away by Act of Parliament, brought into force by proclamation, remained with the Crown. Thus captures made before a proclamation of reprisals or declaration of war had come into force would remain Droits of the Crown; and some other captures irregularly made would suffer a similar fate. Irregular captures were not necessarily unlawful; the court could condemn them if enemy character was established. But the proceeds would accrue to the Crown and any reward to the captors was in the Crown's gift.

Bartholomew James, when war broke out in 1793, was in the West Indies as an unemployed Lieutenant. He commissioned the 40-ton shallop *Marlborough* (otherwise known as *Little Maria*) as a privateer on 1 April and was out chasing prizes almost at once.[17] On 8 April he took the *Bien Aimé* and on the 11th the *Bien Heureuse*, both were brought in to Kingston, Jamaica on 14 April. James appointed agents and bought in his crew's shares for $40 a man, but it turned out that no official letter of marque had been issued so the prizes were Droits of the Crown (James uses the word 'admiralty' which surely cannot be correct in this case). This led to money troubles for James which persisted for four years, with at least two spells in debtors' prison.

The most celebrated case of Droits *jure coronae* occurred in 1804. Britain was at war only with France and Holland, but Spain was closely involved with France under the curious régime of the Minister Godoy, the so-called Prince of the Peace. In consequence a close watch was being kept on Ferrol on the Atlantic coast where some seven French ships of force, as well as some Spanish, were refitting. Alexander Cochrane, who had been promoted Rear Admiral of the Blue in April 1804, hoisted his flag in *Northumberland* on 9 May[18] and took over the watch on Ferrol with a sizeable force, including several line of battle ships.

Cochrane used a variety of means to gather intelligence on Spanish (and French) preparations and intentions. Coasting and fishing vessels were frequently boarded and questioned and clandestine contacts on shore were used. Cochrane also had an open correspondence with Texada, the Captain-General of Galicia and senior Spanish military authority in the Ferrol area.

Cochrane's reports back to the Admiralty during the period up to the beginning of October[19] show increasing suspicion of the situation and of Spanish intentions. On 12 July he said French ships had been given priority in docking; and on 19 July he complained to Texada of French army activities in northern Spain, alleging a breach of neutrality. On 3 September he reported 'more than usual exertions' being made to complete French ships for sea, while the Spanish had two seventy-fours ready and two more in an advanced state of preparation. His alarm was expressed directly to Texada on 14 September; he was 'much astonished' that the Spaniards had given instructions to increase their marine establishment and warned that if French or Dutch ships sailed from Ferrol he would attack them. A reassuring letter was received from Texada next day, and on 25 September Cochrane reported the Spanish ships withdrawn to the arsenal; but in the interim he had expressed to Melville, the First Lord of the Admiralty, his deep misgivings and suspicions.

The Admiralty acted very promptly. They formed a squadron of four ships – *Indefatigable, Medusa, Amphion* and *Lively*, of between thirty-two and forty-four guns – under the command of Captain Graham Moore, to intercept a group of four Spanish frigates known to be on their way back to Spain from Monte Video with a very large quantity of treasure. The encounter took place on 5 October off Cádiz, well outside Cochrane's area of operation.[20]

It began with the British ships ranging themselves close to the Spanish squadron, which consisted of the *Fama, Medea, Mercedes* and *Clara*, of thirty-four to forty guns. This close equivalence of force, on paper at any rate, had a critical effect on what followed. For when the British sent an officer on board *Medea*, the flagship of the Spanish admiral, inviting him to submit in order to avoid unnecessary bloodshed, Admiral Bustamente felt that Spanish honour could not brook surrender at such apparently equal odds. Battle was therefore joined, with results that were predictable, for the Spanish ships were scarcely prepared after their Atlantic voyage for action of this kind, while the British were in full fighting trim. Three of the Spanish ships were captured; the fourth, *Mercedes*, blew up with great loss of life, only 40 of her crew of 280 being saved.[21]

The action undoubtedly hastened the entry of Spain into the war, though the consensus of history is that that would almost certainly have happened eventually. By mid-November Cochrane was reporting extensive Spanish war preparations[22] including orders to seize British vessels in Spanish ports. Spain declared war on 12 December[23] and the British declaration of war and general reprisals followed on 11 January 1805.[24]

There is evidence of much British public unease at this action, which had taken place in advance of any declaration of war or reprisal. Even near-contemporary historians such as James say such things as 'Many persons, who concurred in the expediency, doubted the right, of detaining these ships; and many, again, to whom the legality of the act appeared clear, were of opinion that a more formidable force should have been sent to execute the service.'[25] The *London Gazette* of 26 January sought to justify the action by stating that the arrival of treasure in Spanish ports was a frequent precursor of war, and the action was therefore a justified precaution resting 'upon every foundation of the laws of nature and of nations'. Lord Hawkesbury said in the House that the action was not the cause of the outbreak of war, but Charles James Fox in the Commons took the opposite view.[26]

Alexander Cochrane was not immune from criticism. The *Naval Chronicle* diarist noted that allegations had been made against him that 'he was desirous of involving his country in a war with Spain, from the sordid motive of obtaining prize money . . . greater crimes could not be imputed than these'.[27] The diarist's defence of Cochrane was robust, and certainly there is little in the despatches from the watching force off Ferrol to indicate anything other than a very conscientious commander desperately anxious to report any sign of change in the preparation of a potential enemy. The Cochranes were known, of course, to be very interested in prize money – it is not for nothing that a later chapter in this book is devoted to their relationship with the prize courts – and that no doubt sharpened the allegations, but in this case base motives cannot be attributed.

In any case, there was no prize money as such. The ships and the treasure – amounting to a million sterling – were a Droit of the Crown, since they had been taken before the issue of letters of reprisal or declaration of war. A grant was made to the captors which according to one account[28] amounted to a quarter of a million – rather less than the general run of such 'rewards'. That may have been due to financial stringency: Britain was embarking on a war that was bound to be long and costly. It may also have had something to do with the controversy surrounding the action. The only reference to the affair in the Doctors' Commons file is a scrap of paper from George Gostling dated 26 May 1805, saying 'The Spanish frigates detained before the order for Reprisals have been condemned to the Crown.'[29] There is a marginal note from Marsden, then Secretary of the Admiralty, 'Appropriate them to the service of the Royal Navy.'

One can only speculate how many of the crews, or captains for that matter, of the British ships involved realized that they would not be entitled to the full proceeds of the action. For many it would have been of little concern: a treasure ship was a treasure ship, and even if full value was not given the pay-off would not be negligible, as it so often was for lesser prizes. The captains might have been much more sensitive to the difference between a quarter of the proceeds and the full net value, but at that stage of the war the implications of Spanish neutrality could well not have sunk in for all of them.[30]

On one occasion the full value of such a capture was allowed to the captors. This was the celebrated action of the *Seahorse* frigate against a Turkish fifty-two-gun ship, the *Badere Zaffer*, in July 1808.[31] It was an exceptionally bloody encounter. On 7 December 1808 an Order in Council was issued[32] acknowledging that an Order of 16 May 1807 had decreed the detention of Ottoman vessels but, up to the time of the action, no commission had been issued authorizing the High Court of Admiralty to adjudge and condemn Ottoman ships. The Court was therefore directed to take cognizance and condemn, 'on proof that the [*Badere Zaffer*] was a ship of war belonging to and bearing the flag of the Ottoman Empire' and that the *Seahorse* was to receive the full value of the prize 'as a reward of their distinguished gallantry'. It may have been necessary to issue a separate Order to meet the unusual legal circumstances, but its existence and the specific direction on the scale of reward suggest this was a most unusual, if not unique, case.

At about this time, there was a more sophisticated understanding of the issues involved in Crown Droits. In 1808 an Open Letter, addressed to Sir John Nicholl the King's Advocate at Doctors' Commons, appeared in the *Naval Chronicle*.[33] It was signed 'A.B.' and the identity of the author is unknown; attribution to Alexander Cochrane himself may well be too fanciful, for he was abroad at the time, but the sentiments are in line with his.

The letter began by noting that Nicholl had opposed reimbursement to captors for the expenses of Danish ships and cargoes condemned to the Crown on the ground that His Majesty's Ships had acted 'under the influence of speculation not sanctioned by government'. A.B. denied that the captures were speculative and stated that 'The learned judge [Scott] rejected your notion of speculation, and observed, that if government profited by the capture, it was just to exonerate the captors from all expenses.' He 'warned' Nicholl of the 'consequences of his disposition' towards the captors.

A.B. went on to make a more general point. The old style of trade warfare had been that no captures were made before the declaration of hostilities. Now, however, the Crown could 'derive to itself an immense profit from captures effected prior to a declaration'. The effects might be hidden: '. . . it is somewhat difficult to make the public conceive what a declaration to the Crown means', but 'the interests of the navy are very materially injured by this proceeding. By such a *manoeuvre*, Ministers deprive the navy of their rights.'

The writer had moved on from the point about expenses to the more general question of proceeds. But on both issues, he was clear that extensive blame rested with the King's Advocate: 'sole management of the causes, both on behalf of the Crown and of the officers of the navy, though their interests are in these instances opposed to each other, is of necessity under the sole management of one individual, the King's Proctor' – who in turn came under Nicholl. In consequence, argued A.B., a petition by naval officers was unlikely to get an unbiased hearing, since the King's Advocate and Proctor would be advising government on it. He asked Nicholl to act 'with consistency and decency, by declining to offer any further opinion on the subject'.

Nicholl made no reply in the pages of the *Chronicle* and it is doubtful if one was expected. There is no doubt that the Court as a whole was worried about speculative capture, which was something which if condoned could not only reward opportunists unjustly, but cause incidents which could most seriously affect relations with neutrals at sensitive times – and most times were sensitive. Scott had personally intervened on the subject some years before; in 1804, rebutting a complaint by Captain Rutherford, he inveighed against 'experimental captures' which Rutherford had made 'with the expectation of their proving beneficial to him. It has turned out upon fair examination, that they cannot be made beneficial to him without a violation of that justice which this country owes to the subjects of other states'.[34] But on that occasion, he had recommended some repayment of Rutherford's expenses.

So Nicholl had plenty of backing in making a stand against an abrogation of Droits of the Crown to favour opportunist capture. It was up to the Crown to decide on any action in anticipation of war and run the attendant risks, and therefore the main beneficiary from that action should be the Crown itself. On the expenses of proceedings, however, he was on less firm ground. It is not certain how frequently he did oppose the granting of costs from public funds to captors; in spite of A.B.'s strictures he might have done so only in what he believed were flagrant cases. For there were, in general use, ways of reimbursing the expenses of captains of capturing vessels who had brought in prizes in good faith.

A common one, which may seem curious to those used to modern practice, was for the claimant to pay the costs of the captor even if the vessel and cargo were restored. Scott in *The Hoffnung*[35] represented this as the penalty for imprudent action in an area of 'notorious' blockade, even though in this case the blockaders had been driven off by force and the blockade thereby rendered ineffective and invalid. There were also many instances where some parts of the prize property were restored while others were condemned and provided ample cover for the costs.

However, there was another source and it was a logical one. The Droits of Admiralty fund (which covered Droits of the Crown as well) was administered by Claud de Crespigny, a member of Doctors' Commons considerably senior to anyone else mentioned in this book; he had joined the College in 1763 at the age of thirty.[36] In May 1808 he provided to the House of Commons an account of Dutch, Prussian and Spanish condemnations to his fund totalling three and a half million pounds.[37] Of these about three quarters had gone to the Crown and the remainder to the captors. But it became clear that a proportion of the Crown's moneys had gone to reimburse the costs of captors whose prizes had been restored.

The practice came to public notice in the House of Commons in January 1812.[38] Henry Brougham, a liberal lawyer and notable opponent of the Orders in Council, introduced a motion to subject the Droits fund to parliamentary control. He estimated that the Fund might now amount to £8 million and, though not disputing that 'all prize vested in the Crown', questioned how Droits were appropriated. They 'never went into the exchequer'; if they were not controlled by Parliament, the Crown would have an incentive to make a 'war of plunder'. He cited the case of the Spanish treasure frigates in 1804.

He went on to allege that the Fund had been used to supplement the Civil List and, more relevant to this study, to complain that it was also drawn upon to pay the legal costs and damages of captors whose prizes had been restored. 'If officers who have detained vessels improperly should have such heavy costs awarded against them by the Courts of Admiralty as almost to ruin them, is it fit they should be remunerated in any other manner than by Parliament?'

The proposal was not well received except by those of Brougham's persuasion. Several members argued that captors' confidence could not be undermined by the threat of ruinous costs whose only recompense lay in the gift of Parliament; they would have more trust in their own administrative authority, the Admiralty. The government, in the person of the Chancellor of the Exchequer, argued that all was governed by Proclamations acknowledged by Parliament, which thus was fully informed as to the basis of prize-taking and of hostilities. The motion was negatived.

The relief of George Rose, Treasurer of the Navy, can be imagined. He had been in control for some years of what in its most unkind interpretation was a slush fund; a more just way of putting it is that it was a means of adjusting anomalies in a complex and potentially unfair set of circumstances, where competent officers were faced with difficult decisions that had consequences affecting not only themselves, their crews and their families, but the balance of alliances and allegiances that governed the progress of the war. The use of Droits of Admiralty and of the Crown to defray the legal costs of those who had brought in prizes *bona fide* was a sensible measure, and it is understandable that the Treasurer of the Navy was anxious to keep control in his hands.

But it was Brougham who had the last laugh. Three years after the war ended, the persistence of Parliament drew from the government a complete summary statement of the income and disposal of the Droits Fund for the years 1793–1815.[39] Total receipts, including interest and investment, amounted to £5,692,960 0s 4d. Of this the captors had been paid £2,914,074 8s 0d – about 51 per cent. Administrative and legal costs had amounted to another £537,202, and claimants had been paid £272,011 6s 5d. Some of these amounts are likely to have included meeting the costs of unsuccessful captors in non-droits cases, as indicated above, but it is not clear what the proportion was; and the suggestion of an official financial cushion is enhanced by otherwise unexplained items of £150,000 to the Treasurer of the Navy and £100,000 to the Treasurer of the Ordnance.

But the most telling outputs of the Droits Fund, and those with which most political play could be made, were £1,239,000 to the Civil List; £209,848 15s 9d to 'the Royal Family', which presumably meant members outside the Civil List; £14,579 2s 4d to 'Visits of Foreign Princes'; and no less than £58,360 10s 0d to the Prince Regent's pet project, the Brighton Pavilion. This added up to over 26 per cent of the total, and naval officers and men in enforced and impoverished retirement in 1818 could be forgiven more than a little bitterness. In a later time, those looking at the fancies of the Brighton Pavilion may speculate on which were financed by the hard-driving, eager, risky and sometimes disappointed aspirations and efforts of their maritime forebears.

NOTES

1.   ADM 1/3894; Chapter 2, p. 15.
2.   C. John Colombos, *International Law of the Sea*, 6th edn (Longmans Green, 1967), p. 814.
3.   Lt-Cdr Peter Kemp, *Prize Money* (Gale and Polden, 1946), p. 12.
4.   HCA 2/358, ADM 1/3898.
5.   1 C. Rob., p. 227 [1799].
6.   ADM 1/3894.
7.   ADM 1/3894, 28 February 1799.
8.   3 C. Rob., p. 109 [1800].
9.   *Notifications, Orders and Instructions relating to Prize Subjects during the Present War* (Strahan, for Butterworth and White, 1810), p. 16; *London Gazette* (1806), p. 419.
10.   *Notifications*, p. 75.
11.   Ibid., p. 78.
12.   ADM 1/3895.
13.   ADM 1/3897.
14.   ADM 1/3898, letters of 11 and 17 April 1806.
15.   XXVI NC, p. 264.
16.   ADM 1/3900, Scott to Croker, 12 March 1812.
17.   John Knox Laughton and James Y.F. Sulivan (eds), *The Journal of Rear Admiral Bartholomew James 1752–1828* (Navy Records Society, 1906), p. 212.
18.   ADM 1/126.
19.   Ibid.
20.   William James, *The Naval History of Great Britain*, vol. III (Bentley, 1847), p. 281.

21.   Ibid., p. 282.

22.   ADM 1/126, despatches of 13, 25, 29 and 30 November 1804.

23.   James, *The Naval History of Great Britain*, vol. III, p. 283.

24.   XIII NC, p. 70.

25.   James, *The Naval History of Great Britain*, vol. III, p. 283.

26.   XIII NC, pp. 149–50.

27.   Ibid., p. 134.

28.   James Henderson, *The Frigates* (Adlard Coles, 1970), p. 124.

29.   ADM 1/3897.

30.   Patrick O'Brian in *HMS Surprise* (Fontana edn, 1976), pp. 5–11, gives a fictional account of a discussion in the Admiralty on this case, which, like all this author's work, is based on historical study and shows deep understanding of the factors that may have governed Their Lordships' decision.

31.   XX NC, p. 330.

32.   *Notifications*, p. 109.

33.   XIX NC, p. 390.

34.   ADM 1/3896, 10 July 1804.

35.   6 C. Rob., p. 112 [1805].

36.   G.D. Squibb, *Doctors' Commons: A History of the College of Advocates and Doctors of Law* (Clarendon Press, 1977), p. 193.

37.   XIX NC, p. 412.

38.   XXVII NC, p. 164.

39.   HCA 30/161.

CHAPTER NINE

Vice Admiralty

Given the slow speed of communications in the late eighteenth and early nineteenth centuries and the relative rapidity of events, no single court could be expected to deal efficiently with prize matters worldwide. In consequence, local or Vice Admiralty courts were set up where needed.

They had already been a feature of the system for a century and a half. The first mention of such a court outside the British Isles occurs in 1630[1] in the Charter of the Company of the Isle of Providence off the Mosquito Coast; the wars of the middle of the seventeenth century accelerated development and a document of 1662 makes it clear that a court in Jamaica was well established at this time.[2] By 1793 the system was flexible enough to be responsive to the changing patterns of war, but major modifications such as the setting up of new courts were constitutionally controlled from London. Authorization could come only from the King in Council, an enabling Act sometimes being used to ensure that an Order in Council establishing a new court could be issued speedily.[3]

This did not stop British authorities abroad seeking to set up Courts of Vice Admiralty when and where they thought the situation demanded, nor arrogating to themselves in other courts a jurisdiction over prize matters which they did not properly have. In 1794 General Grey and Admiral Jervis set up an unauthorized prize court in the Leeward Islands to adjudicate their captures there,[4] and it was one of the factors that lost them favour at home when the extent of the plunder, and the damage done to relations with the United States of America, was realized. The Law Officers of the Crown, no doubt with the advice of Scott who was then King's Advocate, declared the Court's condemnations null and void.[5]

One of the first squabbles with which Scott as Admiralty Court Judge had to deal in 1798 was an attempt by Jonah Barrington of the High Court of Admiralty in Ireland (which was an instance court, empowered to try only administrative and commercial cases) to exercise Droits of Admiralty in the case of Dutch Indiamen, and neutral vessels carrying Dutch goods, driven into the River Shannon in 1795–7.[6] Barrington argued that 'a very serious injury arises both to neutral nations and to His Majesty's Kingdom of Ireland by the restraint of a naval-military jurisdiction in that country'. But Scott rebutted the argument: Barrington had been granted no jurisdiction in prize and therefore could determine no question of Droits either.

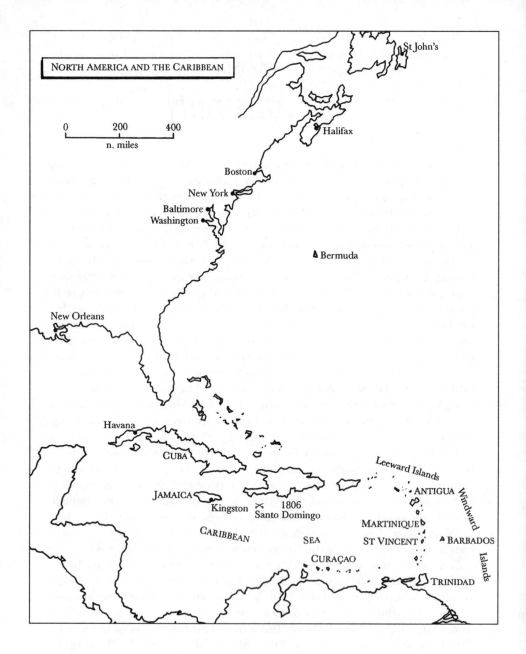

He adopted a similarly purist line throughout his tenure, though it was often severely tested and he sometimes had to give ground. During the River Plate operations in Spanish South America in 1806, for example, Sir Home Popham had set up a 'Prize Commission' without authority and in *The Rolla*[7] Scott implicitly condoned this as he explicitly condoned the blockade declared by Popham. And in July 1810, after a correspondence notable for polite but pained letters on either side, he eased the way for the permanent establishment of a court in Demerara set up without authorization by Governor Bentinck: 'a natural mistake', wrote Scott, but authority could only come from the King in Council; 'It is highly proper that the thing should be done, but it must be done in a proper manner.'[8]

The structure of the Vice Admiralty Courts mirrored that of the High Court of Admiralty at home. Each had a judge; some were men of great experience, others much less so. Sewell in Malta was actually a long-standing member of Doctors' Commons. That was rare; the qualifications of locals, or those prepared to go out and serve locally, were often much shakier. In September 1805, Scott wrote to Marsden the Secretary of the Admiralty about the Vice Admiralty Court at St Vincent: 'it is certainly desirable that the offices of Judge of the Court of Common Law and of the Judge of the Vice Admiralty Court be kept distinct . . . yet highly improbable that a person could be found upon the Island more respectably qualified than Mr Otley . . .'[9] – so Mr Otley got the job, at a salary of £2,000 a year with other 'Profits and Emoluments' limited by statute to the same figure.[10] Mr Otley would have had to render each year to the Commissioners of the Navy an account of those profits and to carry over any surplus to the succeeding year.[11]

Other court officials included a Registrar who kept the books and regulated court proceedings, a Marshal who handled prize goods and duties, and Proctors who brought cases on behalf of the Crown and the captors. Quite often these offices were held by local people of some standing and executed by deputy. This might be good or bad news for the conduct of the courts; sometimes the deputies were much more expert than their principals could possibly have been, but there was always a danger that they might be inefficient or corrupt. Advocates of varying quality would be available to represent claimants and many courts had up to half a dozen interpreters on the strength to deal with language problems. Finally, wherever there were prizes there would be agents: some would be purely local, but the larger English firms had representatives abroad.

The system was perceived as far from perfect. Collingwood wrote to Sir Hew Dalrymple in 1808: 'The Admiralty Court in Gibraltar appears to me to be very oddly constituted, and wants regulation'; his particular complaint was that unqualified people were making legal judgments.[12] There is evidence that faced with an influx of cases at the start of the American War in 1812, the courts at Bermuda and Halifax took a considerable time to establish the right procedures or even make the appropriate judgments; for example, the Bermuda court had to reverse its own decision on ships taken before the declaration of war and condemn them as Droits of the Crown when they had already been condemned to the captors.[13] The Vice Admiralty Court at Malta was the one that achieved most notoriety of all, so much so that it will occupy much of the next chapter in this book.[14]

This variability in the quality of the courts' work is apparent from those appeal papers which survive. Appeals against Vice Admiralty Court judgments were somewhat more numerous than those against the High Court of Admiralty[15] and a higher proportion of Vice Admiralty decisions were probably reversed by the Lords Commissioners of Appeal in Prize Causes. But it was inexperience rather than slackness or negligence that was the prime cause of error. Interrogatories were conscientiously taken and legal instruments fully drafted. Indeed, the fulsome style of many of these, compared with the streamlined work of the London Court, is one of the principal indicators of the outliers' inexperience.

The reaction of naval people to this perceived inefficiency and malpractice was predictable. They sought to circumvent the system whenever they thought it safe to do so. In January 1800 William Henry Dillon was a lieutenant in the *Crescent*:

> we took a Spanish schooner . . . the *Meleager* was with us . . . our chiefs thought it would be worthwhile to send a flag of truce in to Carthagena to the owners of the vessel we had taken, and allow any one of them to come to us to repurchase his own vessel. By this means we should not have to send her to Jamaica, and all the expenses of agency, Admiralty Courts, etc. would be avoided. This was not a very correct proceeding, but had been frequently practised by our own cruiser, and the Captain of the *Meleager*, who had been some time on the station, advised the measure.[16]

Dillon was right that the procedure was 'not very correct'. In fact it was ransom pure and simple and specifically prohibited by all the Prize Acts.[17] But there is little doubt that he was correct in saying the practice was common, and that did not apply only to the West Indies. In May 1798 no less a person than Captain James Saumarez sought to solve the problem of a Spanish brig laden with corn, captured in the Mediterranean, in the same way: 'It was in contemplation to set fire to her; but we, however, finally determined to send the people on shore, and, if they bring off the value of the corn, we shall restore her to them.' Two days later, 'The Spaniard not having come off as expected, the Admiral [Nelson] determined on sending the prize to Gibraltar.' A second prize, taken a week later, really was ransomed; this was a Spanish ship coming from Genoa, 'not very valuable'. 'Our prize requiring more men than I can conveniently spare to navigate her, I have consented to her being ransomed for 10,000 dollars, although, I dare say, worth more than 5 times that sum.'[18]

These were isolated cases. More serious was the allegation of what amounted to a protection racket in the Northern Adriatic between 1805 and 1809. Surgeon Mant, late of the *Unité*, asserted that Captain Patrick Campbell and his squadron had detained some twenty-five ships during that period and Campbell had directed that Mant, who spoke Italian, should 'compromise' with the merchants of Trieste to arrange terms for their release. The shareout was arranged by Campbell 'without adjudication or any legal investigation into the merits'. Campbell had also issued licences and accepted presents from Trieste merchants.

Mant claimed he had attempted to expose the practice to Collingwood when the latter was Commander in Chief, but had been prevented from doing so by circumstances. He had subsequently, he said, been victimized by Campbell, being put ashore on grounds of incompetence, in particular for not conducting a medical examination of the Women of the Town as instructed by his captain.

All this was sent to Pellew when he was Commander in Chief in the Mediterranean years later, in 1812 in fact, with Admiralty instructions to carry out an investigation.[19] No record of the result has been found by the author, but it is likely it was inconclusive; Patrick Campbell was made a Companion of the Bath in 1815 and died a Knight and a Vice Admiral of the Blue in 1841.[20]

There would have been some sympathy in the Navy for Campbell's motives if not for his methods. A letter of April 1812 from Thomas Cochrane to Croker, the Secretary of the Admiralty, though confused in its wording, implies as much: Cochrane was 'not surprised' if Campbell had acted '*in terrorem* to neutrals to induce them to pay, rather than carry on litigation *there*' (i.e., in the Vice Admiralty Court in Malta).[21]

Systematic practices of the kind alleged against Campbell were rare, but isolated instances of ransom or unauthorized sale continued to occur right up to the end of the war. In February 1813 Dillon, now in command of the *Leopard*, brought out two Spanish settees from Vinaroz: 'Weighing in my mind what to do with the Prizes – which were not of any value – I supposed that the circumstances alone of their having been cut out was sufficient proof of their being enemy property . . . I therefore thought I should be justified in selling them to the highest bidder when opportunity offered'.[22]

It is impossible at this stretch of time, and with incomplete documentation from foreign stations even for the lawfully brought in and tried prizes, to say how widespread the irregularities were and what proportion of the captures were sold rather than brought in. There were many factors which would have encouraged a more free-and-easy style on the foreign stations than in home waters.

Distance was one. It could be a long way to the nearest British-controlled port and if a prize was not kept with the capturing vessel a competent prize master had to be found, with sufficient hands to work the prize and control the prisoners, to navigate her there. If a neutral or even enemy port was to hand, with authorities who would be glad to have their ship back, the temptations to take a short cut were great.

Agents were another. A captain familiar with the station would no doubt have built up a network of persons willing to act; Henry Digby in the *Aurora*, capturing some fifty vessels in 1797–8, employed at least six different agents and that in a relatively small range between Lisbon and England.[23] But a captain new to a station might have had little time to establish such links.

These two areas of uncertainty, distance and the availability of agents, were sharply illustrated in a set of circumstances surrounding the capture of the *Admiral Drury* by the *Doris* in Macao in September 1813. Captain O'Brien of the *Doris* gave detailed instructions to Midshipman Edward Wallis Ward, the prize master:

> with nine men proceed to Penang, where if there is a Vice Court of Admiralty you will give the vessel with her papers to Messrs Forbes and Brown as agents for the *Doris*, requiring them to go through all necessary forms for her being speedily brought to Tryal in the said Court . . . but if there be no such Court of Admiralty at Penang you will then proceed with her to Point de Galle [some 2,400 miles] . . . if . . . there is an Admiralty Court at Colombo, . . . having found out the most respectable merchants willing to act as agents for the *Doris* . . . conduct the bringing to adjudication this said *Admiral Drury*.

If there was no Vice Admiralty Court at Colombo, Ward was to proceed to Bombay, another 1,900 miles. Calcutta, on the other side of the sub-continent, was an alternative but not favoured because of prevailing winds.[24]

The case was a long and very complicated one. The owners claimed the *Admiral Drury* was British; though the master was born in Rhode Island, he claimed British citizenship. They alleged that dollars had been removed by the crew of the *Doris*, and all sorts of malpractice against Midshipman Ward. The Court at Bombay by interlocutory decree pronounced the ship 'to have belonged as claimed, but declared there was just cause of seizure, and decreed the same to be restored to the claimant for the use of the owners and proprietors thereof on payment of costs incurred on the part of the captors'. Seeing that these stemmed from a voyage of a good 5,000 miles, they may well have been extensive.

The reputation of some Vice Admiralty Courts was a deterrent to correct practice. The special case of the Malta court will be dealt with in more detail in the next chapter, but it is worth noting that many of the irregularities mentioned above had to do with the Mediterranean. It was not the only suspect area, however. Right at the end of the war, in December 1814, Byam, the Judge at the Vice Admiralty Court in Antigua, complained that Admiral Durham, the Commander in Chief on the Leeward Islands station, had instructed his captains not to send in prizes to the Antigua court for adjudication on account of the excessive fees charged there.[25]

This caused an unholy row that rumbled on in London and on the station for months. Durham's letter, on file for January 1815, explained his action: 'I took upon myself, as the guardian of the sailors in the Squadron under my command, not to suffer them to be any longer wronged . . .'. Croker, the Secretary of the Admiralty, had minuted on the original complaint that there could be no law to prevent Durham's action and now found a further reason for ducking out: 'Their Lordships do not think it necessary to interfere further in this matter as all Prize Commissions in Vice Admiralty Courts have ceased with the War.'[26] This was something of a short cut in itself, as residual jurisdiction over cases in hand must have remained.

In any case, it was not the end of the affair. Scott, always reluctant to be drawn away from his judicial work and into the toils of administration, finally pronounced in a letter to Croker on 16 May 1815. He accepted that the charges in the case first cited by Durham, that of the *Decatur* captured by the *Barbadoes*, did 'seem to be enormous'. But he pointed out that they were not court fees, but fees charged by advocates and agents. He deplored the practice of charging high fees for successful cases and nothing for unsuccessful ones: it was 'extremely incorrect'. (This early example of opposition to contingency fees has been echoed by many British judges to this day.) If, Scott went on, Admiral Durham had had objection to the fees of the advocate and proctor, both of whom were Crown employees, he could have refused payment to the advocate and represented excessive proctor's fees to Their Lordships. He should not have taken jurisdiction into his own hands.

It is unlikely that Durham got more than the lightest rap on the knuckles over this business. Indeed, in November 1815 he made a further complaint against a Vice Admiralty Court, this time at Tortola; again it had to do with excessive fees and this time he was on firmer ground, for non-conformity with the established scale of fees was admitted.

In fact, there had been much agonizing over the fees of Vice Admiralty Courts in Doctors' Commons since 1811. Up to that time there was no standard scale of fees, though legislation existed allowing the government to regulate them.[27] Parliament had however expressed some alarm at the allegations of excessive fees in some of the courts and Scott set up a Commission to look into them. He had already expressed his own concern about at least one Vice Admiralty Court, that in Newfoundland, in the matter of the capture of the *Belisarius* by the

Rattler: the charges were 'excessive and disproportionate in the extreme to charges on the like account made in the High Court of Admiralty'.[28]

The Commission was a very high-level body; the names are a roll-call of the dignitaries of Doctors' Commons, saving only Scott himself: Robinson, Arnold, Swabey, Adams, Farquhar, Bush and Bishop. Its first report on 27 February 1812 gave specimen tables for Malta, Antigua and Ceylon[29] and these were followed up in August 1812, February and April 1813 with scales for all the other courts. More detail on the financial aspects will be found in Chapter 16. Only one protest from the courts appears to have been made: in January 1814 Croke, the judge at Halifax, claimed that his Court could not do its job properly on the new scale. But his protest was rejected by the Commission on 17 May: 'We do not see reason to recommend any alteration in the general scale of the table'.[30]

A final incentive for capturing vessels to break the rules was the desire to avoid bureaucracy and delay. An acute example arose in the Mediterranean in December 1805. Captain William Hoste of the *Eurydice* complained of oppressive conduct by the Malta Court in not allowing him to release prizes which had been brought in but, on his own subsequent investigation, turned out to be innocent or to be of doubtful enemy character. Sewell, the Judge of the Court, argued[31] that once a prize was brought in it fell under the jurisdiction of the Court and that every commander was bound to proceed to 'the solemn adjudication of whatever . . . he may take'.

Failure to do so, went on Sewell, would render a commander liable to penalties under Section 20 of the Prize Act.[32] This was the section dealing with 'collusive capture' and was inserted precisely because a captor could not be permitted to exercise coercive control over the captured vessel outside the law, to the extent that the master of a prize could 'even enter into terms for his dismissal'. Sewell said the true position of a captor was that 'though a party he is also a Trustee, and not a trustee merely for the interests of his officers and crew but for the rights of his Sovereign . . . .'. If the captor's conduct was fair and moderate, he need have no fear of costs even if the prize was restored. Hoste's complaint was therefore frivolous and vexatious.

Sewell missed the human point. Hoste was an officer of great dedication and his principal concern in this issue was without doubt to avoid time-consuming and fruitless litigation to the detriment of his first duty of seeking out and annoying the enemy. But in the generality, and in law, Sewell was quite right. The section of the Act forbidding collusive capture was necessary to make illegal the kind of practices later alleged against Patrick Campbell in the Adriatic: in effect, protection rackets. It is hard to see how it could have been shelved to accommodate an exceptional commander like Hoste.

One further example of the difference between the bureaucrat's and the commander's view is to do more with administration than law, but it has a place in this chapter. It had to do with the taking into service of suitable ships captured on foreign stations. Traditionally, this function lay with the Commanders in Chief of the stations and it was regarded by them as an important part of their powers for two reasons. First, it was a way of augmenting the forces available to them; they always saw themselves as chronically short of ships and the addition of well-found vessels to their inventory was more than welcome. Second, it was a fount of patronage. Deserving officers could be promoted into commands or berths in the vessels taken into service and their careers made, or at least enhanced.

Up to 1806, the method by which this had been done was in practice entirely on-station. Surveys and valuations would be made by officials regarded as competent – most stations boasted a dockyard or base where the necessary staff existed – the prize would be condemned by a Vice Admiralty Court, she would be bought in to the service at the Commander in Chief's discretion, prize and where appropriate head money would be paid to the captors, and a crew formed often giving new opportunities to officers of the captor and their following, but sometimes also to the Commander in Chief's own favourites.

There were, of course, chances of intrigue both personal and financial in all this. There are indications of unease in the Admiralty about it from the turn of the century. Nor was the Law entirely happy. In a dispute between the *Nereide* and the *Abergavenny* in 1802, over the capture of Curaçao, it emerged that a captured vessel, renamed the *Active*, had been fitted out as tender to the *Abergavenny* and the Lords of Appeal 'considered this usage . . . not founded in law'. Marsden, the Secretary of the Admiralty, noted 'The practice of fitting out tenders in the manner described has never met with the sanction of Their Lordships.'[33] It is likely that the *Abergavenny*'s was a purely local action anticipating the approval of the Commander in Chief and therefore more suspect than the regular practice, but the reaction to it indicates sensitivity on the whole issue.

No general action was taken, however, until 26 July 1806, when an order issued from the Admiralty over the signature of John Barrow, then Second Secretary. Commanders in Chief abroad were 'on no account to take in to His Majesty's service any vessel which may be captured from the enemy by the ships or vessels under your orders, but when any vessels may be captured which may appear to you to be fit for His Majesty's Service, you are to cause them to be surveyed and valued and the reports thereof to be transmitted to me for Their Lordships' information, when they shall give such orders on the subject as they shall think proper'.[34]

The furore which this raised can be imagined. The order undercut a huge slice of a Commander in Chief's authority, operational flexibility and patronage. Moreover, it was quite unworkable; even in the Mediterranean, three months was likely to elapse before Admiralty approval could be received to bring a prize into service, while for more remote stations the time could stretch to nearly a year. It is no surprise that the order was repealed on 6 February 1807.

The independence of foreign stations, which persisted to the end of the war, was an outgrowth of slow communications in the days of sail. Viewing the records and recalling the time needed for despatches to go to and from England, it is indeed astonishing to see how much control actually could be exercised by the issue of general instructions and the choice of subordinates capable of interpreting them with a due sense of policy and strategy. This applied to the courts as well as to the operational authorities. They may have been less precise than those in London, more inclined to go their own way, sometimes more venal; but in general they followed the established procedures and principles. In exactly the same way, the commanders and crews of ships on these remote stations adopted a more free-and-easy approach to prize-taking than they could have done at home, but in general conformed to the rules of the game.

NOTES

1.   R.G. Marsden (ed.), *Documents relating to Law and Custom of the Sea*, vol. 1 (Navy Records Society, 1915), p. 408.

2.   Marsden, *Documents relating to Law and Custom of the Sea*, vol. 2, p. 43.

3.   41 Geo. III c.96, Prize Courts in the West Indies.

4.   Michael Duffy, *Soldiers, Sugar and Seapower* (Clarendon Press, Oxford, 1987), p. 111.

5.   Ibid., p. 112.

6.   ADM 1/3894.

7.   6 C. Rob., p. 364 [1807].

8.   ADM 1/3899.

9.   ADM 1/3897.

10.   41 Geo. III c.96 ss.1 and 4.

11.   45 Geo. III c.72 s.35.

12.   G.L. Newnham Collingwood, *Correspondence and Memoir of Lord Collingwood* (Ridgway, London, 1829), p. 285.

13.   NMM HUL/4, pp. 6 and 12.

14.   See Chapter 10.

15.   HCA 30/466, 42/438, 42/441.

16.   Sir William Henry Dillon, *A Narrative of my Professional Adventures* (Navy Records Society, 1953), p. 372.

17.   Thomas Hartwell Horne, *Compendium of the Statute Laws and Regulations of the Court of Admiralty relative to Ships of War, Privateers, Recaptures and Prize Money* (W. Clarke and Sons, 1803), p. 22.

18.　　Sir John Ross, *Memoirs and Correspondence of Admiral Lord de Saumarez* (Bentley, 1838), pp. 197–200.
19.　　NMM PEL/22.
20.　　David Syrett and R.L. DiNardo, *The Commissioned Sea Officers of the Royal Navy 1660–1815* (Scolar Press for the Navy Records Society, 1994), p. 71.
21.　　RNM 197/301, Cochrane to Croker, 28 April 1812.
22.　　Dillon, *A Narrative of my Professional Adventures*, p. 233.
23.　　Papers in the possession of Lord Digby.
24.　　ADM 1/3903.
25.　　ADM 1/3902.
26.　　ADM 1/3903.
27.　　45 Geo. III c.72 s.37.
28.　　ADM 1/3899, Scott to Croker, 21 March 1810.
29.　　ADM 1/3900.
30.　　ADM 1/3902.
31.　　ADM 1/3897.
32.　　45 Geo. III c.72 s.20.
33.　　ADM 1/3897.
34.　　ADM 2/1081.

CHAPTER TEN

The Cochranes and the Courts

The Royal Navy of the wars of 1793–1815 was not short of characters. But few were so colourful or controversial as the Cochranes: Alexander and Thomas, uncle and nephew, godfather and godson. These Scotsmen, tempestuous in nature, always aspiring to brilliance in professional performance and often achieving it, difficult and demanding colleagues, inspiring and often beloved leaders, were at one end of the spectrum of talent and temperament. As such, they were not always appreciated.

'Cochrane' wrote Lord Keith about Alexander in 1804, 'is a crack-headed, unsafe man . . . and his nephew is falling into the same error'.[1] But that same autumn, newly promoted to flag rank, Alexander Cochrane was in charge of the watch on Ferrol in still-neutral Spain, a station demanding the subtlest intelligence-gathering and diplomacy as well as straightforward naval vigilance, and carrying out the duty, as has been shown,[2] with both zeal and skill.

St Vincent's views were not far from Keith's: 'The Cochranes are not to be trusted out of sight. They are all mad, romantic, money-getting and not truth-telling.'[3] Yet St Vincent must have approved Alexander's appointment to the Leeward Islands station in 1805 and, for Thomas, condoned (after some 'penance' in a converted collier called the *Arab*)[4] a series of appointments in the middle of the decade that would give boundless chances to enhance both fame and fortune. The fact was that even if they were all their critics said, they were also highly successful operators and Britain and her navy needed their operations.

Before going into their relationship with the Prize Courts, which is the main theme of this chapter, it will be worth outlining the career of each of these men.

Alexander made his name in the War of American Independence, being made post in 1782. In 1790 he was in command of the *Hind*, moving to *Thetis* on the North American station in 1793. He made numerous captures there, including two French frigates armed *en flûte* in 1795. From 1799 onwards he was in command of line of battle ships, first *Ajax* and then *Northumberland*. In the former, he supervised the disembarkation of troops in Egypt in 1800; in spite of his subsequent grumbles, Keith greatly approved this service. Alexander Cochrane was promoted Rear Admiral of the Blue on 23 April 1804 and sent in charge of the watch on Ferrol, already described in Chapter 8. In 1805 he pursued a detached French squadron under Missiessy to the West Indies; it was a squadron intended to link with Villeneuve's larger force, and Cochrane had no greater success in catching it than Nelson had with Villeneuve. While in the West Indies, Alexander Cochrane was informed of his appointment to the Leeward Islands station and, on being released by Nelson whose flag he had joined, remained in the Caribbean. He was Commander in Chief there until 1814, when he took over the North American station for the remainder of the American war. He was a Member of Parliament for Stirling Burghs from 1800 to 1806, was knighted in 1806 and made GCB in 1815. He died in 1832.[5]

His nephew and godson Thomas, Lord Cochrane and later Earl of Dundonald, is more celebrated, having been the subject of numerous biographies, including his own.[6] The son of a nobleman impoverished by his own enthusiasm for invention, he entered the navy with a desire not only for glory but also for gain. In command of the tiny sloop *Speedy* as a commander in 1800, he worked in the Western Mediterranean, making thirty-three captures in ten months[7] and establishing himself as more than a nuisance to the Spanish authorities.

An end should have been put to these depredations by the encounter of the thirty-six-gun xebec-frigate *Gamo* with the *Speedy* on 6 May 1801. The *Speedy*, with only forty men and fourteen 4-pounder guns, was no match for a ship with eight times the manpower and weight of metal, yet she gave battle and after a gun action closed to board with a fury that carried the Spanish ship. Cochrane's ostentatious calling for reinforcements, when he knew there were none, may well have turned the action at one point.[8] The exploit, probably the greatest victory against the odds in any single-ship action ever, became legendary and made Cochrane's name as a daredevil commander.

His luck ran out temporarily two months later when *Speedy* was captured by three line of battle ships under the French Admiral Linois. But after a brief period of captivity he was exchanged and returned to naval service.

He had by then been made a post captain, some months after the *Gamo* action, a delay which rankled with him to the end of his life, along with many other grievances. Nevertheless, his career through the next eight years was marked by a succession of frigate commands, the sort for which he was so clearly suited and in which he was likely not only to distinguish himself in action – which he did, frequently and with conspicuous courage and skill – but to make spectacular amounts of money.

The most lucrative was the cruise of the *Pallas* in the spring of 1805. This was blatantly advertised as a money-getting expedition[9] and Cochrane would normally have had no difficulty gathering a crew, but he claimed in his autobiography that his service in the *Arab* in 1804 had 'operated against [me] in the minds of the seamen' and he had initially to resort to impressment.[10] He was reputed to have made £75,000 on his own account and he certainly returned to harbour with a gold candlestick at each masthead, taken from one of the Spanish treasure ships that were the chief source of the booty.[11]

In the *Imperieuse* in the Mediterranean in 1808, however, he found little joy in prize-taking – his explanation for this will emerge later – and much more in amphibious operations, for which he showed almost as much aptitude. His exertions in the raids on and defence of the castles of Mongat and Trinidad (Rosas) were particularly praised.[12] But his inventive mind, inherited no doubt from his father, was busy on further ways of confounding the enemy – on which, give him his due, he was always at least as keen as he was on prizes. His notion of exploding his way in to the Basque Roads was put forward and accepted by London and the results with their aftermath have already been covered in Chapter 6.

From this time onwards Cochrane's reputation and fortunes, so far as the Royal Navy was concerned, declined. He was regarded as an uneasy bedfellow, a troublemaker professionally as well as in his parliamentary and public life, which occupied an increasing part of his time. Though still nominally in command of a ship, he found it difficult to reconcile this with his activities in London and a surrogate captain was frequently employed; this gave his enemies an opportunity to attack his reputation. His conviction for a conspiracy involving dealing on the stock exchange, and his striking-off from the navy list in consequence in 1814, may well have been the result of a trumped-up case – which he always maintained[13] – but might not have surprised the establishment as a whole. He had been a Member of Parliament since 1806, and remained so until 1818, with a brief gap during the time of his one-year imprisonment in 1814–15.

He had further glories to come, but they were in South America and not in Britain. The independence of Chile and Brazil owed a great deal to his activity in the years up to 1825; no doubt it would have occurred eventually, but its speed and relative ease were due in large measure to the way he took charge of the emerging naval forces of these two young nations. It was no doubt the merit of these activities, as well as some feeling that he might have been unjustly treated, that led to his reinstatement as a Rear Admiral of the Blue in 1832.[14] He died an Admiral of the Red in 1860.

The appearance of the Cochranes so frequently in this book, and the devotion of this chapter to them, rests however on a more specific issue. They developed an antipathy to the Prize Courts, Admiralty and Vice Admiralty, which emerged time after time in both public pronouncements and correspondence. It was associated with their radical political stance, which sought to challenge the establishment at any point of weakness, but this particular issue had its own personal edge. Whether

Nelson's line of battle ship prizes. A plate showing the line of battle ships taken by forces under the command of Lord Horatio Nelson up to, but not including, the Battle of Trafalgar. The plate indicates not only the scale of Nelson's victories as a fighting admiral, but the fame brought by captures of the enemy's major forces. (RNM V3395)

Dutch prizes in the Medway, October 1797. Duncan's comprehensive victory over the Dutch at Camperdown brought much-needed acclaim for the Navy after the mutinies earlier in the year. (RNM 1976/207)

Vice Admiral Cuthbert Lord Collingwood. Though markedly less interested in prize money than most officers, Collingwood regarded it as 'a comfortable thing', and later in life thought he had been shabbily treated over the proceeds. (RNM 1984/476)

Edward Pellew, Viscount Exmouth.

Admiral Edward Pellew, Viscount Exmouth. A prolific prize-taker, as well as a great fighting seaman, Pellew may well have made over £200,000 in prize money, the equivalent of over £40 million today. (RNM 1980/298)

Capture of the Guillaume Tell, *31 March 1800. This was the final French survivor of the Battle of the Nile, captured off Malta eighteen months later. The picture shows Blackwood's* Penelope *manoeuvring to delay the French ship to enable the British ships of the line to close. This joint capture took eight years to settle in court, by which time many of the protagonists were dead. (RNM 1987/222)*

Capture of the Furieuse *by the* Bonne Citoyenne, *June 1809. The* Bonne Citoyenne *was a British ship, captured from the French on a previous occasion. She out-manoeuvred the* Furieuse *and reduced her to the condition shown on the left of the picture. In spite of this the* Furieuse *was bought in to the Navy, with corresponding extra return for the captors. (RNM 1976/247)*

An exchange before the Battle of Trafalgar. **Officer**: *Why, Starboard! How is this, at prayers when the enemy is upon us: are you afraid of them?* **Sailor**: *Afraid? No – I was only praying that the enemy's shot may be distributed in the same proportion as prize money, the greater part among the officers.* **Aside by the gun's crew**: *Why don't you sing amen to that, Tom?* (RNM 1984/4885)

British Tars towing the Danish fleet into harbour, September 1807. Gambier's expedition technically did not take the Danish fleet as prizes, but 'on temporary deposit' to prevent their falling into French hands. A good deal of Copenhagen was burnt in the process. (RNM 1973/275)

Thomas Phillips, R.A. pinxit   Emery Walker Ltd. ph. sc.

William, Lord Stowell
Judge of Admiralty 1798-1828
Treasurer 1807

Sir William Scott, Lord Stowell. Judge of the High Court of Admiralty from 1798–1828,
Scott was a dominant figure in the law and administration of prize. 'Treasurer' refers to the
office he held in the Middle Temple, his Inn of Court. (Author's collection)

G INTERROGATORIES,
*...istered on behalf of Our Sovereign
...ge the Third by the Grace of
...of Great Britain, France, and Ireland,
King, Defender of the Faith. To all commanders, masters, officers, mariners, and
other persons found on board any ships and
vessels, which have been or shall be seized or
taken as prize by any of His Majesty's ships
or vessels of war, or by merchants ships or
vessels which have or shall have commissions
(L. S.) or letters of marque and reprisals, concerning
GEORGE R. such captured ships, vessels, or any goods,
wares, and merchandize on board the same,
examined as witnesses in preparatory, during
the present hostilities.*

LET each witness be interrogated to every of the following
questions, and their answers to each interrogatory written
down.

I. INTERROGATE. Where were you born, and where have
you lived for these seven years last past? Where do you now live,
and how long have you lived in that place? To what prince or
state, or to whom are you, or have you ever been a subject, and
of what cities or towns have you been admitted a burgher or freeman, and at what time and in what manner were you admitted a
burgher or freeman, and at what time and in what manner were
you so admitted? How long have you resided there since you
were admitted a burgher or freeman, or where have you resided
since? What did you pay for your admission? Are you a married
man, and if married, where do your wife and family reside?

II. INTERROGATE. Were you present at the time of taking
and seizing the ship or her lading, or any of the goods or mer-
chandizes concerning which you are now examined? Had the
ship, concerning which you are now examined, any commission?
What, and from whom?

*The Standing Interrogatories. By law, this thirty-two-point questionnaire, the first page only
of which is seen here, had to be put to the master and other officials of a captured vessel,
normally by the captor's agent. The questions were searching and if answered honestly would
generally establish whether the vessel and its cargo were lawful prize. (Author's collection)*

it was a concerted campaign, or a series of actions that as it were broke surface from an undercurrent of resentment, is not certain. The points made by both, at different times, were often similar, to the extent that some common line might have been worked out, but since no biography or collated correspondence of Alexander has been published, the evidence for that remains to be gathered.

The first recorded evidence of the Cochranes' struggle with the courts comes in February 1799, when Sir William Scott wrote to Evan Nepean[15] about complaints from Alexander Cochrane, then a captain. There were three: first, that it was compulsory for captors to employ the King's Proctor to represent them in contested cases; second, that the King's Proctor was in close association (Cochrane called it 'partnership') with the representatives of the claimants on the other side of the case; and third, that these officers effectively conspired to arrange that cases were contested, in order to enhance their fees.

Scott's rebuttal was on the following lines. First, he contended, the organization was founded upon principles of law. The 1708 Act had indeed gifted to captors the proceeds of prizes, but only after they had been lawfully condemned. Up to that point, the interest of the Crown was not transferred. Captures were an act of state and foreign governments constantly required explanations of the state's actions. Thus it was important that Crown employees should be involved in the Court's proceedings. Agents were all very well: but 'upon the whole, a better protection is afforded the King's cruizers by entrusting their interests to the Publick officers of the Crown'. On the second point, Scott pointed out that this was no secret. The legal profession generally organized itself so that individuals in the same house could take different sides in a case. But to make the position clear, Heseltine the King's Proctor had dissolved his formal partnerships *bona fide*. On the third point, Scott was indignant. There was no collusion; cases were 'sincerely and successfully defended'. He cited numerous instances. As a sting in the tail, Scott wryly congratulated Cochrane on being 'deprived of the opportunity to injure himself' by pursuing a certain appeal.

Nothing further can be found for the next four years, but Alexander Cochrane was clearly simmering. When in 1803 St Vincent set up his celebrated Commission of Enquiry into many aspects of naval administration, the Fourth Report was devoted to the activities of Prize Agents, and Cochrane saw his chance. He first wrote to Markham, one of the Naval Lords, with a 'petition from the admirals and captains of his Majesty's Fleet' that the investigation should be broadened to cover 'the manner in which prize causes have been conducted both at home and abroad'.[16] This was rejected. He then submitted a memorandum to the Commission[17] alleging that appeals had been contrived by agents in collusion with court officials, in order to keep money in agents' hands and earn interest. He quoted specific cases, with alleged inducements. The Commission, and its recommendations, are more fully covered in Chapter 14; it is enough to say here that the problem of moneys in agents' hands during drawn-out proceedings was recognized by the authorities, partly as a result of Cochrane's remonstrance, and continued efforts to solve or ameliorate it were made up to the end of the war.

Alexander Cochrane was not mollified; in August 1807 he was writing to Markham 'If I am spared till next winter and can get to town for ten days, Sir W. Scott shall have another battle to fight.'[18] But by that time, Thomas had come into the frame.

On 7 July in the same year, as a relatively new Member of Parliament (he was titled Lord Cochrane, but only as the son of an Earl, and therefore entitled to sit in the Commons), he moved for a Committee to enquire into, *inter alia*, 'the fees in any courts of law or equity, admiralty and ecclesiastical, or any other court . . . held . . . by any member of this House'.[19] This was a clear knock at Scott, Nicholl the King's Advocate and Laurence, a prominent member of Doctors' Commons, all of whom were Members of Parliament. The motion was negatived, as was another of Cochrane's three days later moving for papers on virtually everything naval: an example, perhaps, of the penalty for protesting too much and too widely. It was a pity, for some of the points made by Cochrane – particularly the dangerous state of ships kept too long on station watching the French Atlantic ports – were of the first importance and needed following up.[20]

From this time onwards the main burden of the struggle against the courts was carried on by Thomas. On the Leeward Islands station Alexander was not entirely silent, but his language was generally moderate as befitted a Commander in Chief and often in tones of genuine enquiry. He was not clear whether the Orders in Council allowed American vessels to carry French merchandise and produce from America to French and Spanish colonies and asked an Opinion, which he got from Doctors' Commons but which unfortunately has not survived.[21] And later in 1808 he sent some captured sword blades to the Admiralty Procurator, an act which looks almost like a peace offering. But in 1810 the old Adam seems to have broken out again: Scott's reply to a list of complaints from the Leeward Islands included the remark that it was 'hard to avoid the risque of breaching civility' in the face of Cochrane's 'unbridled freedom of expression'. Needless to say, Scott made no concessions: the decisions of Law must be accepted unless and until reversed on appeal.[22]

But it was Thomas by this time who was in the forefront. Mainly this was because of a row between him and the Vice Admiralty Court at Malta which was extensively chronicled at the time and in numerous biographies since, including his own memoirs. But it does not appear from any of these that the Malta Court's side of the matter, as it emerges from the Doctors' Commons files, has been fully taken into account and it may be worth going into some detail on the whole business.

The facts of the quarrel itself are well established and corroborated by independent witnesses.[23] On 20 February 1811 Thomas Cochrane, then on leave but still nominally captain of the *Imperieuse*, had entered the Vice Admiralty Court at Malta and torn down the table of fees which was hung up in the Registry (some later accounts, including his own, say it was on the back of the door in the Judges' privy). This was regarded by Sewell, the judge, as an outrageous contempt, and he gave orders for Cochrane to be arrested.

After several abortive attempts at arrest, during which Cochrane was alleged to have assaulted and threatened armed violence to court officials, Cochrane allowed himself to be carried downstairs from his lodgings in a chair and appeared in court. He defended himself against the charges of contempt by saying that the court's own actions were unlawful: the court was not a court of record and therefore incompetent to try him; and the table of fees should have been hung up in public view in the court room as required by the Act,[24] so their display in the Registry was unlawful and therefore his act in taking them down was not in contempt.

Cochrane was committed to prison, but his many friends in Malta made life a misery for the legal authorities while he was there and he added to this by first refusing to pay for any food and then, when order was given for its free supply, by holding a series of dinner parties.[25] In fact, his sense of humour was given a free rein and that of the court, limited in any event, was severely tested. His escape from detention, from which he was not pursued, was almost certainly condoned and may even have been arranged.[26]

But what lay behind all this stretched back to November 1807.[27] In that month, off the coast of Corsica, *Imperieuse* had encountered a ship called the *King George*. Her identity was not clear to the British frigate, but in fact she was a Maltese letter-of-marque. She wore British colours but these could not be distinguished because it was flat calm and a union flag draped over the side was regarded as a ruse; Cochrane assumed she was French or Genoese. Boats from the *Imperieuse* boarded and carried the *King George*, with casualties on both sides, and brought her in to Malta.

The captors' monition was on three grounds: *King George* had offered resistance; she was not navigated according to law; and her letters of marque were irregular. Against this, however, it was argued that the *Imperieuse*'s own actions were precipitate and unjustified. The boats had worn no colours and were 'rowed in the French manner'; *Imperieuse* was herself French-built and had a French name; no assurances were given to the privateer of the real character of the frigate. The court noted that

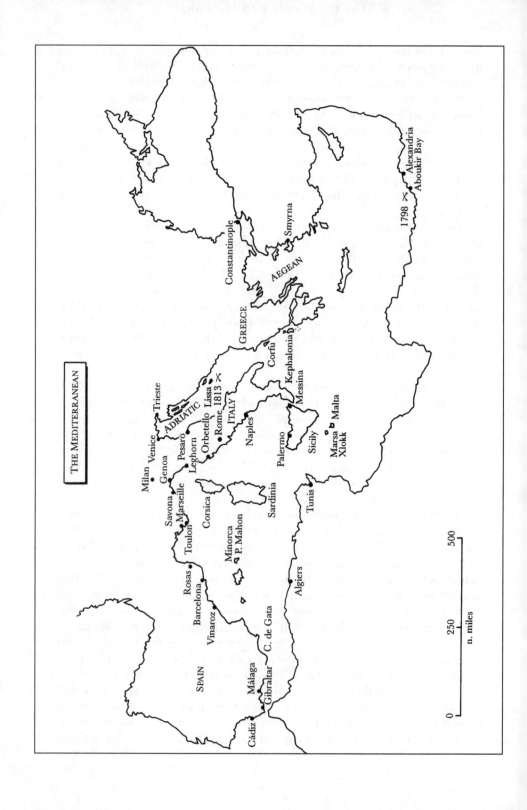

THE MEDITERRANEAN

Milan Venice Trieste
Genoa
Savona Marseille
Toulon
Pesaro
Leghorn
Orbetello Lissa
Rome 1813
ADRIATIC
ITALY
Naples
Corsica
Sardinia
Rosas
Barcelona
Vinaroz
Minorca
P. Mahon
C. de Gata
SPAIN
Málaga
Gibraltar
Cádiz
Algiers
Tunis
Palermo
Sicily
Messina
Kephalonia
Corfu
Marsa
Xlokk
Malta
GREECE
AEGEAN
Constantinople
Smyrna
1798
Alexandria
Aboukir Bay

0   250   500
n. miles

most arms had been thrown down in the privateer as soon as the boarding parties were known to be British and concluded that the loss of life had been 'wholly imputable to the rash conduct of those belonging to the frigate'. So far as the *King George*'s status was concerned, the court recognized that misrepresentation did exist as to the letters of marque but concluded this was 'of a harmless description'. There was also some allegation of pillage against the *Imperieuse*'s people and, after hearing witnesses, the court held that there had been some forcible separation of the *King George*'s crew from their property, in spite of Cochrane's contention that his orders on the subject were absolute.

Because the *King George*'s letters of marque were irregular, in particular because her ownership did not tally with that stated in her commission, she was in fact condemned. But it was a condemnation to the Crown and not to the captor; and all prize goods onboard were condemned as Droits of Admiralty. The expenses of the captors were refused; in Cochrane's estimate, they 'brought him 600 crowns in debt'.[28]

In summary, the Court's finding was that Cochrane had unjustifiably committed what in the late twentieth century would be called a 'blue-on-blue', an attack on a friendly force. The Court's sentence ensured that he would get no benefit from his action and in fact would suffer financially, but it could not of course impose any formal penalty much less disciplinary action; that would have been for a military tribunal and none was convened. Cochrane, in his post-action letter to the Commander in Chief and subsequently, presented the *King George* as little better than a pirate, manned by the riff-raff of the Mediterranean and preying on all and sundry, whose activities had been notorious.[29] However, there is no evidence to suggest that even if this were true, he knew anything about it before he made the attack.

There is no suggestion in the Court's report that the *King George* had committed piratical acts, nor (as Cochrane and Marryat, then a midshipman in the *Imperieuse*, subsequently asserted) that a reward of £500 had been offered for her capture. This may simply have been a rumour going round Malta; no documentary evidence can be found.

Whether Cochrane knew much about the composition of the Malta Vice Admiralty Court before the *King George* case is not known. However, he certainly began investigating it soon afterwards, and what he found gave him ample opportunity for what he regarded as justified retaliation.

The officers of the court were peculiarly constituted. One Jackson was the Marshal; he was also the Proctor. This meant that the man responsible for administering prize cases was one and the same as the man representing or arranging the representation of those cases in court: he was in fact employing and paying fees to himself. At the very least it was highly irregular and contrary to the letter of the Prize Act[30] as well as its spirit. At worst it was a recipe for all sorts of corruption.

As Sewell the Judge subsequently argued,[31] he had in 1805 represented to Doctors' Commons that Malta was a special case where the rule could be waived, since there was 'only one marshal, and without any hope that another . . . might be coming out from England . . . the only expedient seemed to be to permit Mr Jackson to execute the office of proctor' – and Scott had been so informed and by silence consented.

If Cochrane knew this dispensation existed, he took little notice of it, and indeed the way in which the situation had been allowed to jog along for years must have suggested to him that it was altogether too comfortable for the officers concerned. Collingwood might privately have agreed with him: in 1809 he wrote that Malta was 'the most gossiping, gormandizing place I ever heard of. The merchants are suddenly become exceedingly rich . . .'[32] – and he might have added, the court officials too.

For court fees were the other principal abuse Cochrane believed he had uncovered. He would have found many allies among the ships based on Malta at the time. Many of them regarded the fees of the Malta court as excessive; Cochrane's campaign was simply the sharp end of a general thrust of unrest. Sewell had his windows broken at least twice by unruly mobs of junior officers.[33] It was in vain for the judge to aver that the scale of fees in Malta was lower than that usually charged in Admiralty Courts, and that a full scale of fees had been deposited in Doctors' Commons in 1804; the perception in Malta was that the court was making a pretty penny out of captures and the navy was suffering accordingly.

So that was why and how Thomas Cochrane came to his quarrel with the Vice Admiralty Court at Malta in 1811. It is clear from his subsequent statements that a sense of injustice over the *King George* case was the prime mover; the more generalized crusade against the malpractice of the Court followed. The Basque Roads affair, and the Gambier court martial, had intervened;[34] but Cochrane's memory for any wrong he thought had been done to him was a long one.

After Cochrane's arrest, escape and return to England the matter was brought up in London, both administratively and politically. The political forum was the House of Commons.[35] On 18 July Thomas Cochrane moved for an investigation into the fees of Vice Admiralty Courts and in a long speech went into detail on the composition and irregularities of the Malta Court. He was particularly scathing on the processes whereby Jackson the Proctor reimbursed Jackson the Marshal and on the 'unmerited emoluments' enjoyed by court officials to the detriment of the navy. There was a good deal of sympathy in the House for this *démarche* and no doubt more in the navy itself, where the proceedings were closely followed. As was seen in Chapter 9, Scott was forced to set up a Commission to establish scales of fees for the Vice Admiralty Courts throughout the world; Cochrane's efforts had not been in vain.

His conduct in Malta in February 1811 was in the meantime being considered administratively. Scott had as early as May in that year given his opinion that a complaint from Cochrane about the Malta Court was 'extremely proper' to be submitted to the Law Officers – not to the Admiralty Court, since it involved matters beyond maritime jurisdiction – and he held to this line throughout the affair. The Law Officers finally reported in May 1811 that the proceedings of the Malta Court against Cochrane 'were justified by the circumstances of the case, and that the conduct of the noble Lord was marked throughout by a spirit of contempt which it was the duty of the Judge to repress for the vindication of the jurisdiction over which he presides'.[36] Scott, unsurprisingly, concurred.

A pencilled note by the secretary to Croker, Secretary of the Admiralty, appears on the flyleaf of this document to the effect that Their Lordships' 'high displeasure' be communicated to Cochrane; but there is a further note, 'Not executed'. Perhaps their Lordships felt Cochrane had suffered enough in other ways; perhaps they themselves had some sympathy for the cause he had, albeit over-zealously, pursued; or perhaps they judged that the feeling in the navy against Vice Admiralty Courts was so strong, and support for Cochrane in this cause at least was so marked, that they thought it inexpedient to say the least to put any disciplinary measure into effect.

The aftermath in Malta was curious to the point of being bizarre. First, Jackson's position in both offices was clearly untenable; but instead of going quietly from the post of Marshal, while retaining that of Proctor, he astonishingly recommended that the Marshal's post should go to his brother, whom he represented as being well qualified for it.[37] If corroboration for Cochrane's campaign is required, this is a powerful piece of circumstantial evidence.

Jackson's suggestion was rejected and one Norcott was appointed Marshal. Alas, things went from bad to worse; in May 1813, Sewell had to explain to Croker that Norcott had absconded with the proceeds of several prize sales and was thought to be living in Smyrna 'under the name of Smyth'.[38] This was not the end of it; Stevens the Assistant Registrar (whom Cochrane had particularly criticized in the House of Commons) made off with the proceeds of the *Mahi Ali ben Murad* later in the same year. Times were difficult in Malta; there was plague about and the defectors made great play with their personal safety and health. But the picture persists of court machinery not under control. Pellew knew all about it, as Commander in Chief: 'The Court at a stand still', he wrote to Keats in September 1813.[39]

So the Vice Admiralty Court at Malta ended its wartime work, as probably it had gone on for some time, messily. Whatever the genesis of his quarrel with it – and it seems not to have been too creditable to him – Thomas Cochrane had uncovered a poor state of affairs and had brought matters to a head in his own inimitable way. It was no fault of his that once the boil had been lanced, it came to a head again.

That fault can scarcely be laid at any door but that of Sewell, the Vice Admiralty Judge. He comes out of the correspondence as a rather fussy man, meticulous in small details, anxious to uphold the dignity of his Court, yet unable to see or correct its glaring shortcomings. His sense of humour, if he had one, was subject to frequent failure – though one is bound to say it was frequently tested. It is doubtful if he himself was corrupt and technically he was a more than adequate judge. But above all, he failed to take charge of his subordinates: the strains of administration were too much for him. In July 1814 he set out for England. Little about him comes to light after that; he was knighted in 1815, along with several other Vice Admiralty Court judges, and died in 1833.[40] He rates no entry in the *Dictionary of National Biography* and no known record of his life exists. Thomas Cochrane, with a dozen or so to his name, was a posthumous winner of that as of so many other battles.

NOTES

1.   Sir Clements Markham (ed.), *Selections from the Correspondence of Sir John Markham* (Navy Records Society, 1904), p. 153.

2.   See Chapter 8.

3.   Warren Tute, *Cochrane* (Cassell, 1965), p. 58.

4.   Thomas Cochrane, Earl of Dundonald, *Autobiography of a Seaman* (Constable, 1995 edn), vol. I, p. 166.

5.   XI DNB, p. 159.

6.   Tute, *Cochrane*; Cochrane, *Autobiography of a Seaman*; Donald Thomas, *Cochrane* (Andre Deutsch, 1978); John Knox Laughton, entry in XI DNB, p. 165.

7.   XXII NC, p. 8.

8.   William James, *The Naval History of Great Britain*, vol. III, New Edition (Bentley, 1847), p. 145n. Patrick O'Brian, in *Master and Commander* (Fontana, 1971), at p. 332, gives an account which is legitimately embroidered for the purposes of fiction, when he makes the surgeon Stephen Maturin the recipient of the order *otros cincuenta*. The ships are given different names but the action is clearly the *Speedy* v. *Gamo*.

9.   The well-known recruiting poster for the *Pallas* says she is 'built on purpose' to take Spanish galleons bringing treasure from the Plate.

10.   Cochrane, *Autobiography of a Seaman*, vol. I, p. 172.

11.   Tute, *Cochrane*, p. 61.

12.   XX NC, p. 326; XXI NC, pp. 165–8.

13.   XI DNB, p. 169.

14.   David Syrett and R.L. DiNardo, *The Commissioned Sea Officers of the Royal Navy 1660–1815* (Scolar Press for the Navy Records Society, 1994), p. 87.

15.   ADM 1/3894.

16.   Markham, *Selections*, p. 366.

17.   XI NC, p. 222.

18.   Markham, *Selections*, p. 369.

19.   XVIII NC, p. 66.

20.   Cochrane, *Autobiography of a Seaman*, vol. I, pp. 226—33.

21.   ADM 1/3898, 30 June 1808, Gostling to W. Pole.

22.   ADM 1/3899, letter dated 13 August 1810.

23.   XXV NC, p. 300.

24.   45 Geo. III c.72 s.38.

25.   Cochrane, *Autobiography of a Seaman*, vol. II, p. 174.

26.   Tute, *Cochrane*, pp. 126–8.

27.   For Cochrane's version of the incident, see Cochrane, *Autobiography of a Seaman*, vol. I, pp. 234–6. Sewell's memorandum, written on 30 October 1809 in answer to a letter from Doctors' Commons of 10 August 1809 asking for comment on the case (triggered apparently by Cochrane's representations to the Law Officers), is in ADM 1/3899.

28.   Cochrane, *Autobiography of a Seaman*, vol. II, p. 188.

29.   Cochrane, *Autobiography of a Seaman*, vol. I, pp. 234–6; Pope, pp. 84–5; XI DNB, p. 167.

30.   45 Geo. III c.72 s.41.

31.   ADM 1/3900, letter of March 1811.

32.   G.L. Newnham Collingwood, *Life and Letters of Lord Collingwood* (Ridgway, 1829), p. 495.

33.   ADM 1/3900, letter of 18 June 1812.

34.   See Chapter 6.

35.   Cochrane, *Autobiography of a Seaman*, vol. II, pp. 181–214.

36.   ADM 1/3900, Scott to Croker, 30 May 1811.

37.   Ibid., Jackson's Memorial to Doctors' Commons, 28 December 1811.

38.   ADM 1/3901, Sewell to Croker, 27 May 1813.

39.   C. Northcote Parkinson, *Edward Pellew, Viscount Exmouth* (Methuen, 1933), p. 405.

40.   G.D. Squibb, *Doctors' Commons: A History of the College of Advocates and Doctors of Law* (Clarendon Press, 1977).

CHAPTER ELEVEN

Disputed Waters

In the late summer of 1800, Admiral Dickson, commanding at Yarmouth, was advised by the Admiralty that several enemy letter-of-marque vessels were in the Elbe: he was instructed to send over 'such cutter or lugger' as seemed to him to be fit, 'to keep a watchful eye . . . but not to commit any act which may be considered a breach of neutrality unless the said vessels or any of them should commit or attempt to commit any depredations on the property of his Majesty's subjects'.[1]

This instruction highlights the sensitivity of the British government to breaches of sovereignty in neutral waters. The right of visit and search on the high seas was one thing and in that very period was being vigorously and successfully upheld, as *The Maria* and other cases showed;[2] but the violation of the territorial sea of a neutral was quite another.

The law apart, it was politically extremely sensitive. There was a high price to pay if a state in amity with the British sovereign was unnecessarily offended by a British ship's rash action in neutral waters; for this reason the proclamations of reprisal as a matter of course included a provision that prize-taking was not to occur in waters under the jurisdiction of such a state.

Moreover, there was general agreement as to the principle by which the demarcation of such waters was to be governed. If there was one tenet of international law that was generally known to seamen, it was the dictum of Bynkershoek that 'the dominion of the land ends where the force of arms ends', *terrae dominium finitur, ubi finitur armorum vis*: in other words, a rule that water within cannon-shot of the shore was under the jurisdiction of the shore. Even if they could not spell, much less pronounce, the name of the great Dutch publicist, they could say what it meant to them: the territorial sea extended 1 league, or 3 miles, from the coast.

Sometimes, it was that simple. In December 1799 the Spanish Ambassador in Lisbon complained to Admiral Duckworth that the British schooner *Netley*, commanded by Lieutenant Bond, had committed a breach of Portuguese neutrality by capturing the Spanish schooner privateer *Virgen del Carno* under the guns of the forts between Cascais and the Rock of Lisbon – and that therefore the Spanish ship should be released.[3] Duckworth reserved his position to both the Spanish and Portuguese authorities, but 'recommended to Lieutenant Bond to give the privateer schooner up as a compliment to the Court of Portugal, though the infraction complained of seems to be doubtful'. Bond initially was reluctant to give in: he maintained that the *Virgen del Carno* (which he called the *Nuestra Senora del Carmen*, but it was almost certainly the same vessel) was taken out of gunshot of the fort, and that no shot had been fired nor flag displayed by the forts.

As so often occurs in documents of this nature, the final outcome does not appear in the record, but it is more than likely that Bond acceded to his senior's 'recommendation'. Moreover, his case was weak; no shot may have been fired by the forts, but he did not suggest he was outside their range, much less that the capture had taken place more than 3 miles from the coast.

Perhaps the most significant aspect of the whole affair is Nepean's marginal note: 'Send copies of the papers to Lord Grenville'. To have involved the Foreign Secretary personally in this incident, concerning the activities of one very small craft against another on the fringes of Europe, shows a sensitivity that would not be inappropriate in apparently more complex and fraught situations concerning sea jurisdiction two centuries later.[4]

Geography, hydrography and operational factors were not always so straightforward as they were in the approaches to Lisbon. A particularly knotty case was *The Twee Gebroeders*.[5.]Four Dutch ships were taken on 14 July 1799 in the Western Eems by boats from the British cruiser *L'Espiègle* and four other British ships, then lying in the Eastern Eems. Prussia, then neutral, claimed restitution on the ground that it was a capture made 'within the protection of Prussian territory'.

The case is unusual in several aspects. Scott took two bites at it, on 29 July 1800 and 27 November 1801. This sort of thing quite often happened, when a case 'went to further proof' because further and better particulars were required; the delay between the first and second hearings was long, but not unprecedented. What distinguished the *Twee Gebroeders* case was that Scott actually gave a judgment in terms, restoring the ships, at the end of the first case; and reversed that, condemning them, at the end of the second. Some plea or injunction by the captors must have been entered, and been allowed, staying the restoration of the ships after the first hearing, but no record of it has been found. The other unusual, indeed unique, aspect is that this is the only case in Robinson's *Reports* where a map or chart is inserted. The marginal notes on the map suggest that it was drawn specially for Robinson's book, but it must have been drawn up from maps and charts that were available to the Court during the hearings and were indeed frequently mentioned in the judgments.

The first of the two judgments was much the shorter. The evidence before Scott at that time was that *L'Espiègle* was lying in the Eastern Eems, in water which on an inspection of the charts . . . was . . . within the limits to which neutral immunity is usually conceded . . . a distance of three miles, at most, from *East Friesland* [Prussian territory]: an exact measure cannot be easily obtained; but in a case of this nature, in which the Court would not willingly act with an unfavourable minuteness towards a neutral state, it will be disposed to calculate the distance very liberally . . .[6]

Therefore, asked Scott, were the actions of *L'Espiègle*, from this position, acts of violence that violated the neutral territory she occupied? He concluded that they were: 'nobody will say, that the very act of sending out boats to effect a capture, is not itself an act directly hostile . . . If this could be defended, it might as well be said, that a ship lying in a neutral station might fire shot on a vessel lying out of the neutral territory.'

Later in this first judgment, Scott showed himself again as sensitive to politico-military as to legal factors:

Many instances have occurred in which such an irregular use of a neutral country has been warmly resented, and some during the present war; the practice which has been tolerated in the northern states of Europe, of permitting French privateers to make stations of their ports, and to sally out to capture British vessels in the neighbourhood, is of that number; and yet even that practice, unfriendly and noxious as it is, is less than that complained of in this instance; for here the ship, without sallying out at all, is to commit the hostile act. Every government is perfectly justified in interposing to discourage the commencement of such a practice; for the inconvenience to which the neutral territory will be exposed is obvious; if the respect due to it is violated by one party, it will soon provoke a similar treatment from the other also; till, instead of neutral ground, it will soon become the theatre of war.[7]

This was strong stuff, and it is on the face of it astonishing that Scott found it possible seventeen months later to reverse the judgment. But the evidence brought in the meantime was detailed and novel enough to put a different complexion on the case.

The operational story was told in an affidavit from Commander James Boorder, in command of *L'Espiègle*. He testified that the orders to the British ships involved – *L'Espiègle, Circe, Pylades, Courier* and *Nancy* – were to send their boats into the Groningen Wat and bring away as many vessels as they could find there. The Wat was a stretch of water close to the Dutch shore with a depth of only a few feet at low tide; indeed the crews of ships lying there often walked ashore into Holland.

Boorder's affidavit went on to say that the Dutch had stationed gun vessels at the eastern end of the Wat, as he 'verily believed' to protect shipping lying in the Wat itself. And indeed the boats at first deployed by the British force found the Dutch cover too strong for them, being driven back to their ships by sustained fire. The British accordingly decided to mount a heavier assault, the boats to be supported by the ships themselves so far as the depth of water would permit. This plan was put into execution some days later, after the British ships had been 'fitted out at sea', as Boorder was careful to state. It was enough to dislodge the Dutch gunboats, which cut their cables and retired towards Delfzijl. The British ships thereupon anchored, by the senior officer's direction, in exactly the same positions as the Dutch guardships had previously occupied.

When the boats were sent away up the Wat, however, things began to go wrong. Even the well-practised British oarsmen found an 8-mile pull against a flood stream and strong wind too much for them. They even tried to wade towards the potential prizes, but 'the flood tide drove them back' and the boats and their crews returned to the ships. They tried again next day, but

> most of the vessels had run off on the night tide, except those proceeded against in this Court; which not being able to escape the vigilance of the British forces, were taken possession of, and secured and sent to Yarmouth, except one vessel, which was destroyed, owing to her not being seaworthy, and some few which they did not think worth detaining; and at the time of the capture of the said vessels, His Majesty's said forces were lying at anchor in, or very near the exact place in which the said Dutch gunboats had been before laid, and from whence they had been as aforesaid driven.[8]

Two other new affidavits were by Prussians from Emden or thereabouts, giving evidence about the status of the water immediately off the Dutch coast in the region of the Wat, where the captures were made. These asserted that Dutch water was generally accepted as extending only so far as a horseshoe could be thrown from the shore, all the rest being Prussian. But one admitted that when markers were put down to show the limits, the Dutch would take them up and throw them away.

All this new evidence turned what had previously seemed a simple case into a very complex one, and the second judgment occupies eighteen pages of Robinson's *Reports* where the first took up only five. Scott did not refer at any point to the first judgment, which in itself is surprising. A large part of the second judgment consists of an analysis of the status of the waters off the coast of the Dutch province of Groningen, of which the Wat where the capture took place forms part. This analysis is scholarly and much of it turns on where river becomes sea: words become important at this point. The history of grants from 1454 onwards is investigated and discussed, as is the actual practice in respect of those claims. Scott's conclusion after this discussion is not entirely clear, but seems to be leading towards the view that both construction and practice could not sustain the Prussian claim to sovereignty over water so close to the Dutch shore.

Then, however, comes a clinching passage in the judgment:[9]

> ... there is a most material fact arising, that the Dutch not only had guard-ships in the Groningen Watt, but that they exercised actual hostilities there; certainly this exercise of hostility is not conclusive evidence, that the place where this happened was not Prussian territory; because it might be an irregularity on the part of the Dutch, and a subject of complaint on the part of Prussia; but as far as it appears on this evidence, it stands a naked fact; it does not appear to have been complained of, as an irregularity or encroachment on the Prussian territory; and therefore it is not to be presumed by this Court, that it is so to be considered.

So, ruled Scott, the actual captures had not been made on Prussian territory. Had then Prussian waters been passed over in order to effect the capture? After several pages of further discussion, in which geographical and historical parallels were widely drawn, he concluded: 'Where a free passage is generally enjoyed, notwithstanding a claim of territory may exist for certain purposes, no violation of territory is committed, if the party, after an inoffensive passage, conducted in the usual manner, begins an act of hostility in open ground.'[10] Since those criteria had been fulfilled in the case before him, he pronounced that 'the ships must be adjudged lawful prize to the captors, being bound to Amsterdam in breach of the blockade'.

When they are read carefully, the judgments in the two *Twee Gebroeders* cases are not inconsistent. The first rested on the assumption, which was justified on the evidence then before the Court, that the capturing boats had been despatched from a station in Prussian waters and this was an unlawful breach of neutrality; the second, taking into account further evidence, found that most of the relevant activity had been in enemy waters and any passage through neutral water had not been directly connected with the capture. The principle set out in the first case had not been dented by the finding in the second. It is interesting that the first case, and the principle laid down there, is the one that has been most quoted by publicists.[11]

What all this meant to Commander Boorder of *L'Espiègle*, and the captains and crews of the *Circe*, *Pylades*, *Courier* and *Nancy*, is not easy to judge. The financial proceeds were not great, and the legal niceties probably passed them by. They had been involved in an operation which, though conducted with more than usual hardihood and determination, had not been particularly successful. It was not of course Scott's business to reward military prowess; his concern was with the law. However he might privately have admired the conduct of *L'Espiègle* and her consorts, he made no comment on it. The case was not, so far as can be found, reported in any periodical available to naval officers and no evidence has been discovered of its finding its way into Admiralty directives.

The other great case concerning neutral water was *The Anna*.[12] In July 1805 a British privateer, the *Minerva*, had captured an American ship, bound from the Spanish Main to New Orleans with a cargo of logwood and 13,000 dollars on board, in the delta of the Mississippi, and brought the prize home to England. The United States claimed that the ship had been taken within the territory of the USA and the capture was therefore invalid. The case was heard in November 1805.

On the part of the captors, it was argued that the *Anna* had first been sighted well clear of the mouth of the river and had been chased to the position of capture, over which it was admitted there was dispute, particularly as to where it was relative to Fort Balise, acknowledged to be the American administrative post at the mouth of the river. The captors contended that the islands of mud and driftwood which occurred in the estuary, and were alleged by the Americans to govern the limits of their sovereignty, were temporary 'spots of an equivocal nature' that could not be held to possess the 'ordinary requisites of territory'. In any case, argued Arnold and Robinson representing the privateer, that did not necessarily matter. If the initial contact had been made outside neutral jurisdiction, it was lawful for the privateer to chase the *Anna* into neutral water and capture her there.[13]

The claimants' case was led most unusually by the King's Advocate, seconded by Laurence. They argued that the privateer had systematically violated neutral water for some weeks by 'standing off and on' the mouth of the river; that the chase had started within neutral territory; that even if it had not, the right of a chasing vessel to effect a capture in neutral water was a great deal less clear-cut than the captors had argued; and that the unlawfulness of capture had been aggravated by the privateer's bringing the prize back to England instead of sending her to 'a convenient port' under British control, as laid down in the Prize Act.[14]

Scott in his judgment released the ship without delay. Whatever the questions of jurisdiction and neutral water surrounding the case, he said, the grounds for suspicion about both ship and cargo were too slender to sustain a case for condemnation. 'To bring a vessel so much out of her way . . . is an act of indiscretion which, I hope, will not often be committed by those who are entrusted with his Majesty's commission'.[15]

On a subsequent day, returning to the case, he expanded on this theme, dealing one by one with the reasons given by the captors for bringing the *Anna* to England and dismissing them all: 'there is more reason to suspect that the real cause of seizure proceeded, not from what she had not [a full set of papers], but from what she had, the 13,000 dollars which were on board'.[16]

He then went on to discuss the question of territorial limits in much detail. Strictly speaking he did not need to do this since the restoration was settled, but clearly the problem had caught his imagination. He had done a lot of work on it, consulting charts in detail. Clearly he did not want this work to be wasted and believed his ruling would be useful to posterity.

He began by rehearsing the general rule of law on the subject: the distance of the force of arms 'has usually been recognized to be about three miles from the shore'. But, he went on,

> it so happens in this case, that a question arises as to what is to be deemed the shore, since there are a number of little mud islands . . . which form a kind of portico to the main land . . . I think that the protection of territory is to be reckoned from these islands; and that they are natural appendages of the coast on which they border, and from which indeed they are formed. Their elements are derived immediately from the territory . . . Consider what the consequence would be if lands of this description were not considered as appendant to the main land . . . if they do not belong to the United States of America, any other power might occupy them; they might be embanked and fortified . . . the possibility of such a consequence is enough to expose the fallacy of any arguments that are addressed to shew that these islands are not to be considered as part of the territory of America. Whether they are composed of earth or solid rock will not vary the right of dominion . . .[17]

The remainder of the judgment deals with the activities of the *Minerva* privateer in light of this ruling, in particular her 'standing off and on', in other words using American waters habitually to effect captures, and her setting prisoners on shore in violation of the Instructions to Privateers.[18] Scott concluded that he could 'perceive strong traits of bad faith running throughout the whole conduct of the captors' and made a decree of costs and damages against them.

Several strands of these important judgments stretch down to international law in the twentieth century and indeed to the present day. The misuse of neutral territorial waters and the ill- or neglectful treatment of prisoners have been the subjects of both case law and international legislation. But the most unbroken strand is that from the 'little mud islands' to the present United Nations Convention on the Law of the Sea,[19] where Article 13(1) states that where low-tide elevations are situated wholly or partly at a distance not exceeding the breadth of the territorial sea from the mainland or an island, the low water line on those elevations may be used as the baseline for measuring the breadth of the territorial sea. The principle is exactly the same as Scott enunciated, and is of real value in determining jurisdiction in estuaries and shallow coastal seas. International lawyers still refer to *The Anna* as 'the Portico Case'.[20]

NOTES

1.　　ADM 2/140
2.　　See Chapter 3.
3.　　ADM 1/400.
4.　　For considerations during the Second World War, see D.P. O'Connell, *The Influence of Law on Sea Power* (Manchester University Press, 1975), particularly Chapters III and IV.
5.　　3 C. Rob., pp. 162–6 [1800] and 336–54 [1801], and Appendices XI–XIII.
6.　　Ibid., at p. 164.
7.　　Ibid., at p. 166.
8.　　Ibid., at Appendix, pp. 40–1.
9.　　Ibid., at p. 351.
10.　　Ibid., at p. 354.
11.　　C. John Colombos, *International Law of the Sea*, 6th edn (Longman, 1967), p. 588.
12.　　5 C. Rob., pp. 373–85h [1805].
13.　　This was to some extent analogous to 'hot pursuit'. But the twentieth-century meaning of that term is different, meaning chase out of waters under national jurisdiction on to the high seas; see Colombos, *International Law of the Sea*, pp. 167–75 and Myres S. McDougal and William T. Burke, *The Public Order of the Oceans* (Yale U.P., 1962), pp. 893–923.
14.　　33 Geo. III c.66 s.25.
15.　　5 C. Rob., at p. 383.
16.　　Ibid., at p. 385b.
17.　　Ibid., at p. 385d.
18.　　Instruction dated 13 August 1803, noted in 5 C. Rob., at p. 385f.
19.　　UN Convention on the Law of the Sea, Montego Bay, 10 December 1982.
20.　　Conversation with David Anderson, Second Legal Adviser to the Foreign and Commonwealth Office, 1997.

CHAPTER TWELVE

Recapture and Salvage

The title of this short chapter may be something of a misnomer, for in legal terms recapture of a friendly vessel from the enemy is but one aspect of salvage, defined as the recovery of a vessel from any peril or danger.

Recapture was a fairly frequent occurrence in the wars of 1793–1815. It could occur in a variety of ways. A cruiser could come upon a friendly or neutral vessel, captured by the enemy and making her way towards an enemy port; overcoming a prize crew in such circumstances would generally be easy. If an enemy privateer was captured she might well have one or more prizes in company; in this case the only difficulty would be to split the resources of the captor so that none of the ships under enemy control escaped. Convoy escorts might sometimes effect recaptures; a privateer might for example have been operating on the other side of the convoy, or among stragglers, and an alert escort could restore the situation. Finally, on very rare occasions the crew of a captured ship would themselves manage to recapture her. A sample of captures made during these wars suggests that about 10 per cent of the total were in fact recaptures.[1]

The rules governing salvage were different from those governing prize, but were still adjudicated in the Admiralty or Vice Admiralty Courts. They too had their roots in the *Consolato del Mare*, but the *Consolato*'s rule was that recaptures were to be restored to the former proprietors on payment of 'reasonable remuneration for the expense, trouble and danger incurred'.[2] In the late sixteenth century this rule was radically modified, initially by France, to transfer ownership to the recaptor if the recapture had been in enemy hands for more than twenty-four hours. It was still open to the former proprietor to recover the vessel, but only after payment of salvage, and that was the principle that came to be adopted throughout Europe, though state practice varied in detail and that caused some difficulties, as will be seen.

This change in the legal status of a recapture did not greatly affect the issue, because the level of salvage was set so low that proprietors almost always wanted to buy their property back. In general it was one-eighth of the agreed or independently assessed value of the ship and cargo, though in the case of recaptures by a privateer the proportion was one-sixth.[3] The Court could vary the proportions in special cases and in the case of joint recaptures.

As usual, the basic case was not difficult to manage, and many salvage cases settled relatively quickly.[4] It was the harder cases that came to notice, both in the Reports and in the *Naval Chronicle*.

The *Chronicle* in fact found few such to report. In 1799 there was a genuine claim of salvage in the modern sense of the term: the *Minerva*, an East Indiaman in the Downs, dragged her anchor and was helped to safety by HMS *Sparrow*, assisted by the *Pitt* privateer. Pilotage advice had been given, without which, it was claimed, the Indiaman would have grounded and been lost. A claim for £7,000 was entered; the cargo was said to be worth £40,000. Scott, in his judgment, said: 'Pilotage is an act of labour performed at the helm by persons peculiarly bred to that way of life'; he was reluctant to describe the whole operation as salvage, and awarded 2½ per cent of the agreed value of ship and cargo.[5]

Some years later there was a brief note of a case that could have been the basis of many an incident in a subsequent novel. 'One Murdock and some foreign seamen' had daringly recaptured, in a French port, a ship called *The Brothers* and brought her out to safety among British blockading forces. The recaptors were rewarded with a greater proportion of the value than was usual.[6]

The *Chronicle* recorded only court items it regarded as newsworthy and recaptures generally were not. But in the Court, and faithfully recorded by Robinson, some cases important in law were being decided.

The first difficulty was to reconcile British and continental salvage rules. In *The Santa Cruz*[7] Scott was faced with the case of eight Portuguese ships recaptured at different times over the previous few years. Portugal was certainly 'in amity' with Britain; the question of actual alliance was, as so often, hazy. Scott observed that state practice differed; it would be best always to 'apply in the first instance the rule of that country to which the recaptured property belongs', but there must be reciprocity and there was in English law 'a most liberal rule of restitution on salvage'.

Therefore, it was necessary to examine Portuguese practice rather closely. Scott heard policy evidence by affidavit from high Portuguese officials which he dismissed (after many flowery compliments) as incompetent; examined harder evidence from actual cases in Portuguese courts, of Portuguese recaptures of British vessels over the previous few years; and concluded that 'the law of Portugal established 24 hours' possession by the enemy to be a legal divestment of the property of the original owner' and that before 1797 'the Courts of Portugal considered British property coming out of the hands of the enemy as subject to confiscation'. However, after 1797 a more liberal rule had prevailed in Portugal and this enabled the British to reciprocate. In consequence, Scott ordered that Portuguese vessels retaken since 1797 should be restored on payment of the salvage at the scale which Portugal had established.

A case concerning a ship from a state acknowledged as neutral at the time was *The War Onskan*.[8] This Swedish vessel was captured by the French and retaken by a British cruiser on 26 October 1799. Scott in his judgment said that it was not the general practice of the Court to grant salvage on neutral property, since the original captor was legally bound to restore in any case if no enemy connection was proved. However, added Scott, the French administration and French tribunals had vied in 'outrage' to neutral property and neutrals were so thankful for their liberation that they willingly paid salvage to their recaptors. He so decreed.

In two reported cases Scott was kinder to recaptors with shaky qualifications than he might have been in the case of straightforward captures. The *Helen*[9] was retaken by a revenue cutter having a letter of marque, who received one-sixth salvage as if she was a privateer. No commission was necessary, said Scott; it was the duty of every subject to recapture a British vessel if circumstances allowed. In *The Urania*[10] he followed the same principle.

The commanders of ships escorting convoys could have taken comfort from the case of *The Wight*.[11] A convoy in the Eastern Mediterranean, between Kephalonia and Ithaca, was becalmed. An enemy privateer on the fringes of the convoy saw its chance, boarded and carried the *Wight*. The escorting frigate (not named in the case) saw what was happening, lowered boats and within two hours had recaptured the *Wight*.

When the case came to court, Scott had to decide a claim for salvage on the part of the convoy escort and a counterclaim of negligence against him. He did not discuss the latter on its merits, possibly (it is not entirely clear from the judgment) because it would have involved the professional integrity of the commander involved and this was not a matter within the jurisdiction of the Admiralty Court. He therefore confined himself to the question whether the recapture came within the salvage criteria. As so often, Scott's commonsense approach was apparent. The master of the *Wight* had been taken off the ship; the privateer had put a prize crew onboard; so the capture was complete. Salvage was allowed.

A very similar judgment was made in *The Margaret* some years later.[12] The owners in this case claimed that recapture was, in effect, all part of the service they could expect from a convoy escort. But the Court ruled that the *Margaret* had been 'subdued' by her initial captor and salvage was allowed.

An even happier outcome for a recaptor came in the case of *The Ceylon*.[13] This was an East Indiaman captured by the French in the Indian Ocean and fitted out with two carronades. In this form she had taken part in the defence of Mauritius against an English squadron. She had then been refitted as a prison ship there and had been recaptured when the island fell in 1809.

The question was: did the *Ceylon* come under the salvage rules as a recapture, or was she a vessel 'set forth for war' and therefore to be regarded as a normal prize?[14] Scott spread himself rather largely on the development of the twenty-four-hour rule in this judgment; after an exposition full of Latin, he concluded that it meant the 'total obliteration of the rights of former owners' and the question of salvage and prize lay solely within the gift of the Court. In this case, the *Ceylon* had become a vessel of war and she was condemned to the recaptors as a prize, thus entitling them to her full value.

Recapture and salvage were not the most prominent aspects of prize warfare. They were generally low-key affairs and the proceeds tended to match the effort involved.[15] Where special initiative and courage were involved, the Court sought to ensure they were specially rewarded. For the rest, his Majesty's cruisers may well have thought their best recompense was the gratitude of the crews of the retaken ships, for their release from a detention that would have been at least irksome and might for the private lives of many have been catastrophic.

NOTES

1. PRO HCA 2/355–8 and 365–7; some 1,000 captures were analysed.
2. C. John Colombos, *International Law of the Sea*, 6th edn (Longman, 1967), p. 782.
3. 45 Geo. III c.72 s.7.
4. E.g., *Intrigua* by *Indefatigable*, recaptured October 1810 and settled May 1811; *Josephine* by *Volontaire*, recaptured November 1812 and settled January 1813: in HCA 2/357.
5. II NC, p. 337.
6. XXVI NC, p. 59.
7. 1 C. Rob., p. 49 [1798].
8. 2 C. Rob., p. 299 [1799]. Horne thought it worth recording this case, and that of the *Santa Cruz*, in his *Compendium*.
9. 3 C. Rob., p. 244 [1801].
10. 5 C. Rob., p. 147 [1804].
11. 5 C. Rob., p. 315 [1804].
12. XX NC, p. 62.
13. 1 Dods., p. 105 [1811].
14. 45 Geo. III c.72 s.7.
15. See Chapter 19.

CHAPTER THIRTEEN

Conduct Unbecoming

In every activity which is closely governed by statute, minor violations are frequent. This study has already identified numerous examples where the Prize Acts were not followed to the letter, either because they were unworkable in the particular circumstances of the case or the principals thought they could get away with breaking the rules: often both reasons were present. There will be more examples throughout the book. This chapter deals with more blatant transgressions where the spirit, as well as the letter, of the Course of Admiralty were flouted.

Plunder was a constant temptation. In early times there had been a right of pillage: everything found above deck, with the exception of arms, stores and equipment – which were allocated to the appropriate departments of the capturing ship – was the property of the 'finder'. The right inevitably was much abused and was abolished in the reign of William and Mary.[1] But its vestiges remained, in the minds of many and the practice of some.

The case of four seamen from the *Désirée*, flogged for plundering a prize, has already been mentioned in Chapter 6. More common, according to the records, was plunder by the crews of privateers. A complaint by Denmark against an apparent campaign of sea-robbery by privateers in the Leeward Islands was taken seriously by Doctors' Commons in 1800, in spite of strained relations with Denmark at the time.[2] Similar dirty work was claimed against the *Ann*, *Dart* and *Princess Amelia* in August 1804: in their capture of *La Julie*, not only was plunder alleged but their authorization to make captures at all was regarded as irregular.[3] And in 1809 damages were awarded against the master and owners of a privateer for plundering the *Vidia del Carmen*.[4]

A naval vessel accused of heinous robbery was HMS *Hero*. At the outset of the War of 1812 she took an American ship, the *Factor*, whose master stated that 30,000 dollars had been removed. The case is marked in the Vice Admiralty Court report as 'Not yet tried' in December 1812 and no trace can be found of the final outcome.[5]

It is probable that these were simply the more flagrant cases. Many no doubt never came to light, much less to court. The records, however, suggest that the difference between petty pilfering and systematic stripping was well recognized, and the latter was seriously regarded and dealt with by the courts when it could be proved.

Ill-treatment of prisoners was an occasional allegation of claimants in the courts. In *The San Juan Baptista and Purissima Concepcion*[6] all twenty-two of a captured crew were put in irons after making some resistance to search. Scott held that the resistance in this case was understandable since the captured ship had no reason to think her country was at war with Britain and that the restraint was unjustified. Damages were awarded against the captor.

Even the kind of restraint caused by sending in a prize to an inappropriate port could be a cause for a successful claim. In *The Peacock*,[7] a privateer had in 1799 sent in the prize to Lisbon after a capture in 42° North; Scott held that with the wind fair for England she should have been sent to that country: 'Privateers must bring their prizes home to a port in this kingdom as soon as they can. King's ships may reasonably be allowed a greater latitude . . .'. The case was aggravated by other factors: the privateer had fired under false colours and Admiral Duckworth's forces had released the *Peacock* only the day before. It was little wonder, after this judgment, that costs and damages were awarded against the captors.

The same principle, but with reverse effect, was applied in *The Anna*.[8] In this case Scott thought the prize had been brought back to England unnecessarily: 'the instructions to cruisers give something of a discretion to captors as to the port to which they bring their prize . . . it is a discretion which must be cautiously exercised . . .'; it was unreasonable to 'drag a ship across the Atlantic for adjudication'. In this case, Scott was probably swayed by the fact that the adjudication sought was highly speculative, as the case against the *Anna* was flimsy and needed to be put to further proof to have any chance of succeeding. He was quite unmoved by the contention of the captor that it was the end of their cruise and it was ' "time to come home" . . . that the crew were mutinous, will not do – the owner is answerable for his crew, and no legal excuse can be derived to him from their misconduct'.[9]

There was a high degree of difference between this kind of unjustifiable restraint and the precautions necessary to prevent recapture by the crew of a warship taken as prize. Here again the *Speedy*'s capture of the *Gamo*[10] gives an extreme example. The *Gamo*'s very numerous crew could not be taken off into the tiny *Speedy*, so had to be confined below deck in their own vessel. Naturally, chagrined at their defeat by what had turned out to be a very small force and anxious to recover Spanish honour, they could be expected to make every effort to retake their ship. Cochrane arranged for cannon loaded with canister to be pointed at the hatches beneath which the prisoners were confined, and had a slowmatch burning constantly, making sure the prisoners knew all about it,[11] until the arrival of the ships in Minorca.[12]

Very few instances indeed can be found in the British archives of alleged ill-treatment or unlawful action that resulted in death. The best-known case, and probably the most lasting in its effects, was that of Captain Henry Whitby. In 1806 he was in command of the *Leander* on the North American station, examining the trade with 'a most scrutinizing eye'.[13] During one of these examinations, an American seaman called Pierce was killed and it was alleged by the American authorities that Whitby was directly responsible. He was tried by court martial and no less than five American witnesses testified against him. In spite of this he was acquitted, but was not employed again until 1809: his memoir in the *Naval Chronicle* claimed that this was 'to soothe the Americans'.

Certainly, the incident had caused a diplomatic stir in London; Sir John Nicholl, the King's Advocate, wrote an opinion on 'the unfortunate event which took place off the harbour of New York . . . within the limits of the jurisdiction of the United States'; a belligerent vessel could not lawfully visit and search within the limits of neutral territory. Nicholl accepted that the killing of Pierce might have been accidental, but said it was natural that the American authorities had taken matters into their own hands.[14] This had taken the form of a well-orchestrated public outcry, the demand for Whitby's Court Martial and increased American surveillance.

Further evidence, again according to the *Chronicle*, went on to establish that Pierce had not been killed by British fire. This, according to a reminiscence of one of *Leander*'s midshipmen, was half true. A 'casual shot' (itself surely a significant phrase) from the *Leander* struck the American ship's main boom and it was a splinter from this that killed Pierce.[15] In any event, Whitby was reinstated and appointed to command the *Cerberus*, where he distinguished himself at the battle of Lissa. However, the incident was undoubtedly remembered in the United States and, whatever the merits, could have done nothing to sweeten relations.

The kind of humanity generally extended by British ships towards prisoners was not always matched by countries with which they found themselves in alliance. The Aegean was a particularly savage place. Privateering had long been another word for piracy there: the journal of William Davidson, a seaman on board a Russian privateer in 1788–9, gives graphic accounts of prisoners regularly put to death (a rough calculation suggests a total of at least 900, by this ship alone, in less than a year) and prizes plundered and sold, but never brought to adjudication.[16] It was little different when Captain John Stewart was there in the *Seahorse* in 1806; French, Russians and Turks all preyed on the island populations.[17] Stewart, and Adair the Ambassador to the Porte, had a seemingly impossible task which after initial differences they managed successfully; a telling comment in the context of this study is that Stewart 'regarded his instructions to capture and distress the Ottoman trade, rather as a means of bringing a mistaken enemy to his senses, than as a source of emolument to himself'.[18] That did not, however, stop him capturing the *Badere Zaffer* in July 1808, in one of the bloodiest single-ship actions ever, when the Turkish ship disobeyed instructions not to enter a zone from which warships were excluded.

It was not only during and immediately after capture that captors' conduct towards prizes came under scrutiny. The actions of a prize master were often brought in evidence to support a claim for restoration or restitution. Once in charge the prize master – who might be a midshipman or other junior officer – was responsible for the navigation of the vessel, and if he did not measure up the court would have little mercy. *Der Mohr*[19] was taken on 10 September 1799 and sent in to Portsmouth, but was lost on entering the Solent through the Needles Channel. Captain Church, who had taken the prize, had committed her to Captain Talbot with instructions to take a pilot on board. A pilot duly appeared but Talbot refused to accept him. The master of *Der Mohr* at one point urged Talbot to 'brace his yards sharper' and this was corroborated by 'the widow of a British officer' who was taking passage. Scott found that the ship had been ineptly navigated and decreed restitution, with Church, as principal, liable for the damages.

Jersey and Guernsey privateers came in for particular criticism for their handling of prizes in port. In *The Washington*[20] Scott found that Jersey, to which the ship had been sent, was not 'a convenient port' in practical terms; and similarly in *The Principe*[21] for Guernsey. The latter was an aggravated case because the ship was damaged. There was no objection in principle to ships being sent in to these harbours, but account had to be taken of their depths and berthing arrangements (Scott no doubt knew, or was advised, of the phenomenal rise and fall of the tide in the Channel Islands). It was 'no justification to say that it was the port to which the privateer belonged'.

It might be thought a little hard to saddle the captain or master of a capturing ship with the responsibility for the shortcomings of his prize master. Yet it could scarcely be otherwise. Picking the right subordinate to do a job is one of the principal functions of command; training juniors to do jobs that may fall to them is another. If a captain failed in either of these functions, the responsibility had to be his.

It will be noticed that most of the cases discussed in this chapter concern privateers or hired armed vessels. This, as was stated earlier, does not necessarily imply anti-privateer bias by the Court; Scott was a firm and fair stickler for the law and privateers were more free-and-easy in their ways than most naval vessels.

Hired armed vessels were hybrids.[22] They remained under the ownership of their proprietors and were hired out to the navy at a rate of so much per ton, with £5 a man per month paid to the owners who in turn paid the crew. They were almost always commanded by a naval officer though the rest of the crew were technically civilians. Thus their status was quite different from that of privateers. They were commissioned and did not require letters of marque. The regulations for their rights to the proceeds in prize came under the same section of the Prize Act as did those of full-fledged warships; those of privateers came under a different section.[23]

They worked generally under the orders of commanders in chief, carrying despatches and undertaking patrol duties, and their opportunities for individual prize-taking were generally fewer than those of the smaller warships and far fewer than those of privateers. But since they spent much time going and coming, they could fall in with enemy or neutral craft and so prizes could come their way; and sometimes independent action could pay off, as when the *Colpoys* went into Avilas on 21 March 1806 and captured three Spanish luggers.[24]

One abuse that appears to have been general among hired armed vessels in 1799 was the falsification of crew lists. A circular of 1 January of that year[25] spoke of their being kept 'short of the number of men which . . . their complement should consist of' – and for which the Admiralty was paying. Commanders in chief were directed to conduct frequent musters. The instructions were reinforced some months later.

There is evidence of general feeling in the regular navy, for at least the next five years, that hired armed vessels were not earning their keep. One of the first biographies of St Vincent claimed that they cleared their costs in the first year of service and then 'languished in harbour'.[26] Admiral Sir Charles Pole, an assiduous Member of Parliament for Plymouth, said in 1804 that hired armed vessels were 'an arrant job; a job because the men were rarely mustered and the vessels mostly in port'.[27] Thereafter, however, complaints against this type of vessel appear to diminish. It is likely that they came under a more rigorous régime, as commanders in chief and their staffs learned how to make the best use of them.

But if privateers and hired armed vessels came in for most brickbats from the courts, naval ships were subject to stricter discipline from elsewhere. St Vincent was the most severe: his views on prize-chasing to the detriment of the proper business of protecting trade and annoying the enemy were well known. His censure of a commanding officer who was supposed to be protecting the Cornish pilchard fishery and 'found his way to Cape Finisterre . . . with a view to his private emolument' was both sarcastic and savage.[28] Admirals were not immune; in 1806 St Vincent wrote that he had given instructions to Sir Charles Cotton 'to guide the mode of his cruizing'; he believed Cotton had left the coast of Ireland 'naked' by sending frigates 'cruizing in the stream of the Loire'.[29]

Desertion of a station, except under stress of weather or for pressing operational requirements, continued to be looked on with extreme disfavour and tended to be aggravated when prizes were involved. In 1808, Admiral Gardner on the East Coast complained that the *Briseis* had left her station to accompany a captured galliot to Yarmouth: the conduct of her captain had been 'unofficerlike'.[30] There was if anything greater sensitivity about deserting convoy; as has been shown, it was specifically forbidden by the Articles of War. It is noticeable that Horne's *Compendium*, perhaps the nearest book of these times to a comprehensive Prize Manual,[31] is strong on this point, though the case actually quoted, *The Waakzaamheid*,[32] found that a convoy escort was acting on instructions in investigating a strange sail and was therefore entitled to share in a capture on the other side of the convoy.

In any case, the Admiralty Court would not have addressed itself to professional misdemeanours on the part of naval commanders. Scott maintained that the High Court of Admiralty had no power to rule on the fact of negligence on the part of a convoy escort.[33] Occasionally, as in *The Wight*,[34] the question arose; but Scott usually managed to sidestep it, as he did in that case. The reverse case, of merchant ships deserting convoy, was within the Admiralty Court's jurisdiction as an instance court and many such cases were heard in Doctors' Commons.

One misdemeanour by naval officers that could not always be sidestepped, because it affected entitlement to prize proceeds, was the impressment of protected men from privateers. Routine impressment was quite frequently done and when it was kept within bounds complaints were muted. But in the case of *Gibson and others v. Captain the Hon. Henry Blackwood*, heard in the King's Bench Division on 10 July 1807,[35] it was alleged that four men had been pressed into the *Orion*, Blackwood's command, from the *Eliza* privateer when they held protections – documents to prevent their being pressed. In consequence, it was alleged, the *Eliza* had been unable to exert her full force as a privateer and had taken £3,000 less in prizes than she would otherwise have done. Judgment was given for the plaintiffs in the sum of £2,888 10s 6d. It will be recalled that Blackwood had earlier tangled with a privateer in the case of *The San José* and impressment had been mentioned in that case too; but it is not to be supposed that Blackwood was unique in the practice.

Indeed, commanders of naval ships could be forgiven for suspecting letter-of-marque ships of taking their commissions more as a means of protecting key members of their crews from impressment rather than any serious intention to go privateering. The enormous numbers of letters of marque issued on the home station in 1807 – over 1,200 against France alone,[36] – or in the West Indies from 1803 to 1814,[37] suggest the practice was not at all unusual.

One of the most curious pieces of skulduggery to come into Admiralty jurisdiction was the case of the Marquess of Sligo. This young man, not connected with the Royal Navy, owned a private yacht in the Mediterranean, the *Pylades*. Some time in 1811 it came to light that he had suborned a number of seamen from British ships of war to man his yacht; in October the Commander in Chief, Pellew, was instructed by the Admiralty to send to England anyone who might have been involved.[38] The case came before Scott, as cases of crime committed at sea generally did, sitting in the Admiralty Court's criminal jurisdiction at the Old Bailey. It was extensively reported in the press, including the *Naval Chronicle*. It lasted for some months and ended in December 1812 with a sentence on Lord Sligo of a £5,000 fine and four months' imprisonment in Newgate.[39]

The sequel was even more extraordinary.[40] The Dowager Marchioness of Sligo, mother of the accused, had spent a good deal of time in court and interceded with the judge on behalf of her son. Scott may or may not have been swayed by this intervention, but he was certainly impressed by Lady Sligo's personality; a widower of sixty-eight, he married her. It was not a success.

NOTES

1. Lt-Cdr Peter Kemp RN, *Prize Money* (Gale and Polden, 1946), p. 10.
2. ADM 1/3895.
3. ADM 1/3896.
4. XX NC, p. 172.
5. ADM 1/3901.
6. E.S. Roscoe, *English Prize Cases*, vol. I, p. 417.
7. 4 C. Rob., p. 185 [1802].
8. 5 C. Rob., p. 373ff. [1805].
9. Ibid., at p. 385a.
10. See Chapter 10.
11. Thomas Cochrane, Tenth Earl of Dundonald, *Autobiography of a Seaman*, vol. I (Constable, 1995 edn), p. 115.
12. XI DNB, p. 165.
13. XXVIII NC, p. 265ff.
14. ADM 1/3898, Opinion dated 5 June 1806.
15. W.L. Clowes, *The Royal Navy: A History from the Earliest Times to 1900*, vol. 6 (Chatham edn, 1997), p. 16.
16. *The Naval Review*, vol. XII (1924), pp. 592–607.
17. XXVIII NC, pp. 1–47.
18. Ibid., at p. 41.
19. 3 C. Rob., p. 129 [1800].
20. 6 C. Rob., p. 275 [1806].
21. Edw., p. 70 [1809].

22.   See J. Derriman, 'Hired Armed Cutters of the Napoleonic Wars', *Maritime South West* No. 9 (1996), pp. 97–123, for a description of their organization and work.

23.   45 Geo. III c.72, ss. 2 and 9.

24.   XV NC, p. 344.

25.   ADM 2/1079.

26.   E.P. Brenton, *Life of Earl St Vincent* (Henry Colbourn, 1838), p. 166.

27.   Derriman, 'Hired Armed Cutters of the Napoleonic Wars', p. 98.

28.   Brenton, *Life of Earl St Vincent*, p. 195.

29.   C.C. Lloyd (ed.), *The Naval Miscellany*, vol. IV (Navy Records Society, 1952), p. 479.

30.   ADM 1/560.

31.   The copy in the Naval Historical Branch bears Lord Keith's bookplate.

32.   3 C. Rob., p. 1 [1800].

33.   ADM 1/3899, note of 11 January 1810.

34.   5 C. Rob., p. 315 [1804].

35.   XVIII NC, p. 82.

36.   ADM 1/3898, 9 July 1807.

37.   ADM 1/3902, 9 June 1814.

38.   NMM PEL/22.

39.   XXIX NC, p. 169 and ADM 1/3900.

40.   Henry J. Bourguignon, *Sir William Scott, Lord Stowell* (Cambridge University Press, 1987), p. 55.

PART TWO

THE MIDDLEMEN

CHAPTER FOURTEEN

Prize Agents

In 1803 Earl St Vincent, as First Lord of the Admiralty, instituted a Commission of Naval Enquiry to investigate frauds, abuses and malpractice in the administration of the navy, which he had some years before described as 'rotten to the core'. Of these enquiries, the Fourth Report was concerned with the business of prize agency. The whole of this process was followed closely in the *Naval Chronicle*, with extensive verbatim transcripts of the evidence given. Hardly any of the other proceedings or Reports were reproduced in comparable detail; further indication, if any were needed, of the lively interest taken by the Service in the topic of prize money.

Prize agency had, it is true, been governed throughout the war by Act of Parliament[1] but it was generally perceived by naval officers as a system open to widespread abuse. Two officers, both post captains, made submissions on the subject to the Commission: Alexander Cochrane, who as has already been mentioned thought the agents and the courts were in collusion to ensure that as many cases as possible were contested and appealed, thereby keeping funds in the agents' hands and enriching court officials and lawyers; and Graham Moore, who without making specific allegations found the business a 'cause of much dissatisfaction in the Service'.[2]

The agents thus had to defend their position, and they did so at length. The first to testify was James Primrose Maxwell, a prominent prize agent of the day and, it will be recalled, the first agent to be employed in *The Eenrom* case.[3] His lucid description of the agent's responsibilities is one of the best sources for understanding just what an agent did: '. . . on the arrival of a Prize in port, the Agent takes possession and gets the preliminary examinations taken . . . on printed interrogatories prepared by the King's Advocate . . . The examinations are delivered by the

Registrar [of the Admiralty Court] to the King's Proctor, who follows the opinion of His Majesty's Advocate as to taking out a monition . . .'.[4]

But then came more practical considerations: 'If the capture should be a ship of war, or decidedly the property of the enemy, condemnation generally takes place in the course of six weeks; but in regard to ships claimed as neutral property, the proceedings are not so expeditious.' So, went on Maxwell, perishable cargo might be sold by court order. If a case, contested or not, resulted in condemnation, then '. . . after condemnation the agents proceed to sell the prize and within . . . three or four months . . . make up the accounts . . . giving notice twice in the *London Gazette* that the Account of Sales would be lodged in the Court of Admiralty'.[5] Subsequently, the agent would prepare a schedule for the disbursement to the ship's company of the net proceeds, in accordance with the scales of distribution laid down by Proclamation and drawing on the list supplied to him by the capturing ship showing the name and status of every man on board at the time of the capture. He would then publish in the *London Gazette* a notice of where and when the prize money would be paid to those entitled.

Maxwell was closely questioned on the expenses of condemnation. He estimated that court charges for condemnation in the High Court of Admiralty could come to as little as £23 but might in contested cases be as high as £500; while if a case went to appeal, the lowest figure likely was £150. He added that if a prize was condemned in the High Court and an appeal was lodged (for which neutrals had a year and a day allowed), no sale could take place without double the estimated value being paid into court. As for other costs, Maxwell did not go into detail on brokerage and other fees (which, as will be seen later, were sometimes substantial) but did say that the fee generally charged by prize agents was 5 per cent of the gross proceeds of sale. He regarded this as fair.

Maxwell pointed out that an agent had duties and limitations. By statute[6] he had to bring in his accounts to the Registrar of the Court and to submit a copy to the Treasurer of Greenwich Hospital; he had to come to agreement with any other agents appointed by the captain, officers or ship's company of the captor as to how the 5 per cent fee was to be divided between him and them; and he also had to make arrangements for men not paid in the first tranche to have an opportunity to recover their prize money at frequent intervals so long as the sums remained in his hands. Under the current Act that was three years, after which they went to Greenwich for further administration.

How these complexities were worked out was amplified by three other witnesses, Thomas Maude, James Halford and John Jackson, all prize agents of considerable experience with large practices.[7] Both Maude and Halford confirmed Maxwell's estimate of court costs. All three then concentrated on the machinery for distribution. It was customary, certainly in home waters at that time, for agents to go on board ships to make the first payment on any substantial prize. They would sometimes employ a sub-agent, if the ship's port was remote; the sub-agent would of course need his cut of the fee.

What happened after the first distribution was up to the principal agent. He could retain the money and make any late payments, on production of the necessary documents, as 'recalls' at specified times and at a specified address. On the other hand, he could turn over this responsibility to a Recall Agent, who again would have a scale of charges to come out of the overall 5 per cent agent's fee. Jackson, who seems seldom to have used a recall agent, added that in his 'general view, about four-fifths of the proceeds of prizes are distributed in the first month after the commencement of payment; but there remain in my hands a great many unclaimed shares'.[8] This was so, even though payment could be made to wives on proof of marriage, or to ministers of religion at the place of residence of the person entitled, or indeed to anyone holding a power of attorney from that person.

All these principal agents were closely questioned on the amounts of money they actually held. Halford thought it was about £35,000; Jackson about £100,000. They admitted that they put this money out to interest and, tacitly, that they seldom allowed this to go through to the captors. Thus there was an incentive to do just the kind of thing of which they were accused by Alexander Cochrane: to collude with court officials to spin out proceedings, particularly on appeal, so that interest would be maximized. There was, indeed, the provision that Maxwell had mentioned, that in case of appeal twice the estimated proceeds should be paid into court: but it is not clear whether the Commission probed how rigorously this was enforced.

There was inevitably also some suspicion that agents would collude with brokers and auctioneers to fudge the prices made at auction. This was as difficult to prove as a 'buying ring' is among antique dealers today; but there were practical safeguards. There was nothing to stop a captain sending an independent representative along to the auction – which was always in public – to see fair play. Prices would be discussed, too, in the local press; and accounts had statutorily to be produced and published.[9]

The 1793 Statute gave clear instructions on what was to happen to proceeds still unclaimed after three years. Jackson thought these might amount to rather over 10 per cent of the whole. They were to be transmitted to Greenwich Hospital, whose Treasurer was entitled to make full use of them although if anyone entitled turned up even years later he would be able to recover on production of proof of his entitlement. Greenwich Hospital also benefited from shares that were forfeit. These generally speaking were the shares of men who had deserted and were marked 'Run' on the ship's books, or the books of any ship in which they had subsequently served. There was only one way for such a man to recover his entitlement: if he was able to have the 'Run' removed by the Lords Commissioners of the Admiralty by reason of his subsequent rejoining and good conduct, he could claim the prize money previously forfeit.

The Commission, it is clear, heard all this evidence from the main agents with respect; they were, after all, men of substance and had been established in the business for many years. But the respect was tinged with scepticism and this turned to something much nearer suspicion when the recall agent James Poulain was examined.

Poulain was extensively employed by the main agents, whom he charged 1¼ per cent for the recalls of officers and senior ratings and 2½ per cent for junior ratings. He had many contacts further down the line – for the line did not stop with him. He had sub-agents – to one, John Devereux of Gosport, he paid between £4,000 and £5,000 a year – whose function was to collect on behalf of sailors on production of a power of attorney duly signed. Of course, as the Commission well knew, some of the money to which the sailors were entitled would already have been advanced to them by people like Devereux and they would be unlikely to see much of the rest. In fact he was a 'Navy Agent', near the murky end of the agents' line; there were smaller and dingier operators still and they will be treated in the next chapter.

Poulain was extensively questioned by the Commission, and his answers suggest he was squirming a good deal. He admitted that many of the powers of attorney produced by the navy agents were 'not perfectly regular'.[10] When specific cases were quoted his memory tended to be imperfect. The Commission noted that no authority was required for a recall agent to do his work; whereas a main prize agent had to be properly registered by the Court and this was laid down in the Statute,[11] a recall agent needed only to set up as a private individual, and of course a navy agent was not regulated at all. Considerable concern was expressed that 'the seaman's ignorance of his right is an incitement to fraudulent practice' and that 'the powers of attorney given by seamen are frequently general',[12] extending well beyond prize money so that they might be used to support a claim against a sailor's pay, or even his estate on death.

On the practice on foreign stations, the Commission took evidence from two sources. The first was the clerk of Willis and Waterhouse, a leading firm of prize agents in Jamaica. One of his most revealing statements was the amount of prize carried in to that island during the war of 1793–1801. It amounted to over £2,300,000, of which Willis and Waterhouse had the agency for about nine-tenths. It was their general practice to advance money before condemnation; this was not in accordance with the spirit of the Act and was not generally done on home stations. The Commission did not much like the idea of an agent running an 'account current' with his client;[13] perhaps they thought it was a little too much like turning prize-taking into a business, rather than accepting the fortune of war.

The other witness on foreign-station practice was Brouncker, secretary and agent to Vice Admiral Rainier, Commander in Chief of the East Indies Station from 1794 and still in that post in 1801. No Vice Admiralty Court had been set up on the station during that period, and the papers on captures had been sent to England. But only in the case of neutrals had interrogatories been taken. Advances of money to captors had been made; Brouncker quoted one case only, but the practice must surely have been more widespread than that. There had, after all, been extensive captures on that station: at Amboina and Banda in February 1796 a captain's share was said to have been £15,000.[14] The impression given was of a system of administration rather than law[15] not conducted in accordance with the statute but, as it were, touching base with it. The personal involvement of the Admiral and his secretary, who gave every impression of honesty, probably inhibited serious abuse. Rainier was generally an effective commander in chief with a reputation for eccentricity and generosity;[16] he could afford the latter, for his fortune from prize money was said to be one of the largest of all.[17]

Finally, the Commission turned to a well-known scandal. This was the *Requin* case.[18] This prize, worth about £1,500, had been captured by the *Thalia* in February 1795 in sight of a whole British fleet of fifty sail. A proposal had been made that the *Thalia* should be regarded as sole captor but some of the ships had objected. The case dragged on and finally only the flag officers got their share, the shares of the remainder being so tiny that they would have been swallowed up in administration costs.

This was not so much an abuse or fraud as a *reductio ad absurdum* of the rules of payment for individual prizes and of joint capture. Interestingly, there is little or no suggestion in evidence or comment that this is how it was viewed. No one, for example, made a deduction which would readily have occurred in later centuries: that it would be more equitable to pool the proceeds of all prizes on a station and distribute them regularly in proportionate shares.[19] Nor even was the alternative much voiced: that in case of a small capture made on the fringes of a large fleet, ships in sight should automatically relinquish their entitlement to the actual captor. Perhaps the one required organization well beyond the administrative resources of the time, and the other too radical a shift of attitude. The notion of fortune and the rough justice available in the 'in sight' rule went undented for the rest of the war.

The Commission had one more important input. This was from Nelson himself.[20] The main elements of his proposals were that prize agents should continue in business, but they should be backed by an official Prize Agency Office. They should get their 5 per cent commission only if they made distribution within three months of condemnation. After that the proceeds should be paid into the proposed Office and the agents would get only 2½ per cent. The commission should be calculated on the net, not the gross, proceeds. In case of appeals, no distribution should be made until the appeal was settled. Finally, captors should be 'exonerated from all expenses incurred by the onerous decisions of judges'.

There is little doubt that Nelson in the production of this memorandum was advised by John Scott, his secretary and prize agent for the Mediterranean Fleet. Scott's role will be discussed in more detail later in this chapter, but it is worth noting here that his views on, for example, distribution before appeals were settled[21] are faithfully reflected in Nelson's paper.

What then did the Commission make of all the mass of evidence it had taken? Its Fourth Report was signed by the Commissioners [Admiral] Charles Morice Pole, Ewan Law, John Ford, Henry Nichols and William Mackworth Praed on 16 July 1804.[22]

First, it found that there had been 'no copious disclosure of gross and abominable frauds' in the business of prize agency. This might be thought an excellent example of eighteenth-century weasel-wording, but if analysed in the light of the evidence given to the Commission it is about as accurate as can be. At the top end of the business, prize agency was fairly well regulated by statute and generally the statute was honoured in the letter, at least on the home stations.

Whether it was honoured in the spirit was of course more problematical. The imposition of delay either by unnecessary legal process or for reasons of administration; the lurking suspicion that legitimate proceeds, particularly from cargoes, were leaking out at the sides before they reached those entitled; and the disclosure of a network that allowed a large number of fingers into an attractive pie, were perhaps not 'gross and abominable frauds', but the Navy regarded them as indicative of a system where everyone involved could nip a bit and so make a comfortable living, to the disadvantage of those who suffered the discomforts and dangers of the sea life and did the work of capture.

The agents could and did argue that they did a lot for their money. Arrangements for the disposal of ship and cargo were often complex, involving travel which was always arduous; likewise the bringing on of court cases; and accounting and clerical effort was by no means negligible. They could have added, though this was seldom stated, that the system as it existed could not have worked without them. They had a captive market.

The Commission's recommendations sought to change the system quite dramatically, and indeed followed Nelson's proposals in many respects. They were: to set up a Prize Office; to limit the agency for each ship to one person; to require a bond of £5,000 from each agent for registration as such; to limit the agent's commission to 5 per cent of the net proceeds; and to require proceeds to be paid in to the Prize Office after six months from the date of condemnation, if no appeal had been lodged. Notification of all captures must be made as soon as possible to the Prize Office, which would thus have oversight of the whole system and be able to check potential abuse. It would also be a centre for advice to all who required it. The annual cost of the Prize Office, with three Commissioners, ten clerks in the main office and six in the outports, was estimated at £6,860.[23]

The recommendations of the Commission went into considerable detail on the rules to which the Prize Office would work, including very complex provisions for unclaimed shares, the costs of appeal cases and advance payments in cases where there was significant delay. Probably they went into too much detail. It is almost certain that they scared the Board of Admiralty, as they would terrify today anyone with experience of bureaucracy. They probably were not unworkable; they certainly would have been cumbersome.

Hardly any of them were implemented. The Prize Office, the centrepiece of the scheme, was never set up. What did emerge was something quite different: a new Prize Act.[24] 'New' is arguably a misnomer; most of its provisions followed closely the previous Acts of 1793 and 1803.[25] However, in the sections dealing with prize agency it did rather more than tinker with the existing regulations.

First, farming out business to sub-agents was forbidden.[26] This statutorily cut out the recall agent; as subsequent provisions of the Act operated, his function was effectively to die anyway. Secondly, a bond of £5,000 was required of each agent on registration.[27] Thirdly, regulations for the transmission of Prize Lists to agents, with alternative arrangements if they were not transmitted by the captor within reasonable time, were much tightened.[28] Fourthly, the Court was given powers to compel agents to invest the proceeds of a condemned prize for the benefit of captors and to pay a proportion into court in cases of appeal.[29] Fifthly, agents were not to be compelled to distribute until the time allowed for appeal lapsed but were then to make distribution within three months, so far as they were able.[30]

But the two most important changes were, as so often in legislation, contained in a very few words in each case. The first was a provision about agents' percentage commission. No figure was set; but it was to be 'charged upon the *net* [my italics] Proceeds of any Prize or Prizes, Bounty Bills or Salvage'.[31] The other was a change in the time that should elapse before the residue of proceeds was transmitted to the Royal Hospital at Greenwich. This was drastically reduced to four months from the date of first distribution.[32] There were many administrative clauses in the Act which flowed from this change.

Thus the 1805 Act, in the drafting of which Sir William Scott certainly had a hand[33] and the Bill for which he introduced in the House of Commons,[34] did partially implement the recommendations of the Commission. The Bill had not on its second reading received unqualified support; one unkind comment was that it was not for 'The Encouragement of Seamen' so much as 'The Encouragement of Doctors' Commons'. But as it emerged as an Act, it tightened the regulations on prize agents, it abolished the need for one tier of middlemen, and it substituted for the proposed Prize Office a combination of the existing bureaucracies at Greenwich Hospital and the Navy Pay Office.

The agents probably felt they had come out of it quite well. They had escaped an irksome, if not worse, power of oversight from a brand-new institution that would certainly have sought to interfere with their usual mode of conducting business. The change in the timing of transfer of funds to Greenwich cut both ways: agents were relieved of tedious recall arrangements, either their own or using recall agents, but on the other hand they lost the use of money in their hands. Finally, the provision that the agent's fee was to be charged on net and not gross proceeds was less onerous to agents than might be thought, because the question immediately arose: net of what? There were many points in the accounting process where proceeds could be called 'net': after brokerage charges by the auctioneers had been deducted, after court and shipkeeping charges had been deducted in addition, or after all related charges of whatever kind had been allowed for. Examples of all these ways of calculating net proceeds occur in the records, though towards the end of the war a more standard method emerged.

One reason for this was an Act of 1806[35] which laid down that 1⅔ per cent of the net proceeds of each prize – including head money and crown or admiralty droits – was to be paid over to the Treasurer of Greenwich Hospital, and an immediately following Act[36] which stipulated that 3⅓ per cent should similarly go to the Chatham Chest, 'to extend and increase allowances to, Persons maimed or hurt, or otherwise disabled in the Service of their Country'. The Chest, which was an institution of great antiquity,[37] had been administered by Greenwich Hospital for some years[38] so the administration was not too cumbersome. It became standard form for agents to deduct these percentages right at the end of the calculation of prize money, so that it came *after* they had taken their commission but *before* the sum remaining for distribution emerged. Since the deductions were 5 per cent in each case, it made no difference to the captors which way round it was done, but the agents nipped a little more.

Even though no Prize Office had been instituted, agents remained under scrutiny from official sources as well as from their clients. Foremost in this activity was George Rose, the Treasurer of the Navy from

1807 through to the end of the war. Rose was of Scots descent and had himself served in the Navy from 1758 to 1762.[39] He was a highly experienced civil servant, having been Secretary of the Treasury for many years round the turn of the century. From the start of his tenure of office at the Admiralty he seems to have been the champion of the rights of sailors to their prize money and in 1809 he instituted a deep inquiry into the operation of the system.

Rose's Report[40] was transmitted to the Lords of the Admiralty in January 1811 and made sombre reading. His introduction outlined his rationale: 'the probable extent to which the officers and men of His Majesty's Navy have suffered from the want of an active and vigilant officer to watch over their interests'. He emphasized the scale of the moneys involved: 'The net proceeds of prizes distributed in the past year considerably exceeds in amount £1,300,000.'

The Report itself began by saying that 600 agents' accounts had been examined and that in frequent instances agents had been challenged over charges. Rose accepted that the Prize Act was in places not easy to interpret, but agents had often been guilty of 'interested misconception'. His assessment was that perhaps £50,000 must have been over-claimed. He was at pains to point out that he had a robust statistical base to back up his findings; he had employed Samuel Hancock, who had himself been a prize agent in a small line of business, to produce a 'perfect record' of 5,600 cases, as well as 3,000 in the Vice Admiralty Courts, and 600 appeal cases. (Sadly, there seems to be no trace of Hancock's list in the Public Record Office; had it been there, at least one researcher's task would have been greatly eased.)

Rose went on to look at the likely amount of money in agents' hands pending distribution, either because cases were under appeal, or were the matter of other forms of dispute, or simply because agents had been slack over disbursement – a particular failing on foreign stations. He calculated this at £750,000 as a general, ongoing figure. Out of this the captors very seldom saw any interest. Rose saw a need for a 'controlling power' over this serious shortcoming, and the Report says he already had done something about it: a pooled fund of £500,000 had been negotiated and was now earning interest on behalf of captors. The accounts of this fund and evidence on the way it was administered have not come to light.

The Report continued by discussing various other abuses and irregularities, each carefully costed: the charges of double agency, the withholding of reserved sums in joint operations, the lack of control of droits grants after payment over to agents, the loophole whereby, in cases of restitution by compromise, Greenwich and the Chatham Chest received no percentage, and alleged 'great abuses' over head money. Some of these are, in the light of analysis contained in later chapters of this book, surprising; but Rose was looking at specific cases as well as overall statistics, and no doubt he uncovered many nasty little nests. In many cases he claimed already to have checked the abuses, either by individual action or by instituting tighter regulation.

Rose's claim is borne out by the figures. The survey carried out by the author (see Appendix 1) shows that the average proportion of gross proceeds which accrued to captors of merchant vessels as the 'net amount for distribution' steadily increased as the war went on, significantly so after 1811. In the previous decade it had been just under 80 per cent; in the last five years of the war it climbed to 83 per cent, and this, it must be remembered, was after the introduction of the subvention to the Chatham Chest and Greenwich Hospital, which should in theory have worked in the opposite direction.

But the agents were still doing quite well. The established firms – Marsh and Creed, Ommanney and Druce, Sykes, Jackson (with, latterly, Muspratt), Cooke and Halford, Maude – remained in business throughout the war and long after. Though their main function during the war had been as prize agents, they were also bankers and merchants and this diversification allowed them in many cases to move smoothly into a peacetime function. The firm of James Sykes became Thomas Stilwell and Sons in 1816 and was absorbed by the National Westminster Bank in 1923.[41]

What then was the relationship of the captain of one of His Majesty's Ships with his prize agent? This is much the same sort of question as the length of a piece of string, for without doubt it depended on personalities and circumstances. Many captains were seldom on shore and many more could not get up to London where most of the agents' offices were – though some agents were based in Portsmouth or Plymouth and many would keep a clerk there as a link. So much correspondence and communication would be at arm's length.

Trust had to be mutual. Certainly the captain had to trust his agent not to go broke or abscond with the takings; but the agent also had to rely on his captain to render returns, particularly prize lists, when they were required and to keep him informed as to the ship's whereabouts. In fact, so critically was the business of prize viewed and so great was the confluence of interest, that both these criteria were on the whole met. There is no recorded instance of the default of a major agent in the United Kingdom throughout the war, though some lesser firms or individuals may have succumbed, and in previous wars such cases had been more frequent. For example, Captain Andrew Mitchell during the War of American Independence had acquired considerable prize money in the Indian Ocean; but his agent had laid out the money in nursing a Scottish parliamentary constituency and 'scarcely a wreck remained'.[42] Such cautionary tales circulated in the naval community and must have kept prudent captains on the alert.

Agents were well placed to be advisers to their clients on points of law, for although few appear to have had legal training they were necessarily in close touch with Doctors' Commons.[43] Discussion of the principles of prize law and the effect of recent judgments must have taken place when agents and captains met, particularly when no manual existed and law reports, official circulars and publications on the subject were spasmodic and piecemeal. The agent would in effect be acting as solicitor, accountant and banker in addition to his principal and specialized function in matters of prize.

An example of the kind of service expected of agents is in a letter written on behalf of Captain Stanhope of the *Ruby* in January 1798:

> the ships which were concerned in detaining the Dutch East Indiamen and Men of War (in number about 12) in Plymouth Sound, would receive a Gratuity, or reward for that Service. As Mr. Pitt thought proper to appropriate a Million arising from the sale of these Prizes to the purposes of Government, it is I shd. think but right that some little douceur shd. be given the officers and men that forced them into harbour'.[44]

The outcome is not known; seeing that it was almost certainly a droits matter, Stanhope and his men would probably have received something, sometime.

All this held good for the home stations. It was a different matter abroad. In the more settled stations such as Jamaica, the system functioned as a microcosm of the home station, with well-established agents, experienced courts and a steady stream of business. But as the war went on, even on those stations complications and opportunity for widespread irregularity developed. The rash of little Vice Admiralty Courts in the West Indies, which Sir William Scott had tried unsuccessfully to check,[45] led to proliferation of agents and some lowering of standards. Changes in the tempo and intensity of operations, such as at the opening of the American war of 1812, could catch courts unawares and allow inexperienced people into the agency business. And always the tyrannies of time and space, wind and weather, would operate against efficiency and give opportunities for those ashore to give less than adequate service to those afloat.

The Mediterranean was as bad as anywhere, whether before or after the formation of the Malta Vice Admiralty Court in 1803, and Nelson was as aware of the deficiencies of the system as anyone. As early as 1796 he recorded a 'List of Prizes' taken while in command of the *Agamemnon* for the previous three years, showing an estimate of what he thought he should have received against the amounts he actually had had; the figures were £4,349 and £2,227 respectively.[46] Much of the business had passed through the hands of M'Arthur and Pollard, agents in Leghorn, with whom Nelson was on polite but by no means effusive terms.

It was no doubt partly this experience that induced Nelson, when in command of the fleet in the Mediterranean from 1803 to 1805, to nominate John Scott, his secretary, as prize agent. A letterbook of Scott's, consisting entirely of letters written in that capacity, was acquired in 1995 by the Royal Naval Museum at Portsmouth and makes interesting reading.

Clearly, it was impossible for Scott, working as secretary to an Admiral who spent his whole time afloat, to conduct all the business of prize agency. He therefore had to lay off the business to agents ashore. In Britain they were the well-established firm of Marsh and Creed; Nelson's interest in any prizes sent to England was to be dealt with by them.[47] In Malta Patrick Wilkie, Agent Victualler, was employed as agent, as was his counterpart Cutforth in Gibraltar. There were others: Pemberton and Lawson in Malta, Broadbent in Messina are names that occur frequently.

The networking of the system is well illustrated by these letters. Because the Commander in Chief partook, through his 'flag eight' share, in every prize taken on the station, Scott had to be in communication on any matter of prize that raised the least difficulty. Thus when Captain Richard Keats in the *Superb* detained a Ragusan brig, the *Madonna del Rosario*, John Scott wrote at some length to Wilkie; it was clear to his mind, from the 'evasive and contradictory answers' given by the brig's captain, 'that she has been trading for our enemies', and that 'other circumstances, agreeable to Sir William Scott's opinion, would of itself condemn the vessel'.[48] Later, while pressing for Wilkie 'to use every means to condemn the *Superb*'s prize', John Scott accepted that she should not be detained for further proof or appeal unless there seemed to be a good chance of condemnation.[49]

John Scott's approach was at once pushing and cautious, just what one would have expected of this admirable secretary. He was particular on the matter of advancing money in anticipation of the favourable outcome of appeals: even if 'needyness' should intervene, 'as an agent I would say *no*'.[50] He took up the cudgels on behalf of the smaller ships, challenging any apparently high charges on condemnation, expressing pleasure when prizes sold well, and helping with administration such as the provision of prize lists when ships had omitted through no fault of their own to provide them. The care and concern of his Admiral was often apparent: when in August 1804 the *Phoebe* detained the Sardinian ship *Fortuna*, Nelson reversed the decision and allowed her to pass, but he took full responsibility.[51] When Broadbent in Messina showed signs of being in default through failure to pay up on cargoes sold there, Scott, 'exceedingly astonished and disappointed', had no hesitation in bringing Nelson in.[52]

There seems to have been one fly in this ointment, and that was Nelson's relationship with Davison, his friend and chief agent in

England. From about March of 1805 Scott's letters show increasing concern that Davison was meddling in the Mediterranean agency, which he, Scott, had comfortably split fifty-fifty with Wilkie and Cutforth.[53] In particular, Davison was offering himself to all captains on the station as agent. It appears from the correspondence that Scott sought a ruling from Nelson and it went in his favour. In May, he was writing to Cutforth that they would be 'several thousand pounds in pocket' as a result of Nelson's decision.[54]

As is well known, John Scott did not survive Trafalgar to enjoy the fruits of what he had earned. He was killed on the quarterdeck of *Victory* alongside his chief, shortly before Nelson himself was shot down. 'Is that poor Scott?' asked the Admiral as they heaved the body over the side. It had been an extraordinarily close relationship between a naval genius and a highly talented administrator, made all the more effective by an honest and well-conducted prize agency.

Not all flag secretaries were either so conscientious or so comprehensive in the scope of their work. Often it was confined to making sure that the 'flag eight' was secure and this particularly applied on the home stations.[55] On the other hand, some flag secretaries took an even more active part than did John Scott. Of these the best documented is George Redmond Hulbert, secretary to Sir John Borlase Warren from 1807 to the end of the war. Warren was Flag Officer on the North American station at the start of the war of 1812 and because he conducted operations mainly from his shore headquarters, Hulbert had ample opportunity to act directly as agent for most of the ships on the station. Many of his papers have survived and are in the National Maritime Museum.

Hulbert was a conscientious and efficient agent. His accounts are models of clarity and appear to be the first to use printed forms to cover the more usual headings for deductible expenses.[56] A deep study of his papers by Tony Gutridge[57] has estimated that his average charges, including agency and court fees and Greenwich and Chatham Chest deductions, were no more than 15½ per cent, an unusually low figure.

Errors and omissions there certainly were, though, and these are the matters that naturally predominate in the correspondence over things that went right. Hulbert was none too secure on the procedure for head money: he sent to Ommanney and Druce for advice and their 'observations' identified in every case omission to provide one or more of the four elements of information required before payment could be made: the decree of condemnation, a certificate of the enemy crew, a letter of attorney from the captor and the captor's prize list.[58] Many years later the Navy Pay Office was picking up items, some trivial but others less so: for example, what had happened to the prize money owing for a ship which had been lost before distribution could take place?[59] Hulbert was able to make a satisfactory reply, but the date of this correspondence, November 1821, shows just how exacting the Admiralty had become in chasing prize matters. Foremost among the chasers was Samuel Hancock, whose work on Rose's Report had clearly been rewarded with a permanent job in the bureaucracy.

Many individual naval ships appointed someone on board, or a friend or relation of the captain's, to act as co-agent to look after the ship's interest: to chase agents on shore, or to go ashore themselves and do some of the agent's part. Thomas Peckston, Purser of the gun-brig *Pelorus* in the Mediterranean in 1813, was thought to have the potential:

> Captain Gambier . . . and all the officers joined in expressing their desires that I should . . . whenever we make a capture I shall be appointed Agent with some other person on shore, who will have to transact the business, while I remain quietly on board to receive one half of the Agency, [but] If we take prizes of sufficient worth I should certainly remain on shore to see them condemned and their cargoes disposed of . . . I should probably remain at Mahon three fourths of the time.[60]

Peckston was writing to his wife, who had enterprisingly journeyed out to Minorca the year before. His optimism was ill-founded; the *Pelorus* took no prizes. But his letter shows that the practice of shipboard agency was by no means exceptional.

In summary, most naval people regarded prize agents as a necessary evil – the fate of many classes of middlemen. Given the need for every prize to pass through the courts and to contribute in various ways – duty payable, Greenwich, the Chatham Chest – to the exchequer, it would have been out of the question for captains or ships' officers to handle all the necessary transactions themselves. From the beginning to the end of the wars of 1793–1815, the agency system was steadily subjected to increasing control and its worst excesses were checked. For this the 1804 Commission and the work of George Rose in the years round 1810 were principally responsible, always backed by a sub-current of feeling in the Navy to which the leaders of the agency business could not have been insensitive. There were far more structural defects and flagrant abuses at the lower end of the market: they are for the next chapter.

NOTES

1. 33 Geo. III c.66 and 43 Geo. III c.160.
2. XI NC, p. 224.
3. See Chapter 3.
4. XI NC, p. 32.

5.   Ibid., p. 33.

6.   33 Geo. III c.66 ss.59–63.

7.   Survey of Prize Accounts (see Appendix 1), *passim*; the market share was approximately Maude 5 per cent, Halford 3 per cent and Jackson 6 per cent.

8.   XI NC, p. 131.

9.   33 Geo. III c.66 s.60.

10.   XI NC, p. 221.

11.   33 Geo. III c.66 s.51.

12.   XI NC, p. 297.

13.   Ibid., p. 462.

14.   W.L. Clowes, *The Royal Navy: A History from the Earliest Times to 1900*, vol. 4 (Chatham edn, 1997), p. 294.

15.   C. John Colombos, *A Treatise on the Law of Prize* (Sweet and Maxwell, 1926), describes this as a characteristic of the French prize system. To a lawyer it had clear shortcomings.

16.   Robert Gardiner (ed.), *The Campaign of Trafalgar 1803–1805* (Chatham, 1997), p. 22.

17.   Michael Lewis, *A Social History of the Navy 1793–1815* (George Allen and Unwin, 1960), p. 320.

18.   XII NC, p. 23.

19.   Lt-Cdr Peter Kemp RN, *Prize Money* (Gale and Polden, 1946), p. 30, for the system in the First and Second World Wars.

20.   XII NC, p. 29, note.

21.   John Scott to Wilkie, Agent Victualler at Malta, 12 April 1804 (letterbook in the Royal Naval Museum, Portsmouth).

22.   XII NC, p. 221. The *Chronicle* gives the year as 1803, but this must be a misprint.

23.   XII NC, p. 28.

24.   45 Geo. III c.72.

25.   33 Geo. III c.66 and 43 Geo. III c.160.

26.   45 Geo. III c.72 s.55.

27.   Ibid., s.57.

28.   Ibid., s.60.

29.   Ibid., ss.63–4.

30.   Ibid., s.70.

31.   Ibid., s.69.

32.   Ibid., s.80.

33.   ADM 1/3896.

34.   XIV NC, p. 77.

35.   46 Geo. III c.100.

36.   46 Geo. III c.101.

37.   J.R. Hill (ed.), *The Oxford Illustrated History of the Royal Navy* (OUP, 1995), pp. 67, 254.

38.   43 Geo. III c.119.

39. XLIX DNB, p. 226.

40. ADM 1/3657; a printed version also appears in HCA 30/627.

41. Geoffrey L. Green, *The Royal Navy and Anglo-Jewry 1740–1820* (Green, 1989), p. 103.

42. XVI NC, p. 97.

43. Green, *The Royal Navy*, p. 103.

44. NatWest archives, Stilwell/4 No. 242.

45. ADM 1/3898, letters of July 1806 and June 1807.

46. Sir Nicholas Harris Nicolas, *The Dispatches and Letters of Lord Nelson*, vol. II (Chatham edn, 1997), pp. 178–9.

47. John Scott to Marsh and Creed, 5 October 1803.

48. John Scott to Wilkie, 14 November 1803.

49. John Scott, Memorandum of 8 December 1803.

50. John Scott to Wilkie, 12 April 1804.

51. John Scott to Cutforth, 15 August 1804.

52. John Scott to Broadbent, 31 December 1804.

53. John Scott to Wilkie, 27 March 1805.

54. John Scott to Cutforth, 7 May 1805.

55. Tony Gutridge, 'Aspects of Naval Prize Agency 1793–1815', 80 The *Mariner's Mirror* (1994), pp. 46–7.

56. There are many examples in HCA 2/358 and HCA 2/366.

57. Tony Gutridge, 'George Redmond Hulbert, Prize Agent' (unpublished thesis, Portsmouth Polytechnic, 1981–2), p. 67.

58. NMM HUL/7, 15 November 1813.

59. NMM HUL/42 Folio 3.

60. RN Museum Papers No. 1997/65: Thomas Snowden Peckston to Mary Peckston, 16 February 1813.

Navy Agents

Officers generally regarded themselves as having a substantial interest in prize money and would take some pains to maximize and preserve it. They used prize agents as bankers and accountants and were willing to spend considerable time in correspondence and discussion with them. Relationships were close or distant, friendly or not, as personalities and circumstances dictated.[1]

The seamen were in a different situation. The lure of prize money was no less for them than it was for the officers; indeed, Professor Michael Lewis regarded it as 'the most important of all material inducements to a naval career'[2] and Thomas, Lord Cochrane gave it as the 'first motive' for fighting seamen.[3] But their opportunities for administering what came as their share were far more limited than those of the officers.

First, the amounts, as will be shown further in later chapters, were small in relation to those of the officers and often very small in absolute terms. It would be a prize of well above average worth that yielded more than ten pounds to an able seaman; and even though that was equivalent to half a year's pay, it was not the sort of figure that would materially alter his life or his prospects.

Secondly, shore leave was limited and spasmodic. The opportunity simply did not occur to enter into a stable business relationship with a well-established banker or agent. When a ship arrived in one of the home ports, the shore came to its crew rather than its crew to the shore; the memories of 'Jack Nastyface' give graphic descriptions of the Bacchanalian goings-on that ensued on board.[4] This was countenanced by the officers as preferable to allowing shore leave and giving men the opportunity to desert. Leave might be given to trusted men, particularly when there was ship's business to be looked after ashore, but for the average seaman in an operational ship, liberty was rare.

That led to the third factor. When he did get ashore, Jack tended to live up to his uproarious, free-and-easy reputation. Life was for living and sailors wanted to pack many a day's living into a few hours' life on shore. A sharp new suit of clothes, a great deal of liquor and a girl or several were most men's idea of a good run ashore. They might sail tomorrow and be dead the day after. In consequence, prize money when it was made available would be spent freely.

That was the fourth factor: was the money available? Sometimes, after condemnation and due publication of accounts and the appearance of a notice in the *Gazette*, prize agents would come on board to pay the majority of the ship's company their shares; but as like as not the ship would sail on the same day, without any chance of further leave.[5] Otherwise, a call at the agent's office might be necessary and this could be inconvenient or downright impossible. Knowing well that he was due for some prize money, though often not at all sure how much it might be or when he would get it from the regular source, a sailor would be likely to look for a short cut.

It was readily available in the Navy Agent. This was the term generally given to the traders – often publicans or slop-sellers – who negotiated with sailors for authorization to receive their share of prize money in return for advances of cash or supplies in kind.[6] They were of course taking a financial risk in doing so. The money might be a long time coming; the paperwork on which a loan was based might be defective or even forged; there might be clever attempts to pass off one prize ticket to two or more agents;[7] or the seaman concerned might desert and lose his entitlement, leaving the navy agent with a valueless power of attorney. But all the evidence is that they laid off their risk with some pretty spectacular rates of profit.

A judgment on their activities was encapsulated in the Fourth Report of the Commission of Naval Enquiry:

> there exists a set of men, who take advantage of the unsuspicious character of the indiscretion and extravagance which prevail among seamen; and who, in time of war, earn a scandalous livelihood, by supplying them with liquor, clothes and trifling sums, and getting from them wills and powers of attorney for prize money . . . the seaman's ignorance of his right is an incitement to fraudulent practice . . . the powers of attorney given by seamen are frequently general . . .

In other words, extending far beyond prize money.[8]

The Commission pointed out that the matter of navy agents was not strictly within its remit, which dealt only with the activities of the main prize agents, but it did recommend tightening up the law so far as navy agents were concerned. These recommendations were reflected in the 1805 Act, where one long section[9] was prefaced with the objective of remedying the practices whereby

> Petty Officers, Seamen, Marines and Soldiers, in his Majesty's Naval Service, have heretofore been, in many instances, defrauded of their Prize and Bounty Monies, or large proportions thereof, in consequence of their having acted improvidently, and without

sufficient consideration for the same, executed Powers of Attorney, and other Instruments, by which they have transferred their interest not only in all such Prize and Bounty Money, which at the time of executing such Powers of Attorney or Instruments, might have been due to them, but [my italics] *also all Prize and Bounty Money to which they might thereafter become entitled.*

The statute then prescribed a standard power of attorney, for presentation by the navy agent to the prize agent or to the Treasurer of Greenwich Hospital, which specified the prize or prizes for which it was drawn and which included a certificate from the captain, countersigned by a 'signing officer', of the sailor's current ship to prove his entitlement to the prize money in question as well of course as the fact that he had freely executed the instrument. There was even provision for other forms of countersignature in the case of men who had been discharged through invaliding or other cause. It was, in theory, only on production of such a document that a navy agent could be paid prize money.

For the further discouragement of navy agents and encouragement of seamen to go through the proper (but cumbersome) channels, a later section of the same Act[10] made it lawful for the Treasurer of the Greenwich Hospital, if satisfied as to entitlement, to make out duplicate bills that could be presented to a county Receiver of Land Tax, or Customs and Excise official, in order to collect prize money, and prescribed the form for doing so. How widely this provision was taken up is uncertain; it could have been useful to wives living in areas remote from the home ports and there already was a good deal of legislation to encourage allotments of pay,[11] so it may have been more used than popular belief would suggest.

There had been suspicion that powers of attorney were quite widely forged. Certainly the evidence of James Poulain before the 1804 Commission admitted that many were 'not perfectly regular',[12] and that was a euphemism that must have covered some very dubious goings-on. The 1805 Act could not have been more severe in its provisions against such practices: personation, forgery or counterfeit in order to obtain prize or bounty money would result on conviction with the miscreant's 'Death as a Felon, without benefit of Clergy'.[13] In fact this reiterated the provision of an Act of 1758[14] but it certainly rammed the point home. In spite of this sanction, some personation persisted right through to the end of the war. When it could be established that a seaman had suffered financially thereby, he was reimbursed by government.[15]

All the shortcomings that still existed in the system are demonstrated in the accounts for the Trafalgar prize money.[16] Every man in every ship is detailed in these documents, the shares ranging from £973 for a captain to £1 17s 6d for a seaman. The disposal of the money is noted in every case.

The main payment was made in April 1807. Virtually all the commissioned and warrant officers, and a substantial majority of the petty officers, picked up their share in good time. For the seamen the situation was clearly quite different. In one ship, the *Temeraire*, 441 out of 636 were paid their share, though not all in the first distribution and not all, by any means, personally. Agents in many instances signed for the money, having the necessary powers of attorney. Unclaimed shares were marked with a red 'G', signifying that they had been transferred to Greenwich; a few are shown as having been claimed later.

But the *Temeraire*'s list is a great deal better, from the standpoint of the sailor after his £1 17*s* 6*d*, than most of the others. In the list for Blackwood's *Euryalus*, for example, nearly all the seamen's shares are recorded as having gone to Greenwich, only 10 out of 212 entitled being shown as paid. The lists for some line of battle ships other than the *Temeraire*, the *Tonnant* being typical, exhibit another very worrying aspect. Whole pages show names bracketed together with an agent's signature for receipt of the whole, while other pages contain sequences of 'marks', theoretically the crosses made as a form of signature by illiterate seamen, which are all clearly by the same pen and look to be by the same hand. None of this is proof of corrupt practice, but it is highly suspicious.

A less extreme story emerges from the earlier list of the distribution of the Trafalgar Bounty money, the £300,000 voted by Parliament in recognition of the significance of this great battle where so few of the shattered and storm-tossed prizes eventually reached a British port. Here the seaman's share was £4 12*s* 6*d* and the main distribution was made in the autumn of 1806. Far fewer of the shares are recorded as having gone to Greenwich, but otherwise the evidence of payment to agents rather than directly to the men entitled is the same.

These records put into context the prize agent Jackson's evidence noted in the previous chapter, that 'about four-fifths of the proceeds are distributed in the first month after commencement of the payment'. In money terms he was probably right, but – if the Trafalgar accounts are in any way typical – much of the remaining fifth was money that ought to have gone to the neediest part of the ship's company, and either it was never paid at all, or it went to navy agents who pocketed a disproportionate part of it.

Thus, every indication is that widespread abuses at this end of the market persisted. The fact that many navy agents were in the clothing and tailoring trade – slop-sellers in the language of the time – meant that they often provided clothing as payment in kind for the powers of attorney and prices were only too easy to inflate. Myers and Hart of Portsmouth were shown in 1810 to have marked up prices by some 20 per cent above the market rate when supplying clothes as navy agents.[17] Moreover, they were found to have charged a commission of 5 per cent on loans when 2½ was the maximum permitted under the 1758 Act, in a section which had never been repealed.[18]

Thus, when George Rose produced his Report[19] in 1811, he had ample room for criticism of navy agents. But in fact he could point to action he had already taken to check abuses. This had been done in a way which at first looks quite lenient, but proves to have been to a significant degree effective in practice.

Rose had introduced new legislation in an Act 'for the further Encouragement of Seamen, and for the better and more effectually providing for the Interest of the Royal Hospital at Greenwich'.[20] In Section 37 of this Act, navy agents were required to take out a licence in prescribed form. The licence itself cost only 5s, but it had to be backed by a surety of £200 by persons acceptable to the Treasurer of the Navy. The Treasurer had power to revoke licences if in his judgement 'any such licenced Agent hath abused the Trust reposed in him by not duly accounting to any Person or Persons by whom he shall have been empowered to receive any such Wages, Pay, Prize Money, Bounty Money . . .'; there were no provisions for appeal.

This was nailed down by the form of the licence, which was in the name of and to be signed by the Treasurer of the Navy and none other.[21] Licences were to run for three years before renewal, so there was a built-in review procedure. Moreover, they could be terminated at any time, unilaterally by the Treasurer of the Navy, if the provisions of the 1809 Act were breached.

There is a good deal of evidence that this system actually worked. The first list of licensed navy agents was issued in 1809.[22] Rose sometimes held up licences until he was satisfied of the applicant's *bona fides* and revocations did occur. On one celebrated occasion, however, he was persuaded by the mother and wife of a trader that they would be financially ruined by the withdrawal of a licence and he relented.[23] What must have weighed with Rose in that case was the skilful argument of Mrs Myers that the seamen clients of the firm would suffer if it went bankrupt.

It could not have been done by one man, though Rose was clearly the driving factor and maintained a close interest. Indeed, more than half his correspondence was on prize matters and he was extremely sensitive to criticism that he was not doing all he might to uphold the sailors' rights to their money. He could not do more, he frequently wrote, and stay within the law.[24] The main secretarial back-up was Samuel Hancock, who had become the Prize Officer in the Navy Pay Office and was a very vigilant though always courteous official.[25]

Through Rose's organization and constant attention the worst of the abuses of the navy agent system were curbed, while its advantages to the seamen remained. As Geoffrey Green has written, in his fine and too little known study *The Royal Navy and Anglo-Jewry 1740–1820*, 'If the Navy Agents failed, or the Admiralty stopped them functioning without replacing the Agents with an easy method for the seamen to obtain their prize money, then there would have been trouble throughout the Fleet'.[26] For the last five years of the war, this pragmatic, imperfect but workable system-within-a-system was managed in a reasonably satisfactory way.

NOTES

1. See, e.g., RN Museum Ref. 1997/65, Papers of Thomas Snowden Peckston, Peckston to Lark and Woodhead, Malta, *passim.*

2. Michael Lewis, *A Social History of the Navy 1793–1815* (George Allen and Unwin, 1960), p. 316.

3. Thomas Cochrane, Tenth Earl of Dundonald, *The Autobiography of a Seaman,* vol. I (Constable, 1995 edn, 1995), p. 54.

4. W.L. Clowes, *The Royal Navy: A History from the Earliest Times to 1900,* vol. 5 (Chatham edn, 1996), pp. 26–7.

5. See, e.g., IV NC, p. 523: *Nymphe* was paid £30,000 prize money and 'sailed directly on a cruise'.

6. Geoffrey L. Green, *The Royal Navy and Anglo-Jewry 1740–1820* (Green, 1989), Chapter 8. In this book, as in Green's study, the term 'Prize Agent' is used to denote agents who handled the main accounts, negotiations and court appearances, as described in Chapter 14, and 'Navy Agent' to denote those who acted for individual seamen as described in this chapter. Contemporary authorities often used the terms more loosely.

7. ADM 15/2, Rose to Barrow, 21 June 1813.

8. Green, *The Royal Navy*, p. 122; XI NC, p. 297.

9. 45 Geo. III c.72 s.92.

10. Ibid., s.97.

11. 35 Geo. III c.28.

12. XI NC, p. 217.

13. 45 Geo. III c.72 s.121.

14. 31 Geo. II c.10.

15. ADM 15/2, Rose to Treasury, 3 June 1812.

16. RNM 1983/1062.

17. Green, *The Royal Navy*, p. 144.

18. 31 Geo. II c.10 s.30.

19. ADM 1/3657.

20. 49 Geo. III c.123.

21. Ibid., at Form (F).

22. Green, *The Royal Navy*, p. 132.

23. Tony Gutridge, 'Aspects of Naval Prize Agency 1793–1815', 80 The *Mariner's Mirror* (1994), p. 51; Green, *The Royal Navy*, p. 144.
24. ADM 15/2, Rose to Hoste, 25 March 1812.
25. NMM HUL/42 Folio 3.
26. Green, *The Royal Navy*, p. 145.

CHAPTER SIXTEEN

The Officers of the Court

Job descriptions were not a feature of eighteenth-century life. It has not been easy to piece together just who did what in the High Court of Admiralty, nor in Doctors' Commons generally, nor how it was financed. Certain names crop up frequently in the records but individuals are not always accorded the same title, so even if the titles were accurate descriptors of the work people did, it would not be easy to unravel the organization.

The most important person in the High Court of Admiralty was the Judge. It is remarkable that there was only one.[1] The workload in wartime was extremely heavy – 2,286 cases of all kinds were tried in 1806[2] – and hours were long at Doctors' Commons. Clearly, there were legal advantages in keeping the judgments in the hands of one particularly able jurist; consistency and credibility were maximized. Appeals to the Lords Commissioners of Appeal in Prize Causes were by contrast minimized, and very seldom resulted in reversal of the decisions of the court below.[3] The disadvantages lay in the inherent delay in bringing cases on, rather than in obtaining decision once they had come on; Scott did not stand many over.

Sir William Scott was well paid. His salary of £2,000 a year[4] was met from the naval vote and was augmented in wartime. There were peculiarities: 'I recollect', wrote St Vincent to Markham in 1802, 'having doubts whether Sir William Scott's additional salary ended with the war [in 1801 with the Peace of Amiens] . . . if my memory does not fail, the £500 to him was written in pencil at the top of the paper, as if it had been left out by accident . . . some explanation will be required . . .'.[5]

In addition, Scott took judge's fees.[6] These fell into three categories. First were payments for each sentence or interlocutory order: each of these earned him £1. Second were decrees admitting claims and ordering further proof: these came at a rate of 6s 8d each. Finally, Bail orders earned him the sum of a shilling apiece. In a typical year his total fees amounted to some £1,500.[7]

Second to Scott in the hierarchy was the King's Advocate, a post Scott himself had occupied before 1798. From then until 1809 it was in the hands of Sir John Nicholl. The records suggest they were safe and able hands. Nicholl was often asked for opinions on points of both administration and law and his neat writing and concise way of expressing himself command confidence in the reader now as probably they did then. He was quite prepared to approach ministers without going through Scott: in May 1800 he wrote to Lord Spencer pointing out the anomalies and uncertainties surrounding the prize money and distribution arrangements for hired armed vessels[8] and these were clarified in subsequent proclamations.

Nicholl also attended hearings of the Court of Commissioners of Appeal in Prize Causes, often representing the Crown (and therefore the captors) on such occasions. His notebook on these cases survives;[9] the notes are very brief but give a good indication of the points that interested the court, not always those that might be expected.

Nicholl, like Scott, was a member of the House of Commons and appears to have spoken more frequently than did Scott. He was in consequence more taken to task by naval officers; the attack on him in the *Naval Chronicle* in 1808 has already been noted.[10] There is no sign that this criticism did much more than bounce off. Nicholl was not a particular friend of the Navy, nor was he their enemy; he was in favour above all of good order and clarity within the law. He was a relatively heavy gun and when he did fire he was effective. When he left to become Judge of the Court of Arches in 1809 and was succeeded by Christopher Robinson, the latter seems not to have been so influential; it is noticeable that subsequent correspondence, particularly on administrative matters, was handled more by Scott himself – no doubt unwillingly, for Scott clearly disliked administration.

Nicholl does not seem often to have led for the Crown in the High Court of Admiralty. Several other advocates were generally at the Crown's (and therefore the captors') disposal: James Henry Arnold and Christopher Robinson were two of the most prominent in the earlier years. Cases for the claimants were more often than not conducted by French Laurence and Maurice Swabey, though as is the way of British advocates they by no means allowed themselves to be type-cast and would appear for the Crown on occasion.

The advocates' fees were generally modest by twentieth-century standards; a guinea for each appearance plus a 6s 8d retainer seem to have been general.[11] It was the administrative and clerical costs that were more inclined to run away with the money. Many fee books for the period survive in the Public Records Office[12] and were clearly conscientiously kept. In the consolidated fee books, for example, the numerous dated entries are frequently interlined and corrected, indicating a meticulous working document, and each account has been passed and attested by a registry official. In the more complex cases, such costs may run into tens of pounds.

Cases were prepared by proctors, who approximated to solicitors today.[13] They did of course draw heavily on the prize agents for the production of the completed Standing Interrogatories and the papers of the captured ship, including crucially the cargo manifests and clearance papers. They would prepare monitions and ensure they were posted in the appropriate place. If a claim was entered demanding restitution of ship or cargo within the time allowed, the King's Proctor would engage advocates for the Crown (and, *ipso facto*, the captors) while proctors for the claimants would do similarly for their side.

On the completion of a case, if this resulted in condemnation the proctor informed the agent who would arrange for the sale of condemned property and prepare the accounts. When all that was complete the agent would submit them, duly sworn, to the King's Proctor who would then 'bring them in' to the court for formal finalizing, and distribution would take place very soon afterwards; the average time between 'bringing in' and the appearance of a notice in the *London Gazette* was about a week[14] and sometimes the notice actually preceded the formal presentation, though only by a few days.

The fact that only a single King's Proctor was appointed, and that he was nominally the only person allowed to represent Crown and captors in the preparation of cases, was an extremely sensitive point for naval officers. The opposition to this part of the system took two lines. The first, led by the Cochranes, was that captors should be allowed to engage their own proctors and advocates. It was argued that this would avoid any conflict of interest and ensure that the captor felt his interests were being best served by a representative of his choice; there was also an undercurrent of feeling that it might cost captors less. The first time this line of argument occurs is in a letter from Alexander Cochrane in 1799, the last is from Thomas in the House of Commons in 1810;[15] it was a long-running affair which at one time occupied even the busy St Vincent, who in 1803 wrote to Sir William Scott, 'until the officers of the Navy are permitted to nominate their own Proctors, a privilege possessed by privateers, their suspicions will remain'.[16]

It was invariably stalled by two counter-arguments: first, the legalistic one that before condemnation the capture belonged to the Crown and therefore the Crown's representative must bring the case; and second, the practical one that administration was greatly simplified and speeded by having only one representative involved. Moreover, it was argued, that representative was under firm governmental control, expert and experienced, and could be expected to do a better and more economical job for both Crown and captor than an outsider.

The other line of attack on the single King's Proctor came from a more conciliatory naval parliamentarian, Admiral Sir Charles Morice Pole, the member for Plymouth. He was a skilful fighter for many naval causes. On 14 June 1808 he moved for the appointment of three additional King's Proctors in the High Court of Admiralty.[17] Thus a case would still be handled by a single representative for Crown and captor, but he would be one of four such qualified people. The grounds were that a single official was completely swamped by the work and the additional staff would be able to bring on prize cases more quickly. The motion was negatived, but there was widespread sympathy in Parliament.

To judge by the wording of Thomas Cochrane's speech in the House two years later, nothing had by then been done about Pole's *démarche*. However, this is not certain, for whereas in the earlier years only one name appears on the accounts brought in after completion by agents – that of Heseltine, Proctor to 1805 or thereabouts – and only the name of his successor Bishop up to 1809 or so, after that several different names appear on different accounts, even for captures by ships of war (numerous different proctors had always been engaged by privateers,[18] as the Cochranes were at pains to point out). Thus it is apparent that at least more support staff were being supplied and a good deal of monitoring work was being delegated to them.

But particularly in the earlier years, the King's Proctor without doubt had his hands full. In preparing cases of violation of blockade, as mentioned in Chapter 4, he frequently had to consult the Admiralty about the precise wording of the proclamations and whether they were in date at the time of the alleged violation. He sought other information: on neutral trade with Mauritius, any papers held by the Admiralty and establishing involvement of neutrals with the enemy 'might be of essential benefit to the captors if now deposited' with the court.[19] Nepean's response was helpful: 'let all the papers to establish this fact be sent', he minuted. A similarly swift, but perhaps not so welcome, reaction had come some months earlier, when the *Hart* had detained a brig out of Hamburg bound for America with ten thousand stand of arms:[20] 'Let her go', said the Secretary of the Admiralty.

There were other officials attached to the Admiralty Court. One was the Admiralty Procurator, a post held through the greater part of the wars by George Gostling. He was in effect the Admiralty's man at court and was an essential go-between. He made routine enquiries to the Secretary of the Admiralty such as, for example, whether the normal 'reward' should be paid to captors in droits cases.[21] In droits matters it was he, rather than the King's Proctor, who took the 3s 6d for supervising the case. He sought decision as to the restoration of property in captured vessels taken *bona fide* but subsequently shown to have been private property.[22] He transmitted opinions by the King's Advocate concerning contentious captures before the cases could come on; in the matter of the *Benjamin Franklin,* bound for the USA and detained by the *Loire* on the ground that the only passengers on board were French, it was advised that the ship should be released because she was under a cartel flag and therefore protected.[23] Nepean's reaction was swift: 'Send copy of the report to Capt. Newman recommending that he should release her immediately'.

Gostling even on occasion carried out his own investigations. In the knotty business of the *Graff Bernstorff* he himself looked into the papers in 1803 and concluded that they 'proved the ship to be Dutch property'.[24] It was a case that had struggled on for years, the decree as to the cargo having been made as early as June 1800.[25] On the whole, however, he contented himself with stating the facts, setting out the legal advice and looking to the Admiralty for decision.

The sort of complication that could arise was typified by the matter of the *Lennox*, an American ship sold to Spain in Buenos Aires. At that time, in 1801, America was neutral and Spain an enemy. The master of the *Lennox*, one Collins, had remained on board for an onward voyage to Hamburg in order to support the false papers the ship was then carrying. The orders were that the cargo should be delivered to a man called Alsage in Hamburg, but if he did not appear then Lopez, the supercargo, should take possession. This appears to have been too great a temptation to Lopez who in the course of the voyage tried to murder Captain Collins. The attempt was unsuccessful and Collins, not surprisingly, put in to the nearest port which happened to be Falmouth. There the ship was detained as a droit of Admiralty. The King's Advocate gave his view that the seizure was illegal, but Nepean's first reaction was to lay a case for condemnation. However, on further advice from Nicholl, transmitted by the faithful Gostling, Nepean reluctantly minuted 'Let her go'.[26] Unfortunately, the detailed Opinions are no longer on file, so it is not possible to analyse why Nicholl gave the advice he did. The uncharitable view is that it was at the top of his 'too difficult' basket.

Gostling was often instrumental in negotiating relief for captors who had incurred costs when the ships they had captured were restored.[27] This was not an automatic procedure but became commoner and commoner as the war went on and the very understandable complaints of captains about the financial risks they were running became more vocal. It was not Gostling's place to suggest where the compensation was to come from, but as we have seen it is likely to have been met from the droits fund.

In fact, George Gostling's work was an essential lubricant in the machinery linking court and Admiralty. He was a very busy man and it is no wonder that his accounts were many years in arrears. In 1805 he received the most frightful blasts from both Admiralty and Scott for this neglect – Scott alleged that altogether eighteen years' figures were outstanding.[28] But Gostling kept his job; he was far too useful to lose.

Other officials of the Court included the Registrar and his staff, who provided the necessary and extensive administrative support, and the

Marshal. The latter had, as has been shown, heavy responsibilities particularly at a time of embargo, but his underlying function was to see that regularity was observed in all the practicalities of prize matters. It was therefore necessary for him to have close contacts with agents and brokers.

He also had the task of overseeing the recovery of deserters and custody of men alleged to have committed serious offences at sea and therefore subject to the jurisdiction of the Court. These cases of 'Oyer and Terminer' took up a certain amount of the Court's time, but justice was in general fairly swift; it was, however, a curious anomaly that a court administering civil law should have power to impose the death sentence for murder, when that had been committed at sea.

One other aspect of the Marshal's duties was, if conscientiously carried out, immensely onerous for a single official. This was the scrutiny of applications for Letters of Marque. By the provisions of the 1805 and previous Acts[29] any person wishing to acquire a commission as a privateer had to render a comprehensive description of his vessel and its ownership and arrange sureties for his bail, which amounted to £3,000 for ships whose crew exceeded 150 and £1,500 for those with smaller crews.[30] The Marshal or his Deputy were enjoined to 'make diligent Enquiry, and certify him or themselves of the Sufficiency of such Bail or Security, and make thereupon a Report' to the Judge of the Admiralty Court, before any Commission or Letter of Marque was granted. The judge himself, or his surrogate, had to hear the oath of the applicant. However, in the United Kingdom it was not the Court which granted Letters of Marque: that responsibility, once the Court had done its work, fell to the Commissioners for executing the Office of Lord High Admiral, or any three of them.[31]

Abroad, in the Vice Admiralty Courts, the organization was a microcosm of the Court at home. The Malta court, with its extraordinary structure and undoubtedly widespread malpractices, was a special case. More typical was the composition of the court at Jamaica, which in January 1811[32] was reported to be as follows:

Judge: Henry John Hinchcliffe.
Surrogate (to take examinations, grant monitions etc.): Thomas Denness.
Surrogate at Montego Bay: William Grignon.
Registrar: Owsley Rowley, doing his duty by
Deputy Registrar: Nathaniel Marston, who resigned in 1810 and was succeeded by
Deputy Registrar: Adam Dolmage.
Marshal: Sir Mordaunt Martin, doing his duty by
Deputy Marshal: Hugh Wright, standing in for

the regular Deputy Marshal: William Wade, who resumed duty on 1 July 1810 on return from England.

Court Appraiser and Surveyor: Peter Cochrane (no relation, so far as is known, to any naval Cochrane).

Interpreters: two Spanish, one Dutch, Danish, Swedish and German, one French, one Portuguese.

It is noticeable at once that one of the key posts of the Doctors' Commons court is missing from this schedule and that is the King's Proctor. It is clear from other evidence that no permanent appointment to that position existed. There were solicitors in practice in Jamaica and they would take on Admiralty work when offered either for the Crown or for claimants in contested cases. The same applied to advocates; there was seldom any shortage if court work beckoned.

There was nothing very unusual about the use of deputies, who no doubt were glad to get the work even if their more eminent chiefs took a cut of the fees in repayment of the favour. The eighteenth century was an age of sinecures and the nineteenth, with its quite different ethos, was taking time to come in, particularly in places like the West Indies. The slave trade, after all, was not abolished until 1807 and slavery in British colonies not until 1834.

Most of the officials, both in Britain and abroad, subsisted on fees rather than on salary. Indeed, in some Vice Admiralty Courts even the judge had no salary. The consequence was a constant undercurrent of resentment by captors, because the court fees came out of the prize proceeds. The practice gave rise to much rumour, claims of extortion and quoting of particular cases indicating flagrant overcharging.

Thomas Cochrane was the most outspoken critic of the system and in his House of Commons speech on 18 July 1811[33] he quoted a case where the captor had on condemnation a balance of £14 11s against him. He also 'asked the attorney-general whether he did, or did not, receive twenty-two guineas out of the pockets of the navy for every cause which came before the Court of Appeals, though he had attended but once there since the Court commenced sitting in November'. The attorney general was not of course a member of Doctors' Commons, but the barb probably went home.

Cochrane was not a lone voice. In January 1809 the *Naval Chronicle* carried an open letter from 'Admiral Trident' to Lord Mulgrave, then First Lord of the Admiralty, protesting that the court was 'taking from my gallant boys their dearest earnings' and suggesting that the droits fund should finance the fees.[34] The letter is in veiled language but there is little doubt that this was the writer's meaning. It no doubt reflected the general feeling in the naval service that they were being fleeced by rapacious courts.

The survey carried out into the prize accounts (see Appendix 1) presents a somewhat different picture. Though by no means all court charges (generally stated as a total 'proctor's fee') are clear from individual accounts, enough are available to give a good indication of the actual proportion of the proceeds that went to support the courts' work.

Court charges, as a percentage of the gross proceeds, ranged from 40.2 per cent of the gross in the heaviest case, a prize that grossed only £331, to 0.9 per cent in the lightest, which happened to be one of the richest prizes examined, grossing £23,198. When a mean was taken of all the percentages of gross proceeds that went on court charges, the figure was 8.7 per cent. The alternative method of calculating a mean percentage, summing all the gross proceeds and comparing them with the sum of all the court charges, produced a percentage of only 3.4 per cent of the gross.

One particularly significant entry was an estimate of a proctor's fee not yet rendered. This was made by Jackson, a highly experienced agent who was unlikely in his own interests to pitch it too low. The estimate was £150 on a prize grossing £3,912, a rate of 3.8 per cent.[35]

The inferences are twofold. First, the smaller the value of the prize, the greater the proportion of the proceeds likely to be swallowed up in court charges. Second, while proctor's fees generally came to roughly the same amount as the agent's fee, they seldom reached a level that would discourage prize-taking – a spectre regularly raised by opponents of the system.

Some of the cases considered in the survey were from foreign stations. They showed no difference in general level from those in the court at home. It has not been thought wise to draw too many inferences from that fact alone, since the sample of such cases is a small one and their geographical spread is not comprehensive.

The question of course remains: should the system have been as it was? There were two elements that come under question. First, court officials relied much more upon fees than upon salaries and those fees had to come from somewhere. It is to modern eyes an abdication of responsibility by government not to recompense its public servants properly by way of salary. However, practice in the eighteenth and early nineteenth centuries was very different and it would be unrealistic to judge by the standards of the late twentieth century.

Second, the source of the fees was the proceeds of the prizes themselves. This was a different method of funding from that of any other court and it seems a very opportunist way of doing things. The Crown could argue that it was generous in signing away its rights in the first place, under the 1708 Act and its successors; it was only reasonable that the prizes of an expensive war should pay for the proceedings of the court that validated them. On the other hand, 'Admiral Trident' had a point about the droits fund; it might at least have financed salaries for court officials, if not the fees of the advocates.

In the event, however, enthusiasm for prize-taking was not diminished right up to the end of the war. Even during the Hundred Days, Purser Thomas Peckston was looking to be 'off on a good cruise' in the *Pelorus*; later he wrote 'all hands seem to be in good spirits at the Idea of making prize money' – alas for him, that was written a week after Waterloo.[36] Peckston's enthusiasm was misplaced, but the doomsayers had been wrong: the emoluments of the officers of the Admiralty Courts had not destroyed the system.

Sometimes, though, it is necessary to overstate a case to get things done, and the critics of the courts had some effect. This was most noticeable in the Vice Admiralty Courts, and to end this chapter it may be appropriate to quote extensively from the Report on the Jamaica court made in August 1812,[37] which led to a significant rescheduling of fees – a reform that was almost certainly brought on by the work of Cochrane and his allies in Parliament. The Report, signed by a very high-level commission including most of the luminaries of Doctors' Commons, gives some indication of the consideration and care that the question received:

Jamaica

In the Vice Admiralty Court of this Island we have reason to think charges have formerly been allowed, upon some notion of Analogy with those of the Court of Chancery within the Island, a standard in our judgment ill adapted to a Prize Court.

A Table of Fees was brought by the late Judge from the Vice Admiralty Court of the Cape of Good Hope, but we have been unable to ascertain how far it was resorted to by him, during the very short time that he presided in the Court. The present Judge has in some instances lowered the rates of charging in use before, but we think even those which have lately prevailed higher than we ought to recommend.

There are taxes in the Island, which though of less amount than in Great Britain, are by no means inconsiderable. The Rent of Houses and Offices of Business is very high, and the labour of Clerks largely [i.e., generously] paid for. The necessaries of life are dear and the habits of the place are such as render the expenses of Persons far beyond those of the same relative rank in this country.

We have allowed due weight to these circumstances, but as those who engage in the duties of the Prize Court attend likewise to the Business of the Courts of Chancery and Common Law, from which sources considerable Emolument is derived, some deduction has been made from the effect, which considerations of large expenditure might otherwise have had upon a Table of Fees for the Prize Court, by considering them as not to be provided for out of that Court exclusively.

The number of Causes adjudged in the Prize Court has been very great, amounting in part of the last War [1793–1801] to nearly three hundred in a year, and during this War the average, till the present year, has been nearly one hundred and ten. At present the number is very small indeed.

We have thought fit to recommend for the most part an exceeding of one half above the Table of the High Court of the Admiralty. In cases not provided for by the Table, reference must be made to the Judge and not to the former Table, nor to Analogies from the practice of other Courts in the Island.

It will be expedient to discontinue a Practice, which seems hitherto to have obtained, of copying whole Ships Papers into Counsel's briefs. We disapprove also of the practice of copying Papers for the Judge, when the originals with Translations, if made, ought to be in Court for his use.

An opportunity has accidentally been afforded to us of consulting the present Judge [Hinchcliffe had spent the summer in England, by permission] on the subject of this report, which has given us great satisfaction.

There follow principles on which the fees of specific officers are to be based. Of these the most interesting are the passages concerning the Marshal and the Proctors and Advocates, which read:

Marshal: This Office is executed by Deputy. The Fees of the subjoined Table recommended for this Officer, and referred to particular Heads of Duty, must be understood as due to him for such only of those Duties as he shall actually perform. Thus in the Sale of Prize Property, if he shall really conduct the Sale, a Fee is provided for him, but if Prize Agents or other Persons shall perform the Duty, the Fee is not to be considered as due to the Marshal.

Advocates and Proctors: The Duties of Advocates and Proctors in this Island are exercised by different Persons. The Advocates act as Barristers in other Courts, and the Proctors as Solicitors and Agents in the Judicial and other Business of the Island. The Fees of the Advocates, if disputed on Taxation, must be determined by the discretion of the Judge, according to the length and nature of the Cause. The Registrar will thus be able to derive a rule of Taxation as to this Item of charge in future cases.

The *Proctors* in the charges per sheet [of copies of papers to be used in Court], if they have observed any rule as to the number of lines, do not appear to have observed any as to the number of Words, of which the sheet should consist. We consider precision in the charge per sheet as unattainable without defining the number of Words, and have accordingly done so in the table subjoined.

There follows a Table of Fees for the Judge, the 'Judge for Seals' (presumably one of the Surrogates), the Registrar, the Marshal and the Proctors. It is not possible, nor would it necessarily be interesting, to reproduce this in full, but some items give the flavour. The Judge, for example, got £1 10s for every sentence or interlocutory decree. The Judge for Seals received £2 12s 6d for issuing a Letter of Marque, the Registrar no less than £6 6s 6d for its preparation, and the Marshal £1 10s for his investigation into its propriety. If a prize was condemned and the buyer wanted to transfer her to British registry, a Registrar's Certificate would cost him £1 8s. The Marshal was well paid for arranging sales of condemned property: 5 per cent for the first hundred pounds and 2½ per cent for the remainder. Finally, the Proctors received 10s for each court attendance and, on drawing Affidavits, 1s 6d for each folio of ninety words.

Particularly notable is the emphasis on charges for copying. In the days before the typewriter, let alone the word processor or photocopier, this was a business employing large numbers of clerks and attracting considerable fees. Even a routine unopposed case would require some documents to be copied and charges for these could amount to a substantial proportion of the total bill.

Reading between the lines of the Report, it is easy to detect what might have been going on before and what tightening up was required. Nevertheless, there is ample evidence to suggest that, before the reforms and even in the Vice Admiralty Courts where abuse was more likely to flourish, flagrant and widespread extortion by court officials was in fact the exception rather than the rule.

NOTES

1.   Lynne Townley, 'Sir William Scott, Lord Stowell, and the Development of Prize Law in the High Court of Admiralty 1798–1828' (unpublished thesis, University of Birmingham, 1995), p. 66.

2.   Henry J. Bourguignon, *Sir William Scott, Lord Stowell* (Cambridge University Press, 1987), p. 61. Bourguignon notes that these were both instance and prize cases.

3.   4 and 5 C. Rob., Appendices. Two cases out of forty-two were reversed, a record of which any High Court judge could be proud.

4.   ADM 1/3894, Scott to Nepean, March 1799.

5.   Sir Clements Markham (ed.), *Selections from the Correspondence of Sir John Markham* (Navy Records Society, 1904), p. 19.

6.   HCA 2/253.

7.   Ibid.; a sample was taken for the years 1804 to 1806 inclusive.

8.   ADM 1/3895, Nicholl to Spencer, 5 May 1800.

9.   HCA 30/466.

10.   XIX NC, p. 390.

11.   HC 30/627.

12.   E.g., HCA 2/121.

13.   Lynne Townley, lecture to Middle Temple Historical Society, 24 April 1996.

14.   The survey described in Appendix 1 was sampled for the second six months of 1809.

15.   ADM 1/3894 (1799) and Thomas Cochrane, Earl of Dundonald, *Autobiography of a Seaman* (Constable, 1995 edn), vol. II, pp. 112–13 (1810).

16.   David Bonner Smith (ed.), *Letters of Admiral of the Fleet the Earl of St Vincent*, vol. II (Navy Records Society, 1927), p. 221.

17.   XX NC, p. 67.

18.   HCA 30/538; the names coincide closely with those in the HCA 2/215 series.

19.   ADM 1/3894, Heseltine to Nepean, 23 December 1799.

20.   Ibid., Heseltine to Nepean, 26 July 1799.

21.   ADM 1/3897, Gostling to Marsden, 30 August 1805.

22.   ADM 1/3894, Gostling to Nepean, 15 July 1799, 15 November 1799.

23.   ADM 1/3895, Gostling to Nepean, 8 May 1801.

24.   ADM 1/3896, Gostling to Nepean, 19 April 1803.

25.   3 C. Rob., p. 109 [1800].

26.   ADM 1/3895, correspondence between 27 October and 7 November 1801.

27.   ADM 1/3896, Gostling to Marsden, 6 April 1804; and ADM 1/3897, similarly 26 March and 17 April 1805.

28.   ADM 1/3897, Scott to Marsden, 15 and 29 April 1805.

29.   45 Geo. III c.72 s.11.

30.   Thomas Hartwell Horne, *A Compendium of the Statute Laws and Regulations of the Court of Admiralty Relative to Ships of War, Privateers, Recaptures and Prize Money* (W. Clarke and Sons, 1803), pp. 3–9.

31.   45 Geo. III c.72 s.9.

32.   ADM 1/3900, Report of 19 January 1811.

33.   Cochrane, *Autobiography of a Seaman*, vol. II, p. 213.

34.   XXI NC, p. 36.

35.   HCA 2/365, *Nuestra Senora del Carmen (Arriaga)*.

36.   RNM 97/65, Peckston to Mary Peckston, 25 June 1815 off Ile de Bas.

37.   ADM 1/3900.

PART THREE

THE SPOILS

CHAPTER SEVENTEEN

Rich and Poor Lading

From 1798 to 1805 the *Naval Chronicle* included a regular 'Plymouth Report'. Plymouth had all the characteristics of an advanced operational base: it was relatively well supplied with stores and repair facilities, its command structure was well capable of managing the berthing and coming and going of naval and auxiliary vessels, and town and hinterland offered a shoreside life that, if neither so sophisticated as that of Portsmouth nor so convenient for London, had plenty of attraction.

Most of all, though, from an operational point of view Plymouth had a priceless advantage: generally it was well to windward of other major British bases. It was much easier to stretch out for Ushant from there, in the prevailing westerlies, than it was from further up channel. So, in spite of the exposed anchorage in the Sound and the difficulties of getting up the Hamoaze under sail or warps, Plymouth was busy, particularly for the Channel Fleet and the numerous frigates attached to it.

The Plymouth Reports reflect this extraordinarily well. They are a sort of log, with daily entries showing many of the usages of log-writing: 'Arrived the *Indefatigable*, from a cruise . . .'; but they are also gossipy, giving a flavour of the incentives, concerns and anxieties of the time. The gossip was by no means parochial, either, for Plymouth was often the first port of entry for vessels coming from foreign stations and news from abroad was eagerly awaited and freely discussed.

Much of the news was about prize-taking. Thus, when Spain entered the war in late 1804, partly as a result of the treasure-ships affair in October that year,[1] there was much enthusiasm. On 9 January 1805 the Spanish *Santa Maria* arrived, detained by the *Ajax* and *Illustrious*, with *Montagu* in sight, and carrying a 'very valuable cargo': dollars, gold, horn tips, cotton, wool, hides, copper and cocoa.[2] The *Santa Gertruda*, another

Spanish prize, was said to have a cargo worth one and a quarter million dollars; and the *Polyphemus* brought in four more richly laden.

Reports from the other side of the Atlantic were similar. News did not take too long to get forth and back: on 14 February the Report reads, 'Off Jamaica . . . the British Tars in that part of the world in high spirits . . . at the idea of making captures of Spanish vessels laden with dollars'.[3]

It was the time, too, of Thomas, Lord Cochrane's famous cruise in the *Pallas*. On 24 February 1805 reports had already come in of two valuable prizes taken by that ship, indicating that Cochrane 'would fulfil his public advertisement' – a document almost as well known in that day, clearly, as are facsimiles of it in the standard histories now.[4] Better was to come; Cochrane was later reported to have captured *La Fortuna*, well named for according to the *Chronicle* at the time she carried some 300,000 dollars.[5] A local newspaper set the estimate even higher at 432,000, and Cochrane himself did not dispute this in his autobiography.[6] The sterling equivalent was about £130,000, or £26 million in 1998 prices.

This brief description of one of those periods of 'pleasant days' during the wars of 1793–1815 must be set in context. Sailors' ideas of fabulously rich Spanish cargoes really were true. The silver mines of Peru produced great quantities of metal and much of it was minted in that colony, to save the cost of transport either as ore or ingots. Spanish policy was to disperse it in a number of ships, some of them ships of war and others armed merchant vessels, some in convoy and some independent. The figures for captures look impressive, but Spanish historians take the view that statistically and in the long run they were not crippling[7] because a high proportion of ships got through.

That would have been disputed by the Lords of the Admiralty. They were clearly convinced that the interception of Spanish treasure would be a powerful blow against Spain. Even before the formal declaration, they issued a direction 'not to detain any Spanish homeward bound ship of war *unless she shall have treasure onboard* [my italics]'.[8] This was meant to be a deterrent; once Spain was newly come into the war and still vulnerable to shock, a Proclamation of General Reprisal could be issued.

But to British sailors such strategic considerations were of little account. They found more material comfort in the prospect of doubloons. It was part of folklore, after all, backed by historical fact. The richest prize ever taken was the Spanish *Hermione* in 1762, and before that Anson's capture of the *Nuestra Senora de Cabodonga* in 1743 had made fortunes for those who survived that sickly circumnavigation.[9]

But even in the current struggle, before the Peace of Amiens, there had been one tremendous financial coup. This was the capture on 16 October 1799 of the Spanish treasure ships *Santa Brigida* and *El Thetis* by *Triton*, *Alcmene*, *Naiad* and *Ethalion*. The account simply for the captured specie was as follows.[10]

Account of Dollars part of the cargo of El Tetys *and* Sta. Brigida, *sold to the Governor of the Bank:*

1,932,163 ounces of 10dwt @ 64*d* per oz			£515,243	12*s*	0*d*
600,000 dollars sold to govt. @ 67			145,175	4	9
228 ounces 5 dwt of doubloons @ 76*d* per oz			867	7	0
			661,206	13	9
Charges:					
Carriage	£1,720	17*s*	0*d*		
Brokerage	826	9	10		
Bullion Office Clerks	250	0	0		
Porters	30	0	0		
New Bags	55	13	0		
Washing Dollars	88	4	3		
Total Charges	2,979	4	1		
Commission @ 1 per cent	6,612	17	4		
			9,592	1	5
Balance for Distribution			651,694	12	4

It will be noted that some of the figures, particularly that for the 600,000 dollars, do not square with the stated basis for calculation. The account has been copied directly from papers in the possession of a descendant of one of the frigate captains involved, probably in that captain's own hand, and it is possible that '600,000' was an approximation for the exact figure as counted in the Bank. There seem to be one or two minor faults in the addition, too. 'Errors and Omissions excepted' was a fairly common notation on the accounts of the time and needs to be taken seriously.

When the distribution was worked out according to the scale set out in the Proclamation, the shares for the treasure alone were:

To the Admiral	£81,461	16	6½
To each of 4 Captains	40,730	18	3¼
To each of 16 Masters/Sea Lieutenants	5,091	7	3¼
To each of 33 Warrant Officers	2,468	10	9½
To each of 103 Petty Officers	790	17	9¾
To each of 894 Seamen	182	4	9¾

As the *Naval Chronicle* gleefully remarked, there still remained 'the nett produce of the hulls, stores, masts, rigging, etc. of the two frigates to be accounted for'.[11] These might well, at the going rates of the time, have amounted to another £40,000; though it has since been established that the hulls, probably because they were much damaged, were not bought by the navy,[12] so the true figure for the stores alone may have been nearer £20,000.

What all this meant to the individual can be judged partly from the rule-of-thumb multiplier of 200 to reach late twentieth-century values[13] and partly by comparison with going rates of pay. An able seaman got about £20 a year, *when* he was paid; there were some scandalous examples of arrears built up over years, pointed out by Thomas Cochrane in one of his best crusading speeches in the House, but they diminished as the war went on. So, £182 was the equivalent of nine years' pay and probably enough to set up in a small way of business once ashore. It might not have been quite up to the sailor's 'dream figure', which was nearer the three or four hundred supposed to have been paid out for the *Hermione* long before, but it was real riches.

The more senior ratings and the officers saw proportionately more in the way of fortune: £5,000 really would set up a man for life, if he did not squander it on gambling or invest it unwisely – and neither was an uncommon fate for newly acquired wealth. As for the captains, as they bore the overall responsibility for their ships' efficiency and good order, to say nothing of their conformity with the law of nations, so they profited the most. Henry Digby, captain of the *Alcmene*, restored the family house at Minterne Magna and it stands today as a memorial of a highly successful career – distinguished not only by this single incident, but by many other captures in *Aurora* and *Alcmene*, followed by an impressive contribution to Trafalgar in the line of battle ship *Africa*.[14]

The money for *Santa Brigida* and *El Thetis* was paid quickly, too. The engagement was on 16 October 1799; the pay-out on the treasure was in early January 1800. That was quite exceptional. It is accounted for partly by the fact that the sale of the bullion was directly to the Bank, with no auction involved and therefore no tedious preparation of goods for sale, no notices to go out, no agents needing to take interrogatories, no manifests to be examined. The treasure had been stacked in carts and taken to London under guard; it will be recalled that Sir William Scott remonstrated to the Secretary of the Admiralty that this was technically 'breaking bulk',[15] but he was simply making a point; Nepean had long before minuted on the Commander in Chief, Plymouth's initial report: 'Their Lordships have great satisfaction in this very valuable capture'.[16]

Indeed, there is every evidence that the affair was treated to some extent as a public relations exercise. The speed with which the money was handled; the triumphal procession; the publication of the exact amount of each share; the *Naval Chronicle*'s caveats about further riches to accrue: all suggest that the capture was to be regarded as a tremendous success and a great boost for the naval service. Captain Gore of the *Triton* gave a 'splendid ball' in Plymouth late in 1799 or very early in 1800.[17] There had been plenty of triumphs in battle for the Navy since 1796, but here was something else, a real jackpot to gladden the hearts of the fortunate and give the less fortunate new hope.

That incident, then, added to the folklore of prize and the authorities made sure it did. It was one of the bases for the delight that greeted the entry of Spain into the war in 1804 and, as has been shown, that delight was well justified for some. So long as Spain remained an enemy the prospect of doubloons was always there; the prize accounts for ten *Nuestra Senoras*, variously captured in the years up to 1809 when Spain became an ally, grossed a total of £74,056,[18] and that was big money by the standards of that stage in the war.

For, when all was said and done, the average value of an individual prize was well short of anyone's dream of riches. A survey has been made of a substantial sample of agents' accounts throughout the war; the method is shown at Appendix 1. The figures and trends derived from it are remarkably consistent, with one or two explainable anomalies and, of course, occasional wild deviations from the norm – the kind of special cases that are so often used to argue from the particular to the general, in politics, in tabloid journalism and even sometimes, alas, in law.

The figures for cargo-carrying vessels captured suggest that a prize in this category grossed on average £2,472. There was a downward trend in this average as the war went on; the mean for earlier years is nearer £3,000 while towards the end of the war it dips slightly below £2,000.

That trend is accounted for partly by the fact that Spanish ships were richer and takings dropped off when Spain was no longer an enemy; it may well be, too, that towards the end of the war prize-takers were tending to live on scraps generally, wherever they were and whoever the perceived enemy might be. As more and more of the overseas world fell under British domination and the continent fell back upon its own resources and system, ocean-going trade destined for the enemy – unless it fell under British licence – was beginning to dry up. It was no wonder that 'Justicius' complained to the First Lord in 1808 that the commanding superiority of British fleets had 'left them nothing to conquer or to capture'.[19] As it turned out, there was still much to be captured ashore, particularly around the Indian Ocean, but so far as seaborne commerce was concerned there was truth in what he wrote. The outbreak of the American war in 1812 did give one more golden opportunity for ship captures, and it was taken, the total proceeds topping half a million;[20] but in general the law of diminishing returns was operating.

A sum of £2,500 or so for an 'average' merchant prize was not going to make anyone very rich. A captain, certainly, would welcome his substantial share, but much of it would go to pay off his expenses in commissioning his ship and setting her to work, providing his own uniforms and, unless he wanted to be seen as very parsimonious, keeping a good table and dressing his boat's crew in the manner to which the fleet was accustomed.[21] The officers would welcome their shares, to be added perhaps to previous acquisitions if they were prudent, spent if they were not. The sailors, like as not, would want it yesterday and would have borrowed what they thought they were worth from the trader down the Hard.

And that £2,500, it must be remembered, was the gross. It was a natural thing for everyone in the navy, from admirals to boy seamen, to believe they were being fleeced by all the middlemen, from the judges down to the slop-sellers, of their rightful money. The Cochranes were the extreme proponents of this view but it is clear that it was held in varying degrees by many if not most in the navy. Accordingly, it is appropriate in this book to assess how true this might be and one of the most important derivations from the survey of the prize accounts is a comparison of gross with net proceeds.

The first question to be answered was whether 'gross' and 'net' can be precisely enough defined to present a true comparison. The answer probably is that they can. Every account concludes with the unequivocal figure: 'Net sum for Distribution'. That was the amount, clear of all deductions, that would be paid out in due proportion to all those entitled. 'Net', therefore, is well enough defined. 'Gross' can be a little more difficult. The more straightforward accounts show the total of money actually paid by the buyers of ship and cargo – usually separated into those two categories alone. This sum then suffers a succession of deductions: first of brokerage fees, then of charges associated with custody and court fees, then of the agent's fee, then of the Chatham Chest and Greenwich Hospital imposts. Any of these part-way stages can be called 'gross' or 'net', according to the presentation used by the agent. In the figures which follow, only the first of these sums – the amount actually paid at auction – is used as the 'gross'. Thus the gap between 'gross' and 'net' is the widest possible, but it is also the most sensible; anything less is making allowance for the middlemen's turn in a way that is unjustified.

It must be stressed that this part of the survey is properly concerned only with merchant ship captures. Warships came under different rules, principally over the award of head money and the terms of sale, and so did recaptures with the provisions for the award of salvage. They will be for subsequent chapters. Grey areas, of course, there were; the French *chasse-marées* were an example, small coasting vessels often in French government service, used for ferrying small important cargoes along the coast and quite willing to show fight. They did not attract head money and were treated for prize purposes as merchant ships.

The result of the gross/net comparison is not particularly startling, observing all that has gone before in this book, but is a significant rebuttal of the charges of widespread corruption and extortion that are made in some histories. *The average payout to the captor of a merchant prize was 81 per cent of the total received at auction.* Of the 19 per cent that leached away during the period between capture and payout, the main recipients were the brokers, the courts (via the proctor), seamen's charities and the agent. Legitimate charges for pilotage, shipkeeping and insurance were often significant factors.

Clearly, within this global figure there was room for substantial fluctuation. Some prizes, usually those that had hung fire for years owing to appeals, or disputes between multiple captors, or dilatoriness on the part of an agent, realized far less than the normal percentage. Others, that had had an unusually easy run through the process, exceeded the norm. Only one case was found, among close on a thousand, that ended in a negative amount due to the captor,[22] and even that, which was a part-cargo, was offset by a 'plus' on another sale.

What is not a fluctuation but emerges as a definite trend is the increase in the proportion of proceeds that accrued to captors as the war went on. This is on the face of it surprising, for it was in 1806 that the contribution for the Chatham Chest and Greenwich Hospital was imposed and one would have expected that the captors' share would in consequence be less after that. But the figures are clear and it is hard to believe they are not robust. Up to 1808, or thereabouts, the proportion for distribution is around 79 per cent of the gross, after that date it climbs towards 83 per cent. The only explanation that can be made without the most detailed analysis is that agents, proctors and brokers were all being made acutely sensitive to the Navy's concerns and perceptions that they were being done down, and took a close grip on their charges accordingly. The influence of George Rose, Treasurer of the Navy, should not be underestimated.[23]

It would be tempting to suggest the reduction in charges was due to competition, particularly among the agents (the King's Proctor had of course a monopoly in any case). There is some indication that this might have been so, but it is tenuous, based simply on the more frequent occurrence of new names as the war went on. The established agents were a remarkably resilient bunch: the 'big six' – Maude, Sykes, Ommanney and Druce, Marsh and Creed, Cooke and Halford, Jackson – remained active throughout the war. An attempt at a league table for these leaders of the profession yields some interesting but quite inconclusive results:

Ommanney and Druce	83.5% to the captors
Sykes	82.8%
Maude	80.9%
Cooke and Halford	77.7%
Marsh and Creed	76.3%
Jackson	76.2%

The spread could easily be upset by one large prize paying disproportionately well or badly. What is perhaps more interesting is that the big players gave on this evidence no more nor less advantage to their clients than the less well known.

By and large, then, there is little evidence that captors on the home stations were being scandalously cheated out of their rightful money. A merchant prize was, after all, in the nature of a windfall and considerable administrative expense was incurred in bringing in its proceeds. In passing, it would, it is suggested, be a lucky vendor who recovered 80 per cent of the price paid at auction for (say) a piece of furniture today; even though in such a case there would have been no court costs.

Anomalies and aberrations, of course, abounded. On virtually every page of the author's survey are notes such as 'Heavy charges: apparently a complicated sale' in the case of a ship realising only 73 per cent of the auction value,[24] or 'Very high proctor's bill and other expenses'[25] for a ship that grossed only £554 and realized, net, £112 – a paltry 20 per cent.

Cases such as the latter read singularly sadly. Hopes tended to be high whenever a capture was made; even if the prize was small and ill-found, there might be something hidden or unexpected that would increase its value. When it was shown, often years later, that there was no prospect of riches or even a decent return, disappointment was correspondingly great.

This kind of roller-coaster expectation is typified in the letters of George Price, pressed into HMS *Speedy* in 1804 and serving as ship's butcher under the alias of Green[26] during the operations against the Boulogne Flotilla. In May 1805 he wrote to his brother ashore at Southwark: 'I have the Pleasure to inform you that a Ship in our Squadron has taken a Valuable Prize and there is not Above Five Hundred Men to share for it', and on 21 July, 'We are Sure of Geting about 20£ a man and Will impower you to receive mine as soon as I Can'.[27] Yet on 28 August the following letter, signed by John Wolfe, an Irish seaman of the *Speedy*, was sent to Price's brother: 'I have they pleasure to inform you that yr Brother George has eloped from they Ship And I hope By they time you receive this you Will have they pleasure of Seeing him I hope he will doe me they favoure to Rite to Me and let Me know how times goes on in London . . .'.[28]

It is more than likely that Price, who had no previous naval experience, was misled by the euphoria of taking a prize into dreams of relative riches, to be got relatively quickly. The single prize taken in the squadron would have had to be seriously rich to pay £20 a man among 500 and, as will appear in later chapters, joint captures were notorious for delays in settlement. When inevitable doubt or disillusionment set in, desertion must have seemed a reasonable option to Price and the ship's habitual anchorage in the Downs no doubt gave the opportunity.

It is indeed the small captures, often made along the littoral of the enemy, that make the most poignant reading. The effort expended on capturing some miserable little craft, sailed by a couple of men and a boy and either in ballast or carrying little of saleable value, must have seemed quite disproportionate. Time and again the records show the destruction of such prizes, usually by burning, with the comment 'not worth sending in'. In one singularly successful fifteen months' work in 1797–8 the *Aurora* destroyed some twenty of the fifty prizes she took, and returned another three to their crews – though two of those were neutrals, and it is probable that apprehension of a protracted and possibly unsuccessful court case was a factor there.[29]

It was not only cold financial calculation that governed destruction, as opposed to capture, of merchant vessels; sometimes it was operational necessity. Convoys off the west coast of France, particularly, were often driven ashore and there burnt or blown up; it was no place to dally, with a vast tidal range, fierce tidal streams, onshore winds and sometimes shore batteries to contend with. So misgivings about what might have been in the way of prize money would be mingled with relief that British ships and their boats had made their offing safely – if indeed they did: sometimes pursuit was carried too far and rocks or the beach claimed British ships as well as their quarry.

Such operations were overwhelmingly against ships whose enemy character was unquestionable. Destruction of a neutral was very rare. That did not mean that neutral prizes, when taken on grounds of contraband, or false papers, or irregular licence, or blockade-breaking, were necessarily more or less lucrative than enemy vessels. The Swedish convoy taken in the *Maria* incident was said to be worth £600,000.[30] But some neutrals, particularly if only part of the cargo was condemned and the ship restored, would fetch little. Somewhere in the middle came this book's archetypal case *The Eenrom*, and it is to her that this chapter finally turns.

THE *EENROM*: A FINAL VISIT: THE SPOILS

At the end of Chapter 3 the condemnation of the *Eenrom* and her cargo, as lawful prize to HMS *Brilliant* had been affirmed by the Lords Commissioners of Appeal in Prize Causes on 27 March 1802.[31] Now came the reckoning.

The agency had passed from James Primrose Maxwell into the hands of James Sykes. There was some association between these two; in at least one account they are shown as a partnership,[32] so no lack of confidence in Maxwell, on the part of the *Brilliant,* need be assumed.

The account,[33] particularly regarding the charges, is an unusually detailed one and is worth reproducing in full:

Ship Enrom *taken by the* Brilliant *Capt Henry Blackwood on the 28 May* (sic) *1798*

Charges

1799
June 1 Paid Insurance Ship and Cargo, Portsmouth to London
£30,000 @ 2% plus Stamp duty £667 10s 0
Return for convoy 150 0 0 517 10s 0

Ditto £6,000 added £133 10s0
Return for convoy 30 0 0 103 10s 0

July 6 Ditto £5,000 on Ship at Deptford
3 months to 6 October 1799 9 3s 6

Ditto £10,000 on Goods in Warehouse
to 6 June 1800 17 18 6

Ditto at Royal Exchange continued to
21 February 1801 75 0 0
1801
Feby 20 Ditto £6,000 continued to 21 May 1801 7 10 0
1799
April 24 to E. Fennell for coals wood and candles 5 4 4
June to Robt. Yuills order for 4 men assisting navigating
the ship from Portsmouth to London 10 10 0
to do. To pay men for navigating the ship from
Portsmouth to Deptford 70 7 0
to paid Bill to Edward Sherlock Pilotage from
Downs to Gravesend 7 7 0
to Thos Irons assisting bringing the ship
up to Deptford 4 4 0
to ditto for his disbursements for the ship 6 6 0
to ditto for his attendance on the ship 5 0 0
to order for Silmers for Beef etc. 2 1 9
August to Mr. Parkes Disbursements at Plymouth 103 19 6
to Mr. Atkins for Mr. Scarlett ditto 41 10 2

Carried over 987 1 9

1800	Brought Forward		987 1 9	
March 20	Paid Mr Heseltine Proctors Bill in Doctors Commons		434 14 0	
	Paid Fees on giving Bail in Doctors Commons to answer Appeal and obtain Decree, Security Bonds, Marshal, Deputy and Clerks		47 0 0	
	Expences at Lisbon paid by Captain Blackwood		125 6 0	
	Repaid Capt Blackwood for paid by him to 3 men out of the *Enrom* on account of their wages		12 0 0	
	To paid John Porter late of the *Enrom* more on account of his wages		8 0 0	
	To Mr Heseltine's final Proctor's Bill in Appeals	461 13 1		
	Abate to be paid by the appellants	209 0 0	252 13 0	
	Registering Power of Attorney		2 16 8	
	Affidavit inhibiting account proceeds in Doctors Commons		1 11 8	
	Advertising account in Gazette		1 6 0	
	Advertising payment in Gazette		13 0	
	Certifying Prize List Navy Office		1 6 0	
	Making out ditto for payment		1 1 0	
	Stamps for ditto)			
	Recalls)		15 13 0	
	Carriage of Papers, Postage etc.)			

To Agency on £4,600 ship		
£26,138 5 10 cargo @ 5 per cent		1536 18 0
Total Charges		3428 0 1
1802		
May 31 Balance due *Brilliant* carried down		24,845 17 1

Receipts

Ship sold to H. Barke & Co Brokers £4,600		
Prize Duty etc	431 18 0	4168 2 8
Cargo sold as per account	£26,138 5 10	
Prize Duty etc	2,032 10 8	24,105 15 2
		28,273 17 2

1802			
May 31	By balance brought down	24,845	17 1
	Abate one-eighth Admiral Lord Radstock's share	3,105	14 7
		21,740	2 6
	By Interest	1,835	12 3
Due *Brilliant* Captain, Officers and Company		23,575	14 9

Several interesting points emerge from this account, quite apart from the flavour it gives of the practices of the time.

First, the apparent mistake as to the date of capture is almost certainly just that. There is evidence from multiple sources that the capture was made on 28 December, not 28 May 1798 as the account states. It is, however, salutary to remember that an apparent fact written in superb copper-plate is no more certainly reliable than a computer entry in the late twentieth century.

Secondly, the notation 'Return for convoy' needs some explanation. If ships sailed in convoy under the protection of a warship escort their insurance rates for that voyage were correspondingly reduced. As can be seen in this case, the reduction was substantial – rather over 20 per cent. But it appears it was made after the voyage was completed. This would have been a sensible safeguard against desertion of convoy or other misbehaviour.

Thirdly, the *Eenrom*'s was a rich cargo and the associated costs were correspondingly high. But there were economies of scale in the richer prizes and the *Eenrom* in fact realized net 81 per cent of the gross takings, even before interest was allowed – and in this case the charges included insurance over a long period while appeal was pending.

Fourthly, interest *was* allowed. The rate can be variously calculated and Sykes' account gives no indication what basis was used, but a middling estimate puts it at an annual 3 per cent. Observing that the ship was not sold for at least nine months after capture and most of the cargo was held for much longer – the dates for insurance are firm indicators of that – not much money would have been in the agent's hands before 1800 and then he would have had to lodge some in the Court pending appeal. So the *Brilliant* got a good deal. Probably this was at the insistence of Blackwood, who, as has been shown, could be a hard man when it came to money. Interest on merchant prizes, even when these had hung fire for years, was the exception rather than the rule and no pattern has emerged from the survey to suggest the agents had any code of practice about it.

Fifthly, the judgement about Blackwood's attitude to money can be reinforced from his expense claim for the investigations at Lisbon. It is not suggested that this was in any way false: the amount of work put in to find the witnesses, engage the Vice Consul to hear the statements, to have the affidavits made out and sworn, must have been arduous and the costs heavy. But the account is exact and uncompromising: a careful man, at least.

Finally comes an intriguing question to which the answer can only be speculative. Why was John Porter from the *Eenrom* paid so much more than his mates? One clue may be found in the appeal papers.[34] Porter, an American, was the first person to give evidence in Lisbon that the ship was Dutch property and to give an eyewitness account of the flogging of the Goanese John Christian for 'getting the ship into trouble'. Porter would have been extremely unpopular with the owners, more so than any other deponent, and his extra £8 might be regarded more as protection than compensation.

The account is dated 31 May 1802, and was brought in on 23 June. But Sykes had moved fast. On 14 June the following notice appeared in the *London Gazette*:

> Notice is hereby given to the officers and company of His Majesty's Ship *Brilliant*, Henry Blackwood Esq. Commander, who were onboard on the 28 December 1798 at the capture of the ship *Enrom*, that they will be paid their respective shares of said ship and cargo, and the Recalls will be at No. 22, Arundel-Street, on the first Thursday monthly for 3 years.

So, forty-two months after the capture, payment could at last be made. The prize list for the *Eenrom* does not form part of the accounts, so it is a matter of approximation to assess who got what, but taking a typical frigate ship's company the shares would have been:

Captain	£6,736		
Lieutenants and Master (4)	842		
Warrant Officers (8)	421		
Petty Officers (24)	140	6	8
Seamen (200)	16	16	9

The crew of the *Brilliant* would, most of them, have dispersed long since. Blackwood himself had left in the first few months of 1799 to take up a more important frigate command in the *Penelope*.[35] Nevertheless, many past members of the *Brilliant*'s company, knowing the likely value of their prize, would have kept a lookout, and news – particularly news of prizes – was discussed freely in naval circles. It might even, in the uneasy truce of 1802, have enjoyed wider circulation than usual among those in forced (and ill-paid) idleness.

So, it may be hoped, much of the money found its way into the right pockets after all. It had been a long haul, taking up much time and effort from the day of 'fresh gales and hazey' in the Eastern Atlantic when the *Eenrom* was taken, through the (irregular) depositions in Lisbon, the interrogatories in Portsmouth, the Admiralty Court case where Scott had smelt his rat, the final case before the Lords Commissioners of Appeal in Prize Causes, to the rendering of the final account and the opening of the funds for payment. It had employed ship's officers, shipkeepers, temporarily engaged crews, pilots, warehousemen, lawyers, court officials, judges, auctioneers, diplomats, shipowners, insurers, agents and clerks. It was atypical only in the fact that it brought in all the actors likely to be involved in an incident of prize; many of the simpler cases would miss out a few. But as the microcosm of a system, the *Eenrom* has profitably served her turn, as one hopes she enhanced the fortunes of her hard-working and previously unlucky captors.

NOTES

1. See Chapter 8.
2. XIII NC, p. 239.
3. XIII NC, p. 243.
4. J.R. Hill (ed.), *Oxford Illustrated History of the Royal Navy* (OUP, 1995), p. 147.
5. XIII NC, p. 358.
6. Thomas Cochrane, Earl of Dundonald, *Autobiography of a Seaman* (Constable, 1995 edn), vol. I, p. 174.
7. Author's conversation with Spanish historians at the St Vincent Conference, Portsmouth, 14 February 1997. For another view see Leandro Prados de la Escosura, 'The Loss of Colonial Empire and its Economic Impact on Spain', in E. Aerts and F. Crouzet (eds), *Economic Effects of the French Revolutionary and Napoleonic Wars* (Leuven University Press, 1990), p. 82. Prados says that 'Bullion shipments became insignificant during the Napoleonic Wars', though it is not clear just when the sharpest decline occurred.
8. ADM 2/1080.
9. James Henderson, *The Frigates* (Adlard Coles, 1970), p. 119.
10. Papers in the possession of Lord Digby.
11. III NC, p. 79.
12. W.L. Clowes, *The Royal Navy: A History from the Earliest Times to 1900*, (Chatham edn, 1997), vol. 4, p. 526.
13. A figure used by the Jane Austen Museum.
14. Author's conversation with, and papers in the possession of, Lord Digby; and see A.M. Broadley and P.M. Barthelot, *Three Dorset Captains at Trafalgar* (John Murray, 1906), pp. 259–300.
15. See Chapter 2.
16. ADM 1/814, 21 October 1799.
17. III NC, p. 79.
18. HCA 2/365 and 2/366.
19. XXVII NC, p. 462.
20. Tony Gutridge, 'George Redmond Hulbert, Prize Agent' (unpublished thesis, Portsmouth Polytechnic, 1981–2), p. 78.

21. Sir William Henry Dillon, *A Narrative of my Professional Adventures* (Navy Records Society, 1953), p. 119.

22. HCA 2/356, *The Industria.*

23. ADM 15/2: Rose's out-letters show a consistent effort to ensure that all ranks of the Navy received their due.

24. HCA 2/355: the *Jesús Maria y Josef,* captured by *Thalia* and brought in 23 September 1799.

25. HCA 2/357: the *Juliana,* captured by *Surinam* on 24 February 1806 and brought in on 2 May 1810.

26. D.B. Ellison (ed.), *Pressganged: the Letters of George Price of Southwark, 1803–1805* (Ellison's Editions, 1994).

27. Ibid., p. 37.

28. Ibid., p. 48.

29. Papers in the possession of Lord Digby.

30. Clowes, *The Royal Navy,* vol. 4, p. 509.

31. 5 C. Rob., p. ix.

32. HCA 2/355, *L'Impromptu.*

33. HCA 2/342.

34. HCA 42/217.

35. ADM 1/1521.

CHAPTER EIGHTEEN

'The Very French Frigate I Wanted'

In Jane Austen's *Persuasion* Captain Wentworth, describing his activities in the *Asp* to the spellbound Musgrove girls, says '. . . after taking privateers enough to be entertaining, I had the good luck in my passage home . . . to fall in with the very French frigate I wanted. I brought her into Plymouth . . .'.[1]

Jane Austen knew her navy very well. Her brothers Francis and Charles were both naval officers, made post in 1800 and 1810 respectively[2] and both had commander's commands before those dates.[3] Both were successful in the matter of prize money, Francis mainly before the Peace of Amiens and Charles on the North America station after 1805. It enabled Charles to live in Chawton Great House and Francis to buy Portsdown Lodge,[4] both substantial places in Hampshire. It is no wonder that *Persuasion*, Jane's naval novel, is full of talk about prize money and the influence and status it brought.

But why 'the very French frigate I wanted'? Why was it not a Spanish merchantman laden with doubloons?

One reason has already been suggested in Chapter 6. Merchant captures might make one comfortably off, but capturing an enemy in fair fight (and, despite Wentworth's understatements, his was a fair enough fight: it had 'not much improved the *Asp*'s condition', to the extent that she would have sunk in the coming gale had she not made Plymouth in time) was the way to advancement and that might lead to better opportunities for enrichment.

But there was a more direct incentive. This was that the proceeds from a frigate capture, provided the ship was bought in to the navy, were considerably greater than the average merchant prize.

There were four factors at work. The first was the value of the hull. Frigate hulls were constructed for war-fighting and a great deal stouter than those of merchantmen of similar size. There was little point in the government buying a captured merchant ship and trying to turn her into a warship. On the other hand, warship captures were a tremendously important addition to naval strength. The net accretion to the Royal Navy from captures during the wars of 1793–1815 was 367,000 tons, or slightly more than half the warship tonnage built in Britain during that period.[5] Warship hulls were very valuable commodities.

Secondly, stores, armament and rigging were highly saleable items. The government always had first refusal on a warship capture and generally would buy in all items that could possibly have a naval use.

Thirdly, the value to the war effort of warship captures – both for the plus they gave to British naval strength and the minus they gave to the opposition – ensured that the government was not too niggardly over the amount paid for captured vessels and stores. There might be, indeed would certainly be, disappointment if a prize was so shattered or so ill-found that it could not be bought in; it did happen[6] but in many cases quite badly battered ships were purchased for the Navy.[7]

Fourth, there was the matter of head money. A frigate's crew in the Royal Navy was about 250–300; French ships were somewhat more heavily manned. At £5 a head that came to a considerable sum in its own right.

Four cases can be cited to show the benefits from a warship capture when the prize was bought in and head money paid.

The first, in chronological terms, was the *Nereide*. On 20 December 1797 she was sighted by the *Phoebe*, Captain Robert Barlow, in the Bay of Biscay. The British frigate gave chase and brought the *Nereide* to action at 9 p.m. The night action continued until 10.45, beginning with an hour's manoeuvring and ending yardarm-to-yardarm. The *Nereide* then struck her colours, being 'in a very battered condition'.[8] British casualties totalled thirteen, French seventy-five. It had when analysed been an unequal contest, the *Phoebe*'s broadside being half as heavy again as the *Nereide*'s although both were nominally thirty-six-gun ships. Interestingly, though, the French crew was 330 men against the British 261.

The main account, handled by Ommanney and Druce, was brought in very quickly by the standards of the time, on 17 May 1798.[9] Even more unusually, it included head money – often a payment that hung fire. Battered as it might have been, the hull fetched £6,078 and the head money unsurprisingly was £1,650. Stores must have been highly attractive, for they made as much again as the hull; the gross for this main account was £14,444 and the net sum for distribution £13,318.

There was a little more to come, for the ordnance stores took longer to appraise and their account was not complete until over a year later, on 2 July 1799. They brought in another £880 gross, £824 net for distribution.

The concern of the Admiralty to reward distinction in battle is apparent in much of this transaction. The speed of processing, except for the ordnance stores, was impressive, given the small and hard-worked staffs in Admiralty and Treasury. The Court, too, must have stirred itself, though in such a case of course condemnation was a foregone conclusion. The other significant point to emerge, though, was the proportion of the gross that fell eventually to the captors. It was about 92 per cent – far more than would have been expected from a merchant ship capture. The reason for the relatively small overhead was a low proctor's charge – after all, he had little enough to do – and the elimination of the broker and auctioneer, for the ship would have come under the Admiralty Marshal and the fee for appraisal was a nominal one. The agent got his 5 per cent and had probably done enough for it, but that was the largest of the charges. In 1798, of course, there was no impost for the Chatham Chest or Greenwich Hospital.

Sailors in the *Phoebe* would have done well for their hour's hot work. Given 200 in the 5th class, each would have received over £17 – not far short of a year's pay. Captain Barlow would receive £3,535 10*s.*

The second warship capture was even more one-sided. On 3 February 1809 the tedious operations off the Dutch coast in support of the Orders in Council scored one of their more profitable successes when the *Aimable*, 32 guns, Captain Lord George Stuart, captured the 24-gun corvette *Iris*, laden with flour and under orders for Martinique.[10] No resistance is recorded and it is doubtful if there was any, considering the ships' discrepancy in force.

Perhaps in consequence of her undamaged condition, the *Iris* sold well for a corvette. The hull fetched £8,500, stores £4,300 and Ordnance £1,300.[11] Head money came to just over £1,000. The net sum for distribution was £14,871 on a gross of £16,804: 88 per cent of the gross, but it must be remembered that by this time the naval charities were getting their 5 per cent levy.

Sykes, the agent in this capture, had not been so successful in expediting the account as Ommanney and Druce in the case of the *Nereide*. It took some sixteen months to process, being brought in on 4 May 1810. The *Iris* became HMS *Rainbow*.

The third frigate capture to be analysed was the most lucrative. *Le Niemen* (named presumably as a compliment to Napoleon for his negotiation of, or even to Tsar Alexander II for his acquiescence in, the Treaty of Tilsit, concluded on a raft on that river in July 1807) was a substantial forty-gun ship. On 5 April 1809, bound from France to Mauritius with stores and food, she was sighted in the Bay of Biscay by the *Amethyst*, thirty-six guns, which after a well-worked night chase brought her to action at 1.15 a.m.[12] A manoeuvring action was followed by the usual broadside-to-broadside encounter: this was going *Amethyst*'s way when several masts fell at once, inhibiting any further manoeuvre to put in a final raking fire. Fortunately the *Arethusa*, which had steered for the sound of the guns, came up and the *Niemen* at once surrendered. She had lost 47 killed and 73 wounded out of a complement of 339. The *Amethyst*'s captain, Michael Seymour, was created a baronet and his first lieutenant promoted commander with seniority dating from the day of the battle.[13]

This was classed as a joint capture and indeed the *Arethusa*'s intervention had decided it, so it was more justified than some of the more dubious 'in sight' claims. Possibly this complication explains the relative slowness of the settlement, for it was not until 30 July 1811 that the account was brought in. However, Hawker, the agent, had certainly

192

paid attention to detail; the account covers seventeen pages and is one of the most detailed in all the records examined.[14]

The gross proceeds, including head money, were £33,567. Interest amounting to £1,500 was allowed; it was customary by then for interest to be allowed on delayed payments of head money, but the agent must also have contributed some in this case. The net proceeds for distribution amounted to £28,480, or 85 per cent of the gross. It was a smaller proportion than either of the other frigate prizes examined, but still well above what might have been expected from a merchant capture. And in absolute terms the sum, even when split between the two ships, was handsome: given the *Amethyst*'s relatively small crew, a foremast hand might expect about £20 from the night's work.

No other frigate capture approaching *Le Niemen* in value has come to light. She was a new ship at the top of the frigate range. For comparison, one further case concerns a line of battle ship.

This was the *Guillaume Tell*, last French survivor of the Battle of the Nile, caught off Malta on 29 March 1800 as recounted in Chapter 7. Because of the complications of the joint-capture case,[15] settlement did not occur till 18 July 1810; by then many of the protagonists were dead, including Troubridge himself who as captain of the *Culloden* had brought the case and so helped to protract the dispute.

The gross proceeds for the seventy-four-gun *Guillaume Tell* were £37,138,[16] including

Hull	£28,932
Ordnance	6,194
Ammunition	347
Cash paid by Troubridge (an unexplained item)	516
Sails	363
Casks	742

The net proceeds for distribution were £33,017: an 89 per cent proportion and presumably to the credit of Tyson the agent, though there is no specific mention of interest and had full interest been allowed for the extraordinary lapse of time, the net might well have exceeded the gross. But the significant figure is the very small difference between the line of battle ship and the top-of-the-range frigate: the former were more likely to be battered in action, as was graphically shown by the fate of the prizes after Trafalgar, only four reaching harbour.[17]

So a fine French frigate might indeed be the very thing a British cruiser wanted, in financial terms as well as those of honours and promotion. But now this chapter will look at the other half of Captain Wentworth's tale: 'privateers enough to be entertaining'.

Captures of privateers were much more numerous than those of warships. Analysis suggests that of the condemnations by the High Court of Admiralty, about 15 per cent were of privateers and the indications are that on foreign stations the proportion was similar.[18] Their capture was of great importance to the British war effort: not only did it safeguard trade, it increased that trade's confidence. When the Admiralty was able to point out to merchant ship owners and insurers that twenty-seven privateers had been captured in the English Channel and North Sea areas within six months in 1808–9,[19] they must have felt that the Navy was showing real effectiveness in trade protection.

Flag officers frequently reinforced this emphasis on the capture of privateers in their orders to individual cruising ships and in their reports to higher authority which invariably mentioned privateer captures when these had been made. Indeed, captains made sure they did: no captain who took a privateer, however painlessly, would fail to report it to his superior, usually 'with great satisfaction' and mentioning any officer or man who had distinguished himself.

Kudos, regrettably, was sometimes the most tangible result of a privateer capture. For the records suggest that the proceeds from such a capture, including head money, averaged £1,223 gross and £1,063 net.

This small figure, smaller even than the average for a merchant capture, is explained by several factors. First, a privateer was a very different creature from a warship. Though many carried a high-sounding armament – 20 or 24 guns were not unknown, though 14 or 16 were more usual – the guns would not be of the same weight of metal as those of a warship of similar nominal force. A privateer's scantlings would not be anything like the same strength as those of a warship: they were built for speed, manouevrability and a quick getaway if trouble threatened. Often they were beautiful sailers, but that did not greatly help them if brought to close action.

Secondly, privateers, though manned appropriately for boarding and getting prizes back to port, had crews smaller than those of warships of similar nominal force. They seldom topped a hundred. Privateers were built, operated and manned for profit; it was their business to take merchant vessels, not to tangle with warships, though sometimes they fought fiercely when confronted.

Finally, not all privateer actions ended in capture. Many, probably a higher proportion than merchantmen, were driven on shore, burnt or otherwise destroyed. If a certified statement of the number of crew was accepted, they would still be condemned for head money only and appear in the accounts brought in. Such, for example, was the *Nouvelle Mouche*, destroyed by the *Diamond* on 7 March 1801;[20] head money fetched £800 (£714 net), so she was clearly much bigger than the average privateer; disappointment in the *Diamond* at the loss of the ship and stores can be imagined.

But a privateer, even if captured intact, would not make much in the way of proceeds. The hull might be useful as a despatch vessel, in which case it would be bought in to the navy, but at a much lower rate per ton than a warship would have been. More likely would be its disposal at auction, when its lean lines would make it unsuitable for normal commercial work and so reduce its value. And head money on the average privateer's crew of fifty or so would fetch only £250.

There was one compensation. As in the case of warship captures, the proportion of gross proceeds remaining 'net for distribution' was high. It stood at an overall level of 87 per cent for the whole war, being higher in the early period and descending to about 82 per cent after 1810. This was the Chatham Chest/Greenwich effect operating again; it tended to flatten out the differentials between captures of enemy war vessels, both national and privateer, and plain merchant ships.

Some large and lucrative privateer captures, of course, there were. The highest-paying that has come to light is the *Imperatrice Reine*, taken by the *Hotspur* in May 1813, which grossed £11,539 with a net sum for distribution of £10,318.[21] Head money was paid: it is not entirely clear whether the ship should be classed as a privateer or national vessel, but her commander was noted as 'Master' which indicates the former. Several other undoubted privateers grossed upwards of £4,000; but, as has been said, they were the exception.

Capture of privateers, particularly those of limited force, did of course give an opportunity for the smaller ships of the navy to pick up a modest amount of prize money. About half the 140 privateer actions studied were conducted by British ships of 20 guns or less. They were at the lower end of the scale for proceeds, seldom exceeding £1,000, but the crews of these small ships could at least see some reward for their labour and those long days on fruitless patrol.

From 1807 onwards a new and unfamiliar form of head money became available to the navy: but it was to be hard earned. On 23 February that year, after many years' campaigning, William Wilberforce carried the anti-slave trade bill through the House of Commons.[22] The Royal Navy found itself acting first in support of the domestic legislation against British slavers, then against foreign slavers on grounds of 'natural justice and humanity',[23] then in support of treaties concluded with other European powers – though these were slow to mature, only becoming general after the Congress of Vienna in 1815 and even then excluding Spain and Portugal.[24]

Few enough naval ships could be spared for the duty of enforcement on the West African coast. Moreover, the climate was notoriously unhealthy; and the unpopularity of the service was compounded by the ambivalent attitude of some of the officers, particularly those with West Indian interests.

Incentives were thought to be needed. The government settled on a system of head money for each slave liberated. This was set at a relatively high level: men £40, women £30, boys and girls pro rata.[25] Captured slave ships were to be brought in to Freetown, Sierra Leone, where a new Vice Admiralty Court was set up.[26] The staff there had to be augmented in 1814 to cope with the increased workload, particularly the international ramifications: but where, enquired Scott, was he to find suitably qualified people to work in 'such a place'?[27]

Certainly the load was considerable. In 14 months up to June 1813, 26 captured slave ships were sent in to Sierra Leone, with 1,387 men, 430 women, 459 boys and 185 children.[28] This represented a strong effort from a navy still in the middle of a global war and many problems for an inexperienced court dealing with untried legislation.

It does not appear, from a very limited scan, that the financial rewards for the navy's labour were at all substantial. One account that it has been possible to analyse, even though it falls slightly outside the period of this book, is that of the slaver *Neptune* captured by the *Tyne* in September 1816.[29] The gross proceeds were £2,483, including £2,190 head money on the liberated slaves. But the net sum for distribution – five and a half years later – was only £423. The proctor's bill was very high at £312; but the most unjust charge seems to have been £528 for 'victualling the blacks'. Of course this was a proper provision to have made, but to have taken it out of the ship's entitlement to bounty money seems wholly inappropriate: a reversion to eighteenth-century *mores* to deal with the product of early nineteenth-century evangelistic fervour. Remedying one terrible injustice only to commit another, albeit lesser one on the very people responsible for putting the remedy in operation, was an imperfect way of ushering in *pax Britannica*.

NOTES

1. Jane Austen, *Persuasion* (Collins, 1953 edn), pp. 240–1.

2. David Syrett and R.L. DiNardo, *The Commissioned Sea Officers of the Royal Navy 1660–1815* (Scolar Press for the Navy Records Society, 1994), p. 13.

3. J.H. and E.C. Hubback, *Jane Austen's Sailor Brothers* (Bodley Head, 1906), pp. 56, 124.

4. Ibid., pp. 262, 282.

5. Daniel E. Baugh, in J.R. Hill (ed.), *The Oxford Illustrated History of the Royal Navy* (OUP, 1995), p. 125.

6. See, e.g., W.L. Clowes, *The Royal Navy: A History from the Earliest Times to 1900* (Chatham, 1997 edn), vol. 4, p. 520, describing the action between *Prudente* and *Daedalus* in the Indian Ocean, 9 February 1799.

7. Ibid., at p. 521: the *Forte*, taken by the *Sibylle*, was much shattered but bought in.

8. Ibid., p. 508.

9. HCA 2/365.

10. Clowes, *The Royal Navy*, vol. 5, p. 430.

11. HCA 2/357.

12. Clowes, *The Royal Navy*, vol. 5, p. 433.

13. Syrett and DiNardo, *Sea Officers*, p. 220.

14. HCA 2/366.

15. Edw., p. 6 [1808].

16. HCA 2/350.

17. Clowes, *The Royal Navy*, vol. 5, p. 163.

18. XXX NC, pp. 240–4, for captures on the North America station, 1812–13.

19. ADM 1/3993.

20. HCA 2/365.

21. HCA 2/357.

22. Sir Reginald Coupland, *Wilberforce* (Collins, 1945), p. 279.

23. HCA 30/466, Appeal Court note on *The Amédie* (1810).

24. Coupland, *Wilberforce*, p. 333.

25. *Notifications, Orders and Instructions relating to Prize Subjects during the Present War* (Strahan, for Butterworth and White, 1810), p. 91, Order dated 16 March 1808.

26. ADM 1/3898, Gostling to Pole, 17 May 1808.

27. ADM 1/3902, Scott to Croker, 14 August 1814.

28. XXX NC, p. 110.

29. HCA 2/367.

CHAPTER NINETEEN

Salvage Money

Handy to the bridge of Her Majesty's Ships, when at sea, is kept a blank copy of Lloyd's Salvage Form. It has a bold preamble of four syllables which few naval officers ever forget, once they have seen it: 'No Cure No Pay'.

Bringing in a vessel that was in danger of being lost through fire, foundering or stranding still attracts salvage money – so long as the Lloyd's Form was signed by the master of the endangered ship – and so nowadays does assisting in that work, though if more than one salvor is involved the negotiation of the split can be protracted.

It was more rough and ready and governed by simpler law in the case of recaptures during the wars of 1793–1815. The Prize Acts throughout the period had the fundamental rule that 'all Regulations herein contained respecting Prizes, shall apply to all cases of . . . Salvage upon recapture from His Majesty's Enemies'.[1] That said, there was in each Act a special section on recapture,[2] laying down one-eighth of the 'true value' of ship, stores and cargo as the salvage to be paid to warship recaptors, one-sixth to privateer recaptors.

'No cure no pay' was to be liberally interpreted, since there was a provision[3] for a recaptured ship to continue her voyage, provided the recaptors consented, and the master or his agents might then 'unlade and dispose of their cargoes before Adjudication'; and if the vessel remained absent for six months or more, the recaptors might proceed in the Admiralty Court to seek a decree for restitution upon salvage 'upon such evidence as the said Court shall, under the Circumstances of the Case, appear reasonable, the Expence of such Proceeding not to exceed the sum of Fourteen Pounds'.

This provision was very much to the advantage of shipowners and shippers and the evidence is that they did not abuse it. It is negative evidence, to be sure: that is to say, no clear case of complaint can be found from a recaptor that any attempt was made to evade the responsibility to pay up. There were probably two factors at work here: first, recaptors would make very sure documents confirming the recapture were signed on the spot, the equivalent of the signature of the Lloyd's Form today; and second, owners and shippers would be happy enough with the restoration of their property, particularly at the scale of salvage laid down.

Even so, quantum was of course subject to negotiation and here was a situation where an agent was invaluable to a ship's captain and company. There was no possible way for anyone from a ship's crew to haggle with knowledgeable merchants, even if he could get the necessary leave, but an agent would know the market and probably some of the personalities and would be in a good position to get the best deal he could. If the ship suspected he was not doing his best for them, another agent could always be engaged.

Given the one-eighth scale for salvage, the proceeds could not be expected to be very high. Indeed, taking the mean value of a merchant prize, which as has been shown was somewhere about £2,500, it might be expected that a recapture would fetch only three or four hundred pounds.

In fact it was rather better than that. About 100 recaptures were studied in the survey (see Appendix 1) and the average gross figure for salvage was £715. The average net proceeds for distribution were £637: some 89 per cent of the gross. As in the case of warship and privateer captures, the proportion of net to gross declined as the war went on, due almost certainly to the levy on account of the Chatham Chest and Greenwich Hospital.

The reason for the relatively low charges was twofold. Court charges for a decree of restitution ('condemnation' was clearly an inappropriate word for a recapture) were not high, since the documents were likely to be agreed by all the parties. And assessment of the value of ship, stores and cargo would be reached by agreement between agent, owner and shippers without any need for the machinery of shipkeepers, pilots, warehousing and auctioneers that was associated with prizes.

So it was a matter of modest returns for, quite often, a modest amount of effort by the more humble ships. Most recaptors fell into the frigate class, to be sure, but *Gannet* and *Port Mahon*, both sloops, notched up recaptures worth over £1,000.[4] At the other end of the scale of profit came another small vessel, the *Dwarf*: for her recapture of the *Juste* she received £22 1s 9d. The highest return for a recapture in the records covered by Appendix 1 is the *Jeannie*, recaptured by the *Helena* in 1810 or 1811; her salvage came to £3,169 gross, making £2,750 net.[5]

There is evidence of higher figures in exceptional cases. In 1800 the *Naval Chronicle* reported that the owners of a particularly rich recapture had offered one-eighth of £60,000, and that this had been accepted.[6] The very fact that it was reported in this way suggests that a figure of £7,500 for salvage was unusually high, and this bears out the general findings of the survey.

Only one even more generously rewarded recapture has been uncovered. This was the Indiaman *Lord Nelson*, which was captured by the French privateer *Bellone* of 34 guns and 260 men on 14 August 1803 and recaptured 12 days later after a concerted operation involving a British privateer, a hired cutter, the 18-gun brig *Seagull* and 4 ships of the line under Pellew, which came up to clinch the issue.[7] The salvage was settled quickly in spite of the joint nature of the recapture, probably because the powerful East India Company was anxious to show its gratitude; the account was brought in on 19 March 1804.[8] The total of salvage paid out was £24,600 15s 0d for the cargo and £2,061 1s 1d for the ship; this computes at a total value of over £200,000 for the *Lord Nelson*, richly laden indeed. The line of battle ships *Culloden* and *Colossus* each received over £4,000 for being in sight at the recapture.

There is precious little about recapture in the folklore of prize. One or two cases turn up later in the war: the *Ranger*, for example, was effectively retaken by 'the mate and a boy' who had been left on board by the French prize crew, subsequently making the offing to meet a British cruiser. The cruiser got the usual salvage, but the mate received £30 and the boy £10.[9]

Recapture may have been one of the more humdrum kinds of operation in the business of seaborne economic warfare. It was a useful element nonetheless; the very fact that 10 per cent of all captures were recovery of one's own shows its importance. The Admiralty, in answer to a remonstrance from the Committee at Lloyd's, was able to point with satisfaction to the fact that, of seventy-two ships captured by the enemy in the approaches to Britain between 1 September 1808 and 1 March 1809, no less than twenty-four had been recaptured.[10] Recapture may have made no fortunes, but it was a substantial factor in establishing and sustaining the confidence of the merchant marine in Britain's ability to maintain control of the sea.

NOTES

1. 45 Geo. III c.72 s.8.
2. 33 Geo. III c.66 s.42; 43 Geo. III c.160 s.39; 45 Geo. III c.72 s.7.
3. 45 Geo. III c.72 s.21.
4. HCA 2/356.
5. HCA 2/357.
6. III NC, p. 328.
7. W. Laird Clowes, *A History of the Royal Navy from the Earliest Times to 1900*, vol. 5 (Chatham, 1997 edn), pp. 325–6.
8. HCA 2/359.
9. XXI NC, p. 252.
10. ADM 1/3993.

CHAPTER TWENTY

Distribution

For one hundred years after 1708, the scale for distribution of prize money remained effectively unchanged. The proclamations by which it came into effect at the start of each war might vary in detail, but the proportions for shares were the same as between admiral, captain, officers and crew.[1]

The net sum for distribution was divided by eight. Of this the captain of the capturing ship received three-eighths; but if he was operating under the direction of a flag officer, one of those eighths went to that officer. Flag officers generally made sure that ships in their command area were indeed operating 'under their direction', so effectively the captain would expect a quarter of the net prize money for any capture and exactly the same proportion for head or salvage money; all were governed by the same scale.[2]

Another eighth went to be divided equally among the 'sea lieutenants' (to distinguish them from lieutenants of marines or the army), the captain of marines if borne, and the master. A physician, as distinct from a surgeon, if on board at the time of the capture, would have an entitlement in this second class.

The third class, entitled to another eighth of the spoils, consisted of warrant and certain other officers: the boatswain, gunner, carpenter, purser, chaplain, surgeon, the master's mates, lieutenants of marines, any lieutenant or junior officer of land forces, and the quartermasters of both marines and army.[3]

The fourth class were, broadly, the petty officers, but they included midshipmen, the assistants to the warrant officers – boatswain's mates, gunner's mates, clerks – and the tradesmen, the sailmakers, caulkers and ropemakers. Curiously, the master at arms was in this class, since he was a less powerful person in those times: the boatswain was the principal wielder of discipline on board. The fourth class received another eighth to be split between them.

Finally, the fifth class consisted of all the rest and in theory the split of the remaining quarter of the distribution was to be equal between them. These would include some highly skilled and responsible men – captains of tops, tradesmen's mates, corporals of marines – but equally there would be landsmen either volunteer or newly pressed, captain's servants who were aspiring officers of a very tender age, and boys. If there was any differential between these persons of disparate experience and skills, it was not officially recognized.

Some indication has been given in earlier chapters of the way in which distribution would work out in an average frigate's company. One further example shows how much better individuals could do from a relatively modest capture if their ship was small and there were fewer of them to share.[4] The ship concerned was the *Pelican*, eighteen guns, and her prize the *Nancy*, an American ship running contraband and captured in July 1796. The gross proceeds were £4,063 13*s* and the net sum for distribution was £3,872 8*s*. It was split as follows:

Admiral	£484		
Captain	968		
Second Class (3)	161	7	0
Third Class (6)	80	13	6
Fourth Class (14)	34	11	6
Fifth Class (85)	11	7	9

The equivalent of over half a year's pay was no bad return for anyone.

This somewhat crude system soldiered on until 1807. There is little sign in the *Naval Chronicle*, or in officers' correspondence, that it caused any particular concern. There were grumbles, of course, and a well-known cartoon of the time showed a sailor praying that 'the enemy's shot should be distributed in the same manner as the prize money, the greater proportion to the officers'. It was noticeable that the Spithead mutineers did not mention distribution as a grievance, though the more politically oriented ones at the Nore did.[5]

But in 1807, clearly, there must have been some perception in the Admiralty that changes should be made. It might have been murmurings from the fleet: there was much more sensitivity to such things since the mutinies of 1797. It might have been a sense of natural justice: eighteenth-century morality was giving way to nineteenth, 1807 had seen the triumph of the abolitionists of the slave trade and some hierarchies were just beginning to crumble at the edges. Finally, it might have been the accession to two influential posts at the Admiralty of two formidably tidy-minded people, George Rose the Treasurer and John Barrow the Second Secretary, who had come into office within a week of each other in April 1807.[6] Probably it was a combination of all three factors.

What emerged was a new scale of distribution, embodied in a Proclamation of 15 June 1808.[7] It is thought worth giving the operative paragraphs almost in full, since they govern much of the discussion in the rest of this chapter.

Whereas it has been represented to us, by our commissioners for executing the Office of Lord High Admiral, that it will be productive of beneficial effects to the Service, if, instead of three eighth parts of the neat produce of prizes, which have hitherto been granted to the Captains and Flag Officers serving in our Fleet, two eighth parts only shall be allotted to them, and the remaining eighth part distributed amongst the petty officers, seamen and marines, in addition to their present shares . . .

The distribution shall be made as follows: – The whole of the net produce being first divided into eight equal parts,

The Captain or Captains of any of our ships or vessels of war, or officer commanding such ship or vessel, who shall be actually on board at the taking of any prize, shall have two-eighth parts; but in case such prize shall be taken by any of our ships or vessels of war, under the command of a flag or flags, the flag officer or officers, being actually on board, and directing or assisting in the capture, shall have one third of the said two-eighth parts; and said one-third of such two eighth parts to be paid to such flag officers, in such proportions, and subject to such regulations, as are hereinafter mentioned.

The sea lieutenants, captains of marines and land forces, and master, on board, shall have one-eighth part, to be equally divided amongst them: but every physician appointed . . . to a fleet . . . shall, in the distribution of prizes which may hereafter be taken by the ships in which he shall serve, . . . be classed with the before-mentioned officers . . . provided such physician be actually on board at the time of taking such prizes.

The lieutenants and quartermasters of marines, and lieutenants, ensigns, and quartermasters of land forces, secretaries of admirals and commodores . . . second masters of line of battle ships, surgeons, chaplains, pursers, gunners, boatswains, carpenters, master's mates, and pilots, on board, shall have one-eighth part, to be equally divided amongst them.

The other four eighth parts of the prize to be divided into shares, and distributed to persons composing the remaining part of the crew, in the following proportions:

viz. To the first class of petty officers, namely, the midshipmen, surgeon's assistants, secretaries' clerks, captains' clerks, schoolmasters, master at arms, captain's cockswains, gunner's mates, yeomen of the powder room, boatswain's mates, yeomen of the sheets, carpenter's mates, quartermasters, quartermasters' mates, ship's corporals, captains of the forecastle, master sailmakers, master caulkers, master ropemakers, armourers, serjeants of marines, and of land forces, four and a half shares each.

To the second class of petty officers, viz. Midshipmen, ordinary, captains of the foretop, captains of the maintop, captains of the after-guard, captains of the mast, sailmakers' mates, caulkers' mates, armourers' mates, ship's cook, corporals of marines and land forces, three shares each.

The quarter gunners, carpenter's crew, sailmaker's crew, cockswain's mates, yeomen of the boatswain's store room, gunsmiths, coopers, trumpeters, able seamen, ordinary seamen, drummers, private marines, and other soldiers, if doing duty on board in lieu of marines, one and a half share each.

The landsmen, admirals' domestics, and all other ratings not above enumerated, together with all passengers, and other persons borne as supernumeraries, and doing duty and assisting on board, one share each, excepting officers acting by order, who are to receive the share of that rank in which they shall be acting.

And young gentlemen, volunteers by order, and the boys of every description, half a share each.

Before discussing the reaction to the proclamation it will be worth considering its effect in a typical frigate. To make the figures impressive and manageable let us take a rich prize, netting £40,000, and compare the pre- and post-proclamation shares.

Pre-Proclamation of 15 June 1808		Post-Proclamation			
Admiral	£5,000	Admiral	£3,333	6	8
Captain	10,000	Captain	6,666	13	4
Lieutenants, Master (4)	1,250	Lieutenants, Master (4)	1,250	0	0
Warrant Officers (8)	625	Warrant Officers (8)	625	0	0
Fourth Class (24)	208 6 8	6 Midshipmen }			
		2 Surgeon's Mates }			
Fifth Class (200)	50	1 Clerk }			
		1 Schoolmaster }			
		1 Master at Arms }	214	5	9
		3 Quartermasters }			
		3 Master tradesmen }			
		1 Ship's corporal }			
		1 Sergeant of marines }			
		1 Capt of forecastle }			
		1 gunner's mate }			
		2 boatswain's mates }			

1 captain's coxswain } (4½ shares each, total shares 108)			
30 captains of tops, tradesmen's mates, ship's cook etc. (3 shares each, total shares 90)	142	17	2
120 quarter gunners, tradesmen's crews, able and ordinary seamen (1½ shares each, total shares 180)	71	8	5
34 Landsmen and domestics (1 share each, total shares 34)	47	12	5
16 Boys and 'Young Gentlemen' (½ share each, total shares 8)	23	16	2

The total number of shares for the erstwhile fourth and fifth classes was in this case 420, which would have been the first calculation for the agent when he received the prize list – this of course had to be a great deal more detailed than it had been before, for it had to show by name who was entitled to which scale of share. After that the shares could be allocated in the way shown.

The people who benefited most, in this constructed case, were the men in the middle ratings: those who would nowadays be leading hands. They would have been in the fifth class under the earlier dispensation, now they had their three shares. Arguably they were just the sort of people the navy wanted to keep at that stage of the war: staid hands who whatever their origin – pressed or volunteer, gaolbird or solid citizen – had proved their ability to fill responsible positions on board. The incentive given to them by an increased share of prize money was, or should have been, powerful.

No one else did comparably well. The able seamen, to be sure, received a comfortable hike and were able to show a differential from the landsmen, thus putting right what they were bound to have considered an anomaly in the former regime. But the senior petty officers' share was more or less unchanged, and in the example given it had risen by only a trifle. The warrant and commissioned officers' shares were unchanged.

That left the captains and admirals. To deal with the admirals first, the wording of the Proclamation as it appeared in the *London Gazette* seemed to preclude their sharing unless they were 'actually on board, and directing or assisting in the capture'. Previous Proclamations[8] had said 'actually on board, *or* [my italics] directing . . .'. This alteration of one little word, if implemented to the letter of any normal construction, would radically have changed the system from what it had always been: before 1808 it was understood that unless the circumstances were exceptional – typically a capturing ship operating under direct Admiralty control – the admiral under whose direction any capture was made would get, as Pellew called it, his whack.[9] The new proclamation would on the face of it have deprived admirals of most of the gain they had come to expect from a lifetime of service.[10]

But in practice the admirals kept their whack. No evidence can be found, indeed, of any challenge, by a captain, to an admiral's entitlement on the grounds of the wording of the Proclamation. There was a reason grounded in the hierarchical structure of the navy, and there was also a legal one.

The structural reason was quite simple. A captain was normally operating under the direction of his admiral, whether on a foreign or home station, and the admiral had an absolute authority in the orders he gave to cruising ships. If a captain sought to deny an admiral's share of prize money on the ground of some new proclamation, he could expect little preference in the choice of his next cruising ground: indeed, it was likely to be convoy duty without the option. The eighteenth century was not dead, however much people like Barrow wanted it reborn into the nineteenth, and interest still played a most important part in individual assignments.

Captains, too, had to remember that they had prospects. No one in 1808 knew how long the war would go on, nor whether it would be followed by other wars. Promotion to rear admiral when they reached the top of the captains' list was certain; if it was still wartime, an active flag appointment was then a probability; and no one would have wanted to forego the prospect of the 'flag eight' (though now, of course, it was a twelfth) through some injudicious opposition to the practice long ago.

It is significant that in a print of the Proclamation dated 1809, the offending little word 'and' has been replaced by the permissive 'or'.[11] It is hard to believe that this change was made without authority. The differing versions could at the very least have been used in argument if any challenge to a flag share had been mounted.

There was a more respectable legal argument, however, arising from the closing section of the Proclamation of 1808. It contained twelve paragraphs setting out the rules for flag officers' shares, and the very first of these[12] not only contained 'or' rather than 'and', but established that 'directing' a capture meant exercising what nowadays would be called operational command. The moment he arrived within the limits of a station, the commander in chief became entitled to his share of the proceeds of captures made there; though if he was junior to his predecessor he was entitled only to the junior flag officer's share until he assumed actual command. There were further provisions for stations with a number of flag officers and for commodores and flag captains.

These rules were necessary to minimize the chance of squabbles between admirals and commodores over entitlement to prize money, which had so disfigured senior officers' conduct not only in this but most previous wars. The row between Pellew and Troubridge over the Indian Ocean split command in 1806, ending as it did in the loss of Troubridge in the *Blenheim*, was perhaps the worst example.[13] There were numerous other cases, not least the bitterness of Nelson in the Mediterranean when deprived of a 'golden harvest' by Sir John Orde's appointment to the Cádiz blockade in late 1804, where Spanish prizes were aplenty and which had previously been in Nelson's operational area.[14]

These disputes were at the very least undignified and tetchy. At their worst they poisoned relations between officers in neighbouring or supporting commands, who ought to have been working in the closest co-operation, and that poison would inevitably percolate through the ships under their command. Moreover, the controversy would preoccupy the minds of the officers concerned, often to the extent of weakening or distorting their strategic judgement. So clarification of the previous rules – which John Scott, Nelson's Secretary, had criticized in 1803 as 'replete with mysterious doubt'[15] – was needed and the twelve paragraphs they occupied in the Proclamation were not superfluous.

But their presence on the face of the Proclamation added up to a consolidation of the previous system, so far as flag officers' shares were concerned, and in effect overthrew the very straightforward wording 'flag officer . . . being actually on board' in the earlier part of the document as worded in the *Gazette*. Just how the drafting process in the Admiralty went on is, of course, now unknown; it is quite likely that it involved differences of view between officials and their Lordships. But in practice the admirals won, or at least did not lose more than a one-third drop in their prize money.

On many foreign stations, particularly, that was still a fortune. Professor Lewis estimated that 'a good C in C ship' would net £100,000;[16] the Mediterranean in 1813 and 1814, with the captures of Genoa and Naples, must have generated at least that for Pellew and in the same period Sir John Borlase Warren would have done similarly well on the North America station.[17]

It was the captains who felt hardest done by in the 1808 system. At first sight this looks like greed. They still stood to gain much more than anyone else on board – in any normal crew structure by a factor of four; and they would get twice as much as their flag officer or officers. An 'average' merchant prize netting £2,400 would still make the captain £400, a tidy sum.

But against that had to be set the captain's unique position. He would have had to lay out a good deal of money to set up his command: his personal stores, furniture and instruments to be bought, his boat's crew to be properly dressed, his own uniform to be beyond reproach and quite likely sweeteners to be paid to dockyard officials to get his ship to sea in a decent state. Once in commission he was expected to entertain his officers regularly, to keep up his own appearance and standards, to set an example. Frequently he would need to intervene financially to improve the amenities, or even the operational capability, of the ship.

Then there was the question of responsibility. If a captain made a mistake, the whole ship suffered – sometimes to the ultimate extent. That burden was a heavy one and constant, as it is today. But in matters of prize it was financial as well, for a captain making a wrong decision as to capture bore the whole responsibility. There was no point in his blaming a boarding officer for a wrong report on a detained ship's status, nor for omission to discover a paper that would exonerate it from capture. Captain Capel's mistake in the case of the *Actaeon*, however it arose, was his in law, and it was he alone who was liable for the £4,000 compensation.[18]

All these considerations were in the minds of captains when they read the 1808 Proclamation. Years later they were succinctly summed up by Sir William Henry Dillon, Admiral of the Red, in his *Narrative of my Professional Adventures*: 'Prize money . . . made up in some cases for the expenses to which captains were liable'.[19] He added that the First Lord in 1808 was Lord Mulgrave, who with his army background could not be expected to know what a captain's obligations were.

But the captains were in a dilemma as to what was to be done. It would be foolish as well as fruitless to seek a simple reversal of the Proclamation. The new provisions were plainly popular with the lower deck. How the shares would actually work out in individual cases was for the future; for the time being, it was enough that there was more for the petty officers and seamen to share. 'A.F.Y.', a frequent contributor to the *Naval Chronicle* on matters of discipline and welfare, wrote in July 1808 'I must congratulate my naval readers, and the country in general, on the spirit of liberal justice which appears in the new distribution of prize money.'[20]

What the captains did, therefore, was to take an entirely different approach. They requested an increase in their pay. They were not in the best of positions even for this, because pay had been put up two years before, by over £7 year in the case of captains,[21] and pay rises were expected to be few and far between. However, they were able to point to several factors, as well as the reduction in their share of prize money, that suggested a further pay rise. One was the increased cost of living: 'every article of life has in late years experienced an extraordinary rise';[22] another was the income tax.

It got them nowhere. Their Lordships' reply on 6 January 1809 was signed by Wellesley Pole, the Secretary of the Admiralty, and said the request was 'wholly inadmissible . . . the pay of the captains and commanders, in common with the pay of all ranks of officers in his Majesty's Navy, and of the petty officers and seamen, was increased . . . on 23 April 1806 . . . after the most mature deliberation, and nothing has occurred within the very short period that has since elapsed to induce Their Lordships to think it expedient to recommend a further increase . . .'. The reply ended by regretting that so ill-timed a memorial should have been sent.[23]

This was very severe. The captains were not put off and returned four days later with a further submission. It begged leave,

> with proper respect to Their Lordships, both personally and from their office, to express their grief and surprize, that their memorial, couched as it was in respectful language, as well as the matter of it undeniable, should be considered wholly inadmissible; and farther, that it should be stated to have been preferred so recently after the extension of his Majesty's gracious bounty to all ranks of the navy, insinuating thereby that it was indecorous . . . the gracious bounty of his Majesty was in fact putting in one hand what was taken out of the other by the Income Tax, and that a charge of five per cent was made on their prize money paid into Greenwich, and ultimately a third of it taken away altogether without their rank being consulted, except in a very slight degree . . .

After this the matter fell away, though there were some half-hearted returns to the charge. A.F.Y. in the *Naval Chronicle* made one more effort in 1810, when in an open letter to the First Lord[24] he referred to 'the late petition from the captains', but it came to nothing. It was succeeded in later years by more general expressions of misgiving about the administration of prize money, particularly the difficulty of getting it out of the bureaucracy at Greenwich and the complexities of its recovery by widows, children and relatives of deceased seamen.

This campaign was conducted in the House of Commons by Thomas, Lord Cochrane,[25] and Sir Francis Burdett, but it became so entangled with the numerous other schemes and complaints which flowed from

Cochrane that no substantive action was directly taken. It may have had indirect effects in spurring George Rose to even greater efforts on behalf of those entitled; but it is quite clear from Rose's original correspondence[26] that his championship of the seamen in matters of prize money long predated Cochrane's campaigning and Cochrane's assertion[27] that it stemmed from his own work in the House was unfounded.

So the scale of distribution remained on the 1808 standard for the rest of the war. It was not egalitarian, but neither was the navy. And though the enemy's shot might not have been distributed as was the prize money, still the officers did take a higher proportion of the casualties, as contemporary accounts clearly show, and they bore the higher measure of responsibility. In general this was accepted, and there is little evidence of any protest, either from the lower deck or in the country as a whole, that the 1808 scale was inadequate tinkering. It was in the spirit of the age; change was to come gradually; the Reform Bill was still twenty-four years away.

NOTES

1. E.g., Proclamation of 7 July 1803: X NC, p. 76.
2. 45 Geo. III c.72 ss.5 and 7.
3. 'Quartermaster' in the navy denoted, and still denotes, a quite different job from that of a quartermaster in the army or the Royal Marines. In the former, the quartermaster is a responsible rating who steers the ship at sea and keeps watch on the gangway in harbour; in the army, he is an officer who has a whole range of accommodation and logistic functions. A typical culture clash occurred when in 1970 a body of sailors from HMS *Dryad* was accommodated in the Guards Barracks in Chelsea during a dock strike. A rating was stationed at the gate to supervise libertymen and was naturally, in naval terminology, labelled the Quartermaster. A request was made to the army for him to be provided with dinner and he was highly gratified to be presented with a little something, in four courses, from the officers' mess, served with the regimental silver.
4. HCA 2/365.
5. W.L. Clowes, *The Royal Navy: A History from Earliest Times to 1900*, vol. 4 (Chatham edn, 1997), p. 172; the demand was seventh out of eight on the Nore mutineers' list.
6. Ibid., vol. 5, p. 4.
7. *Notifications, Orders and Instructions relating to Prize Subjects during the Present War* (Strahan, for Butterworth and White, 1810), p. 98; LG (1808), pp. 853–6.
8. See, e.g., note 1.
9. C. Northcote Parkinson, *Edward Pellew, Viscount Exmouth* (Methuen, 1933), p. 405, Pellew to Keats, 12 September 1813.
10. Michael Lewis, *A Social History of the Navy 1793–1815* (George Allen and Unwin, 1960), p. 321.

11. Bound book of Proclamations in the Admiralty Library.

12. *Notifications*, p. 105.

13. See Chapter 6.

14. Denis Orde, *Nelson's Mediterranean Command* (Pentland Press, 1997), p. 155.

15. John Scott to Marsh and Creed, 16 September 1803: Royal Naval Museum archive.

16. Lewis, *A Social History of the Navy*, p. 321.

17. Tony Gutridge, 'George Redmond Hulbert, Prize Agent' (unpublished thesis, Portsmouth Polytechnic, 1981–2), p. 78.

18. 2 Dods., p. 48 [1814].

19. Sir William Henry Dillon, *A Narrative of my Professional Adventures* (Navy Records Society, 1953), p. 119.

20. XX NC, p. 27.

21. Clowes, *The Royal Navy*, vol. 5, p. 32.

22. XXI NC, p. 158.

23. XXI NC, p. 197.

24. XXIV NC, p. 39.

25. Thomas Cochrane, Earl of Dundonald, *Autobiography of a Seaman*, vol. II (Constable edn, 1995), p. 284.

26. ADM 15/2.

27. Cochrane, *Autobiography of a Seaman*, vol. II, pp. 313–15.

CHAPTER TWENTY-ONE

The Law's Delays

On 12 November 1795 Captain Horatio Nelson, in command of HMS *Agamemnon* then lying in Vado Bay on the west coast of Italy, wrote to his agents in Leghorn:

> You will herewith receive depositions relative to the taking of a ship laden with corn, bound to a place occupied by the armies of France or to France. If it is necessary, you will send these papers to England, but really I see but little a Court of Admiralty has to decide upon . . . I beg you to consider what is proper to be done in this case . . . our Proctor must have proper notice of how things stand here. The Austrians sell instantly, and share the money; our poor sailors are kept a long time out of their money. Is there no Court of Admiralty established in Corsica? England is a great way off: however, I trust you will be as expeditious as possible . . .[1]

As he so often managed to do, Nelson put into clear language a set of concerns that were a constantly recurring theme of the times. The sluggish operation of a process that depended on slow communication between widely scattered clients, agents and tribunals; the unfavourable comparison with less scrupulous and more arbitrary regimes; and, predictably as coming from Nelson, the concern for those whose gain might be least but whose ardour for gain was as strong as any, the 'poor sailors': all would be replicated over and over again in the twenty years that followed.

In evidence to the Commission whose Fourth Report examined Prize Agency in 1803, James Primrose Maxwell suggested that an uncontested condemnation would take place about six weeks after the prize was brought in and a monition posted, and sale of the prize would then proceed, distribution to the captors being made within another three or four months.[2] So far as is known, the Commission did not challenge these figures, nor did they comment on delay as a feature of the system.

They should have done so. Maxwell's timetable from capture to distribution, even if generous allowance is made for the time taken bringing a prize into port, informing the agent, having the interrogatories taken and posting the monition, is about seven months. Analysis of the data gathered by the method outlined in Appendix 1 shows that this timetable was met only in about one-seventh of the merchant ship captures, one-sixth of the privateer captures and slightly less than half the recaptures.

There was not even a flood of settlements at the eight and nine month points, though they did build up as the year approached. And very many dragged on into a second, third or fourth year. The figures can be tabulated as follows:

Merchant Ship Captures – time from capture to distribution of prize money

0–3 months	2			
4–6 months	22	Total first year	88	26.9%
7–9 months	37			
12 months	27			
13–15 months	30			
16–18 months	21	Total second year	85	26.0%
19–21 months	19			
22–4 months	15			
25–36 months		Total third year	41	12.5%
37–48 months		Total fourth year	44	13.5%
over 48 months		Over four years	69	21.1%

Total sample 327

Warship and Privateer captures – time from capture to distribution of prize and head money

0–3 months	2			
4–6 months	6			
7–9 months	12	Total first year	31	41.9%
10–12 months	11			
13–15 months	5			
16–18 months	2	Total second year	17	23.0%
19–21 months	8			
22–4 months	2			
25–36 months		Total third year	14	18.9%
37–48 months		Total fourth year	1	1.4%
over 48 months		Over four years	11	14.8%

Total sample 74

Recaptures – time from recapture to distribution of salvage money

1–3 months	6			
4–6 months	11	Total first year	31	62%
7–9 months	8			
10–12 months	6			
13–15 months	3			
16–18 months	3	Total second year	11	22%
19–21 months	4			
22–24 months	1			
25–36 months		Total third year	3	6%
37–48 months		Total fourth year	0	
over 48 months		Over four years	5	10%

Total sample 50

The patterns for the three categories are noticeably different. Recaptures had the best chance of a quick settlement and warship and privateer captures had a better chance than did merchant captures.

The reasons for the difference are not simple but are fairly easy to explain. A recapture still had to go through the Court, even though it was a decree for salvage and not a condemnation that was sought. But the procedure was relatively quick and uncontroversial. Then there was no need for sale by auction, only negotiated agreement between owner and agent on the value of the ship, stores and – if it still existed – cargo. A simple division by eight for normal salvage (the Court could vary it by decree); deduction of the relatively modest charges for proctor, agency and after 1806 the naval charities; bringing in the accounts; and the salvage money was ready for distribution.

No wonder therefore that it was relatively quick, and this was just as well, for as was shown in Chapter 19 the absolute proceeds were on average less than a thousand pounds. But it did show what agents could do when unencumbered by lengthy court procedures and administration. There was one further reason, which will emerge later in this chapter.

Captures of warships and privateers were less quickly settled, but even so, half fell for distribution within the first fifteen months after capture. Here the delay in court should have been negligible and condemnation a matter of course. Delay would spring from two other sources. First, survey and appraisal of hull and stores could take many months, particularly if a prize was badly damaged and there was doubt whether she could be taken into naval service. Second, the arrangements for head money might run into bureaucratic problems. However anxious to give capturing crews their due bounty, the Navy department had to have some documentary evidence of the number of the enemy alive at the start of the action; particularly in the case of ships destroyed, burnt or driven on shore this could be hard to come by. In consequence some claims to head money were settled separately, as were some sales of ordnance stores. This has complicated, but not it is hoped distorted, the table above.

Again, there was one other factor that made for delay, but it will be right to deal with this after merchant prizes have been considered.

Here the picture was different from, and a great deal darker than, those for recaptures or warship captures. It took two years for even half the accounts to settle, and the number still outstanding after four years – nearly a quarter of the whole – looks disgraceful.

Numerous reasons can be found. First and foremost was the question of neutrals. By definition, an acknowledged enemy owner was most unlikely to contest a case. But as has been seen, many owners who were enemy subjects, or who were closely connected with the enemy, cloaked the connection with neutral papers of one kind or another and were ready to enter claims for restoration. Genuine neutrals who thought themselves unjustly detained were even more likely to do so. Contested cases might take some months to come on while papers were prepared, and the allowance of a year for a neutral claim[3] was not unrealistic.

Secondly, a contested case, if lost by the claimant in the Admiralty Court, might well go on to Appeal. This usually took years. *The Eenrom* was decided in March 1802, affirming the judgment in the court below which had been made in May 1799.[4] The evidence is that such a time lapse was not at all exceptional; many other cases were decided earlier in the Admiralty Court, and later by the Commissioners for Appeal in Prize Causes, than *The Eenrom*.[5]

Thirdly, the operation of the licence system during the period of the Orders in Council inevitably slowed down the condemnation process and led to numerous contested cases – so much so that Edwards produced a separate book of Reports covering such cases exclusively.[6] This factor has not seriously distorted the figures for the whole of the war, but it certainly makes them look no better.

Fourthly, the machinery of sale by auction could grind slowly indeed. The ship needed to be brought to a proper place, the perishables sold quickly by permission, the rest of the cargo disembarked and kept secure, the ship prepared and probably prettied up for sale, and even the most expert agent and his staff, with the full co-operation of the brokers or auctioneers, might take months to make the arrangements. In ports like Plymouth during a boom time for prizes, as in October 1803, it might be reported that 'sales here went off well . . . and fetched good prices'[7] but it was not always so.

Those were all valid practical reasons why merchant prizes should have hung fire in court and afterwards. This chapter will later discuss whether there were more sinister doings afoot, as many people at the time asserted, and whether, even if there were not, something might have been done to minimize delay. First, however, it is necessary to consider one factor that has emerged with great force from the analysis of all categories of capture and which amounts to a delay that the navy inflicted at least partially upon itself.

This is the business of joint capture. It was possible from the accounts examined to differentiate clearly between captures by single ships and by more than one. Altogether 309 merchant ship captures were considered, of which 222 were by single ships and 87 joint. The differences in time taken to settle and come to distribution were marked and, it is believed, highly significant.

On average (and though the figures presented in this chapter have so far eschewed averages, because they can be distorted by particular cases, they are valid for comparison in this case) joint captures of merchant ships took half as long again to settle as did single ship captures. This proportion is very robust and varies little with the various stages of the war. Particular points that emerge are that under 20 per cent of joint captures settled within a year, while 30 per cent of single-ship captures did; and an almost exactly similar 20 per cent:30 per cent ratio is apparent when comparing those that settled between one and two years after capture.

Captures of warships and privateers were also considered and here too the contrast is marked, though because the sample is relatively small – seventeen joint and forty-nine single-ship captures – it is less reliable. Nevertheless, once again the difference in time for settlement – in this case more than half as much again for joint captures – looks highly significant.

Recaptures did not yield reliable statistics because so few of them were conducted jointly. It is quite likely that if a warship was in sight of, but not actively involved in, a recapture it would not bother to submit any entitlement; it must have been common knowledge that salvage was not going to lead to great fortune. The relative paucity of joint-recapture cases is one reason for the speed with which recaptures in general were settled. However, there were one or two cases of salvage which, while not adding to statistical validity, are indicative of the tangles recaptors could get into.

The *New Concord*, recaptured by the hired armed vessels *Courier* and *Charlotte* on 12 December 1804, finally came to account on 5 August 1808 and the net sum for distribution was £74 4s 10d.[8] One wonders whether they thought the negotiation was worth it – and indeed where the original crews had got to in the intervening time. Similar, but for somewhat higher stakes, was the *Nautilus*, recaptured by *Shannon* and four others on the North America station on 16 July 1812 and settled on 12 July 1815: the net sum for distribution was £2,063.[9] On the other hand, the *Neptunus*, recaptured in October 1813 and shared by agreement between *Zealous* and six others, settled within a year; it came to only £699 net all told, but at least they received the money fairly promptly. So did the sailors of the very mixed force that recaptured the Indiaman *Lord Nelson* in 1803; that relatively rich salvage settled in seven months. There may well have been an element of public relations, as well as the Honourable East India Company's gratitude, in that prompt payment.

These differences point to a possible solution of the flaws in the joint-capture system and it was not of course confined to recaptures. If ships operating together could agree to share prize money, whether they were in sight of one another or not, then they would see the spoils all the quicker. In a large fleet the reverse might be the better way: it could be agreed that spoils should go to the actual captor however many ships were in sight and theoretically entitled to a share. Indeed this sometimes happened: the capture of a *chasse-marée* by the *Pelter* in Sir John Borlase

Warren's squadron produced 'a generous relinquishment of the whole prize to the *Pelter* alone, from the officers and seamen belonging to the squadron'.[10] But the very fact that this incident found its way into a naval memoir suggests that it was an unusual practice. Moreover, a *chasse-marée* was scarcely a rich prize; the best of these vessels that can be found in the records examined fetched just over £1,000.

So by and large the navy stuck to the rule which gave ships 'in sight' the right to share in the proceeds of capture. In consequence horror stories abounded. The *Jupiter*, captured by *Centaur* and *Blenheim* in July 1803, settled in January 1810, by which time the *Blenheim* had been on the bottom of the Indian Ocean for over three years. The *Julia*, taken by *Inconstant, Jamaica* and *Albicore* on 6 May 1807, realized only £209 5s 7d in June 1810. The *Juliana*, captured by *Quebec, Bruizer, Archer* and *Sparkler* took from 25 August 1807 to 26 June 1811, though in this case several advances were made on the final sum of £4,764. All those cases came in a single bundle of accounts in the Public Record Office;[11] they are, to be sure, some of the worst instances in that sample of 175 or so captures of all descriptions, but there is no reason to suppose they are not replicated in similar degree for the 5,000 and more prizes taken during the war.

It could be managed better, and sometimes it was. The capture of the frigate *Junon* of forty guns off the Saintes on 10 February 1809 was a brilliant operation by two British frigates, *Horatio* and *Latona*, and the sloops *Superieure* and *Driver*.[12] All played a significant part in chase, heading-off and capture. The prize process was equally well handled, significantly perhaps by George Redmond Hulbert. The first account was brought in on 26 October 1809, only nine months after the action, and was for £23,000. This was followed on 7 April 1810 with £3,818 for the sale of the *Junon*'s cargo – the ship had been loaded with supplies for beleaguered West Indies garrisons – and on 27 July 1811 with £8,280 for head money and ordnance stores.[13] There was even reference to a fourth part to follow, but this cannot be traced. A pleasant footnote is that the sloop *Asp*, which faint but pursuing had early dropped out of the chase, came in for some of the later proceeds. It showed what could be done by a co-operative and well-knit squadron and an experienced and efficient agent.

There is a curious twist to the *Junon* story. She was commissioned as a thirty-eight-gun ship under Captain John Shortland and on 13 December 1809 took on a powerful force of two forty-gun French frigates and two others armed *en flûte* mounting twenty guns each. There is some suggestion that she was lured into range by false colours in the French ships, which was a standard *ruse de guerre*, and also by their making the correct private signal for identification, which was most unusual. In any event, the conflict was uneven and ended after half an hour and many casualties, including Shortland himself, with the *Junon* striking her colours. She was in such a shattered state that the French immediately destroyed her by fire.[14] There is no suggestion in the records that this development in any way affected the prize money for the original capture, only ten months before, or its distribution. It should not have done, of course, in all fairness, but it is comforting to know that it did not.

The fact that the taking of the *Junon* happened on a foreign station may have something to do with the relatively slick way in which a potentially complicated joint capture was handled. There is evidence of formal sharing agreements in a squadron of ships on the Jamaica station in 1796, extending even to an undertaking to share liability in failed cases,[15] and this precedent may well have led to station practice. In the Mediterranean, sharing arrangements tended to be *ad hoc* but certainly existed; on 26 May 1811 Captain Rowley of the *Eagle* informed his agent in Malta that 'on 22 ulto. the *Eagle's* ship's company agreed to share prize money (neutrals or other vessels liable to litigation excepted) with the *Imogene*' and there was 'a like agreement' with the *Kingfisher*.[16] Rather later in the war, several joint captures were swiftly dealt with in the Gibraltar court and clearly there was an agreement between the capturing ships, *Volontaire*, *Undaunted* and *Redwing*, in each case.[17] They were accustomed to working together, a more usual practice on foreign stations.[18] But when another ship, the *Eclair*, joined the group the crew of the *Volontaire* would not be party to an agreement to share unless ships were within sight of the capture.[19] Old habits and old suspicions died hard.

Joint captures apart, a foreign station with a well-established court could, on the limited evidence available, deliver prize money a good deal more promptly than the court in London. The Halifax and Bermuda courts in 1812–14 did particularly well, the great majority of uncontested cases – mostly of course single-ship captures – settling within a year.[20] However, this figure must be treated with some reserve, for it is known that contested cases were often deferred for further proof – these amounted to nearly one-sixth of all cases in the first few months of 1813 [21] – and some of them were resolved only years later.

Slow payment, then, was a feature of the whole prize system. Given the fundamental rule, the 'guiding star' in the words of one writer,[22] that every capture must be taken through the courts for proper legal process, what might have been done to speed it up?

The Cochranes, drawing on their assumption of a general and conspiratorial corruption throughout officialdom, were in no doubt that lawyers engaged by the capturing parties, rather than those appointed by the Crown, would exert the necessary pressure and look after their clients' interests much more effectively.[23] It was successfully argued against this that the King's Proctor in Doctors' Commons and appointed proctors in Vice Admiralty Courts abroad alone had sufficient expertise to manage cases with the necessary certainty. At this lapse of time, it is hard to make a judgement on the merits of these arguments. Proliferation of lawyers usually results in the lengthening, not the shortening, of legal process, and the introduction of inexperienced lawyers tends to do so even more. On the other hand, an influx of enthusiastic solicitors, acting on the sole behalf of captors and not connected with the Crown, into the cosy atmosphere of the Admiralty Court might have had a galvanizing effect. But one's instinctive reaction is that the process, by becoming more overtly litigious, would have been slowed rather than hastened.

A more rational solution was that of Admiral Sir Charles Morice Pole: to employ more King's Proctors in the High Court of Admiralty.[24] In making this proposal he specifically referred to delay as a weakness of the system as it stood. As has been shown, the help available to the King's Proctor was almost certainly strengthened thereafter, but the legal function remained in the hands of one man, as Thomas Cochrane was able to point out as late as 1811.[25] There is no evidence that the increase in the number of solicitors working on behalf of Crown and captors changed to any marked extent the speed with which cases were concluded and distribution made.

George Rose, the Treasurer of the Navy, champion of the seaman's right to prize money as he was, might have intervened to speed up the process by means of increasing the number of King's Proctors working as such. However, the government was notoriously niggardly in sanctioning increases of establishment, and indeed Rose himself had to defend increases in his own office complement.[26] He was therefore unlikely to seek to interfere with the staffing of the Admiralty Court, even in a good cause.

An even more radical solution would have been to increase the number of Admiralty Courts in Britain. This could have been done either by instituting Vice Admiralty Courts at the outports, probably Plymouth, Portsmouth and Yarmouth,[27] or by providing a second judge with appropriate staff in the High Court of Admiralty. Such courts could have dealt with uncontested cases or the more modest captures. It was possibly this solution towards which Sir Charles Pole was tending when he said in the House that 'all his reflections on the subject convinced him that the Admiralty Court ought to be on a new footing'.[28]

So far as is known, proposals for such enlargement were never put before Sir William Scott. That is some indication of his formidable reputation, because it is probable that he would have argued strongly against any of them. His opposition to the proliferation of Vice Admiralty Courts abroad must have been well known,[29] and there is no reason to suppose he would have taken kindly to dilution of his jurisdiction in the United Kingdom.

Scott was a deeply conservative man, however briskly he developed the law during his long haul in office. His most recent biographer has called him 'a thoroughly eighteenth-century man'.[30] That century had run its justice system in a measured, deliberate style and the civilians of Doctors' Commons, let alone Scott himself, were not likely to be the first to break that mould. Rapid administrative and structural change was not in his terms of reference.

There may well have been one further factor. Scott's judicial work made him a very busy man, as he often maintained.[31] People with a heavy workload and great responsibilities often find it impossible to see how these can be reduced, particularly by the restructuring of their own organization. There seems to them just to be no time to think about that. If they are also people of strong character and unchallenged authority, it is hard to approach them on such matters. Thus, if the Admiralty Court under Scott was culpable for refusing to delegate, the fault is understandable.

However, the facts are plain. Poor sailors, from admirals to boy seamen, were kept a long time out of their money. Sometimes it was denied to them by their own fault in pursuing squabbles over joint capture, sometimes by the dilatoriness of agents and lawyers, occasionally by collusion in delay: but most often it was simply the system, the process of both bureaucracy and law, that slowed matters down. Authority was not imaginative enough to change the system to make it operate more quickly. Research for this book has found that many allegations of abuse in prize warfare and its process, both from contemporary and later commentators, are unfounded or grossly exaggerated; but on this one at least the accusation must stand. The great evil of the system was delay.

NOTES

1. Sir Nicholas Harris Nicolas, *The Dispatches and Letters of Lord Nelson*, vol. II (Chatham edn, 1997), p. 98.
2. XI NC, p. 32.
3. XI NC, p. 33.
4. 3 C. Rob., p. 1 [1799]; 5 C. Rob., p. ix.
5. See 2–6 C. Rob., Tables of Cases Reported and Cases Heard on Appeal.
6. Thos. Edwards LLD, *Reports of the Leading Decisions in the High Court of Admiralty in Cases of Vessels Sailing under British Licence* (Strahan for Butterworth, 1812).
7. X NC, p. 433.
8. HCA 2/366.
9. HCA 2/367.
10. XXV NC, p. 92.
11. HCA 2/357.

12. W.L. Clowes, *The Royal Navy: A History from the Earliest Times to 1900*, vol. 5 (Chatham edn, 1997), pp. 431–2.

13. HCA 2/357.

14. Clowes, *The Royal Navy*, vol. 5, p. 447.

15. NMM DUC/20/1A.

16. RNM 301/77(188).

17. HCA 2/366, *Notre Dame de Rosaire* and *Notre Dame du Carme.*

18. Papers of Thomas Snowden Peckston, RN Museum 1997/65, letter to Mary Peckston, 30 June 1812.

19. Ibid., letter of 27 November 1812.

20. NMM HUL/16.

21. NMM HUL/4.

22. Lt-Cdr Peter Kemp, *Prize Money* (Gale and Polden, 1946), p. 14.

23. Thomas Cochrane, Earl of Dundonald, *Autobiography of a Seaman*, vol. II (Constable, 1995), p. 190.

24. XXI NC, pp. 272, 282.

25. Cochrane, *Autobiography of a Seaman*, vol. II, p. 211.

26. ADM 15/2, correspondence of January and February 1812.

27. Some historians have assumed that such courts did indeed exist. There is no contemporary evidence of this and the fact that there is no mention of them in contemporary material strongly suggests that there were none. Commissions were indeed issued by the Registrar of the Admiralty Court to Mayors of certain cities empowering them to take Interrogatories in prize cases (HCA 30/627), but this in no way amounted to a jurisdiction in prize.

28. XXI NC, p. 272.

29. ADM 1/3898, Opinion of 6 July 1806.

30. Henry J. Bourguignon, *Sir William Scott, Lord Stowell* (Cambridge UP, 1987), p. 115.

31. ADM 1/3900, Scott to Croker, 8 November 1811.

CHAPTER TWENTY-TWO

Attitudes

'I never cared much about Riches' wrote Sir Edward Pellew from HMS *Culloden* in 1805, when he was taking command of the East Indies station.[1] In the light of subsequent events that statement sounds like hypocrisy. Pellew quarrelled with the Admiralty and Troubridge about the latter's appointment to the more lucrative half of the station;[2] he boasted privately in 1807 of the aggregate of prize money he had made, amounting to over £30,000;[3] he gave command to both his sons at a very early age and allotted them tasks that could scarcely fail to bring them large sums on their own account. Later, in the Mediterranean, he had the reputation of placing favourites in areas where prize money was to be made.[4] He may well during his career have enriched himself, by prize and freight money, to the tune of over £200,000,[5] the equivalent at the end of the twentieth century of about £40 million.

Yet viewed in the light of other evidence the words, 'I never cared much about riches' are more convention than hypocrisy. They are consistently replicated in the writing of other participants in the prize system and of their chroniclers. Nelson wrote to his brother in 1796, when in command of the *Agamemnon* on the coast of Italy, 'It is true I have taken numbers of prizes, but I have always shared with my squadron . . . they run away with the greater part . . . As to rewards, I expect none.'[6] Yet his personal accounts show that he received over £2,000 from mid-1794 to mid-1796, and expected as much again from subsequent settlements of prizes taken during that time.[7]

On the other hand, Nelson's letter to Sir William Hamilton in 1798, while he was searching feverishly for the French fleet eventually caught in Aboukir Bay at the Battle of the Nile, owed nothing to convention. He saw two frigates thought to be French, 'and it has been said since that a line of battle ship was to leeward of them with the riches of Malta on board, but it was the destruction of the Enemy, not riches for myself, that I was seeking'.[8] All the surrounding circumstances and correspondence make this ring true. Nelson was focused upon the single objective of destroying Brueys' squadron. He was desperate for frigates, but for the purposes of gathering intelligence, not for prize-taking.

Later on though, in 1804, a different aspect of Nelson's attitude emerged when he was in command in the western Mediterranean conducting the wearying blockade of Toulon. On the entry of Spain into the war the command to the west of Gibraltar, previously held by Nelson up to Cape Finisterre, was given to Admiral Sir John Orde and Nelson's private complaints were many and bitter: to Emma Hamilton, 'this Admiralty takes all my golden harvest . . .' and to Sir Gilbert Elliott, '[Orde] is to wallow in wealth, while I am left a beggar . . . '.[9] By then, it must be remembered, Nelson had two establishments to keep up; and in any case he sought to maintain his dignity: 'I shall never enter into a paper war with [Orde], or anyone else'.[10]

Nelson, of course, was Nelson, and it must be remembered that even then his ideals were well known, his example followed and his failings forgotten or forgiven. But this does not fully explain the very general tendency to disclaim high interest in prize money particularly as the war went on. Both Alexander Cochrane and Home Popham fought hard to protect their reputations against allegations that they instituted operations from the 'sordid motives' of gaining prize money;[11] and when charged with nefarious activity in the taking of *El Trusco*, Popham rejoined that 'the good of his country was nearest his heart'.[12] There were echoes here from previous assertions by senior officers: Calder, in the midst of his dispute with Duckworth about prize-sharing in the West Indies in 1801, wrote plaintively to St Vincent: 'I am sure you who know me will do me the justice to say I have never been grasping for Prize Money and that *Gold is not my God.*'[13]

Sympathy was extended freely to those who were unfortunate in the matter of prize money. Captain George Duff, killed at Trafalgar, was so treated in a memoir in the *Naval Chronicle*[14] while Sir Charles Brisbane, an officer of high operational attainment particularly in the defence of convoys, was said to have sustained a 'very heavy pecuniary loss' by his supersession as governor of Curacoa, and the *Chronicle* reprinted his subsequent petition to the King in full.[15]

Indeed, when there was suspicion of the misfortunate having been supplanted by the favourite of someone in higher authority, sympathy was further extended. Captain George Harding in 1806 had some unprofitable cruises in the *San Fiorenzo* while the *Pitt* (ex *Salsette*), for which he was destined, picked up valuable prizes in the Pacific. Harding was nearly bankrupt in consequence and took on a freighting task for £1,000, but was said to have 'despised wealth'.[16]

Modesty in the actual pattern of prize-taking, as well as in the manner of one's protestations, was commended: 'whatever Captain [Michael] Seymour may have happily added to his fortune, has not been by the casual accident of one rich prize, but by the accumulation of numerous small ones'.[17] So was a modest mode of living: Captain Henry Whitby 'with the hardearned profits of his avocation purchased a small villa'.[18]

Though most of these comments are derived from the *Naval Chronicle*, there is no reason to suppose that that publication was out of line with the public sentiment of the time. Both in the newspapers and in Parliament there was unease about 'wars of plunder' and fortunes being made out of prize money. No less a person than the Duke of Wellington expressed himself severely when commenting on Alexander Cochrane's raid on the American coast in 1814. According to Wellington, 'Plunder was the object', Cochrane was concerned only to carry it off and Wellington's soldier brother-in-law Edward Pakenham was killed in consequence.[19]

Sir William Henry Dillon, Admiral of the Red, recalled in his *Narrative* that on reading one newspaper article six captains were 'all wounded . . . none of us had up to that period received £100'.[20] A note to the 1953 edition of the *Narrative* puts this assertion in its place, however, by explaining that this must have referred to Dillon's experience as a post captain, since he had by his own admission made nearly £1,000 as a lieutenant.

Claims to poverty were, it seems, almost as fashionable as claims to be uninterested in riches. In October 1802 Rear Admiral Sir John Duckworth was writing to Sir John Markham, one of the lords of the Admiralty, that he owed £2,154 and 'ruin must ensue'.[21] Yet, as this chapter will later show, Duckworth's achievement in prize-taking was already far above the average and his prospects exceptionally bright. His financial embarrassment could have been no more than temporary.

In fact, the evidence of ambivalence is everywhere. For every hard luck story in the *Naval Chronicle* there is one of fortune, and for every avowal of disinterest there is, peeping out to be sure, an admission of cupidity.

The reports from Plymouth from 1798 to 1805, with their numerous accounts of captures, sometimes accompanied by an assessment of their value, have already been noted.[22] The 1803 swoop, after the renewal of the war in May, was particularly well reported: on 15 August, for example, 'Captain Prowse's share of prize money for the *Sirius* since the war is estimated at £30,000';[23] and this is borne out by the ship's log, which records four prizes taken in the space of ten days at the end of May and in early June.[24] What the *Chronicle* did not record was the tedious patrolling off Ushant, making sail and chasing, boarding and releasing of neutrals, that *Sirius* underwent for two months to the end of July; that was not news. Neither was convoy, which occupied a great proportion of the time of the smaller ships; references to 'cruise' (which meant the prospect of prizes) outnumber references to 'convoy' in the Plymouth Reports by about eight to one.

However, it is in the *Chronicle*'s articles covering the careers of senior officers – some still serving when the memoir appeared – that the principal evidence of ambivalence, between the lure of prize money and the reluctance to admit it, can be found. Typical is the commentary on Sir John Duckworth.[25] Operating in the Western Mediterranean and

Gibraltar area in 1799, 'The vigilance of Rear Admiral Duckworth was now on the eve of experiencing a very solid remuneration . . .' since on 6 April 1800 he captured a rich Lima convoy: 'It was reported at the time that the Rear Admiral's share would amount to not less than £75,000.'[26]

His fortune continued, for in June 1800 he went to the Leeward Islands station where his 'cruisers were very actively employed, in protecting the trade and annoying the enemy' and later, in the 'important and lucrative appointment' of Commander in Chief Jamaica, he was 'unusually successful in capturing an extraordinary number of the enemy's vessels'.[27] But it was crowned by military glory: at the Battle of Santo Domingo on 6 February 1806, Duckworth's force of six of the line encountered and comprehensively defeated five French ships of the line including the 130-gun *Imperial*.[28] 'Never', crowed the *Chronicle*, 'was victory more complete or decisive'.

This memoir illustrates very well the balance between solid military worth and private gain that might ideally be sought by senior officers. According to the chronicler, Duckworth had done a good job in the Mediterranean: it was his 'vigilance' that was rewarded. Equally, in the Leeward Islands his ships were 'protecting the trade and annoying the enemy', the classic formula, but no doubt the 'annoyance' included taking merchant prizes. Finally, in the battle, his military prowess, including the excellent state of training of his ships, was to the fore: but the captures would have made a pretty penny and the *Imperial*, driven on shore and wrecked, yielded head money.[29] Whether Duckworth, who has been strongly criticized by some historians for his actions before Santo Domingo and even more for his activity or inactivity in the Constantinople mission in February 1807,[30] deserved the praise given to him in the memoir is immaterial for the purposes of this chapter; it is the attitude of the chronicler that is significant.

The pattern is repeated in many other memoirs. Captain Courtney Boyle[31] was a lieutenant in 1793 and almost at once was a participant in the capture of the *St Jago*, condemned 'after a tedious litigation' when each lieutenant received £1,400. In command after 1795, when he was made a commander, he took numerous prizes as well as preserving his ship's company 'quiet and orderly' through the mutinous year 1797, being wrecked off Damietta 'through the great incorrectness of the charts' in 1799, being taken prisoner until released on the peace in 1801, and later commanding one of Nelson's patrolling frigates off Toulon in 1803–04. His ship and her boats took part in two of the cutting-out actions that were a feature of warfare under sail, perhaps more in the Mediterranean than anywhere else; one was costly in casualties and unproductive in captures, the other much more successful, taking a brig loaded with ordnance stores.[32] His memoir records little active employment after 1805, but this was unlikely to have been due to ill-health since he lived to a great age, becoming Commissioner at Sheerness in 1814 and occupying other administrative posts in the 1820s. It is not at all impossible that he had by 1806 made enough from prize money to live in some comfort. A significant number of officers took this course, though little publicity was given to the fact.

The most outspoken record of fortune, with hardly a hint of criticism, was probably that of Vice Admiral James Dacres.[33] He had begun well. In 1762 he was a youngster in the *Active*, which in company with the *Favourite* took what may well have been the most valuable prize ever, the *Hermione*. A seaman's share was £485 5s 4d. Dacres prospered through the next war, that of American Independence from 1775 to 1783, being made commander of the *Ceres*, taking a frigate as prize and then being captured in turn. After release from captivity by exchange, he was appointed to the seventy-four-gun *Sultan* in command, in acting rank, being made post in 1780.[34]

The war of 1793 found him in command of line of battle ships; he was in *Barfleur* at St Vincent. He was made Rear Admiral of the Blue in 1799 and in 1803 was appointed second in command to Duckworth in Jamaica. 'This proved', added the *Chronicle*, 'to be a very lucrative service, though presenting no particular opportunity of acquiring professional distinction. The number of vessels, taken by British cruisers in the West Indies at this time, was astonishing.'[35] He succeeded to the command in spring 1805 and 'the station continued to be very productive'. But Dacres did not live long to enjoy his fortune; he died in 1810.

On the whole, those officers who achieved flag rank fairly early during the wars from 1793 to 1815 were the big money earners. Some, for sure, did not prosper: Collingwood was one. He consistently disclaimed any desire for riches beyond what was necessary to 'keep a good fire in winter'[36] and when he said 'I do not consider [being rich] as a thing that has any relation to our happiness'[37] it was entirely consistent with the genuine modesty that shines through the record of this estimable man. But even he could be stung by the thought that he was not getting a fair deal. A dispute about the flag shares for Santo Domingo dragged on; in 1808, a judge in the High Court (the King's Bench Division) found that Duckworth, who had left his station blockading Cádiz to pursue a French squadron and had, fortuitously, found another which he defeated in that battle, was still then under Collingwood's command. The Court's decision was therefore in Collingwood's favour to the tune of some £5,000, but the case went to appeal and was still not decided a year later. Wearily, Collingwood wrote 'I am treated very shabbily on all hands about prize money. It is very difficult for us who are always at sea . . .'.[38] Within a few months he was dead, worn out with exertion, having not set foot on shore for two years.

Those more junior, who came to flag rank late on in the war, had in the event little time to make fortunes. They might, of course, have done well as captains. One such was Thomas Byam Martin, who in the *Fisgard* in 1798 captured the French frigate *Immortalité*, fetching him some £3,500,[39] and who went on to a highly successful two years in the Channel Fleet. It was hard weather and hard work, much of it off Ushant, with many chases and at least two notable boat actions against convoys close under the land.[40] The *Fisgard*'s log[41] shows the wear and tear on materiel and people. November and December 1799 were notable for split sails; either Byam Martin drove the ship unconscionably hard, or the canvas was old; it may have been both. In any event, the hands were often turned to repairing sails. The work took its toll: poignantly, on 26 December the departure from this life of the sailmaker is recorded.

Martin was promoted rear admiral in 1811. Much of his correspondence has been preserved by the Navy Records Society[42] and it is not difficult to gather the picture of a highly conscientious, professional officer, one who after the war was Comptroller of the Navy[43] and guided its material development for no less than fifteen years of studied and well-directed retrenchment. In some ways he can be regarded as the first truly nineteenth-century admiral.

His attitude to prize money is not easy to discern because little of his published correspondence is connected with it: possibly that in itself is significant. But those ashore took a keen interest in the details: in 1799 the Dowager Lady Martin was writing to a relation, 'I send a list of the prizes taken last cruise. In some of the ships sent in while under Sir John [Borlase] Warren was flour that sold for £1,600; the gum ship lately taken has 4 cwt of ivory besides 60,000 weight of gum. The *Venus* frigate has 5 cwt of flour; as it was not for sale it is hoped it will not prevent head money. Byam and all his people agreed to give up their shares to the poor here . . .'.[44]

Whether the last observation referred to the proceeds of one prize or many, it is an interesting one. But generosity of this sort was not uncommon. Nor was it confined to the poor of the village; often it was extended to persons from the captured ships themselves. 'Private ventures', that is to say small parcels of cargo carried on the master or supercargo's own account, were customarily restored,[45] and personal property likewise.[46] This was official policy, often endorsed by the Court. But generosity could extend further at the whim of the captor; Thomas Cochrane, with the full agreement of his crew, gave from the coffers of the captured *Fortuna* 5,000 dollars to both the captain and supercargo of the prize, when he heard that they had lost heavily not only from their venture on the present voyage but on a previous occasion in the 'war of 1779'.[47]

A charming example of this kind of generosity is found in a letter from Captain George Mundy of the *Ardent* to his agent,[48] asking for £100 to be expended to provide instruments for a Neapolitan band that had deserted from Barcelona: '. . . a serpent, a French horn, and F trumpet and seven tones, and octave flute and two clarinets'.

To judge how captains spoke in private – as opposed to writing in ways that might be made public – about their prize-taking, one can do no better than turn to Jane Austen's *Persuasion*. There Captain Wentworth, 'as high in his profession as merit and activity could take him',[49] tells of his happy time:

> Ah, those were pleasant days when I had the *Laconia*! How fast I made money in her! A friend of mine and I had such a lovely cruise together off the Western Islands. Poor Harville, sister! You know how much he wanted money: worse than myself. He had a wife. Excellent fellow! I shall never forget his happiness. He felt it all, so much for her sake . . .[50]

Wentworth, with £25,000 from prize money, ends the book marrying Anne Elliot, an outcome which would not have been possible without his good fortune as well as his professional reputation. Even then the marriage meets with nothing more than a grudging 'no objection' from Anne's father, the 'foolish, spendthrift baronet' Sir Walter Elliot; for Sir Walter had earlier said he found the navy 'offensive' as 'the means of bringing persons of obscure birth into undue distinction'.[51] While Sir Walter comes as near caricature as any of Jane Austen's characters, this attitude cannot be thought of as a flight of fancy; in her circle she would have come across not only the navy's standpoint from her brothers – expressed no doubt in uninhibited terms like those of the fictional Captain Wentworth – but the jealousies of country gentry and others who had no access to that particular source of wealth and resented the social mobility it represented.

There were fewer constraints in the discussion of prize money among the more junior officers. Many of the memoirs of officers who later achieved high rank place more emphasis on prize money during their days as lieutenants than as captains or admirals.[52] In some ways this is understandable; as a lieutenant, promotion was uncertain, a successful encounter with the enemy being the likeliest way – though it was also the likeliest way to get killed. Consequently, the immediate, rather than the distant, prospect of prize money was the more alluring.

This tendency to frank declaration of interest in financial gain became more marked among the warrant officers. The papers of Purser Thomas Snowden Peckston, which came to light in 1997, are valuable here.[53] Peckston was in the Mediterranean from 1812 to 1814 in the frigate *Volontaire* and then the gun-brig *Pelorus*. The papers consist mainly of letters to his wife Mary, who enterprisingly journeyed out to Malta and then Minorca. There was a domestic reason connected with Peckston's sister Becky, who was engaged to another purser on the station, but that forms a separate story unconnected with this book.

Peckston was distinctly a man of the early nineteenth century. The letters are about one-quarter religious homily, one-quarter conventional protestations of love for Mary and one-half reports of the ships' and personal business with occasional accounts of places visited.

Much of the ships' business relates to prizes. The *Volontaire* under Captain Waldegrave did fairly well. On 27 November 1812 Peckston reported:

> Since I joined . . . we have taken one French vessel laden with deals and pots – another laden with corn – a Spanish recaptured brig laden with corn . . . and since we sailed from Tunis on the 21st of this month we have captured a large French xebec laden with wool and dates . . . together with three thousand five hundred dollars' worth of coral . . . my share of *Le Bonne Conseil* (*sic*) will amount to upwards of £100 which will settle the whole of my affairs in Malta.

In fact, as the record shows, he was optimistic: his share was £85 2s 4d.

But in the *Pelorus* under Robert Gambier, Peckston did not fare well. His brother officers clearly thought highly of his business acumen, since they proposed he should act as the ship's prize agent.[54] But the opportunity never arose. Her patrol station off Cape da Gata yielded nothing. 'I trust', he lamented on 22 February 1813, 'we shall soon get to a prize making station'. On 14 March an American brig was boarded, but 'she was in ballast and had a licence'. Months later, after further complaints of the 'unfairness' of a year without a single day in a lucrative spot, he thought the luck had turned: 'We fell in with two vessels on Wednesday evening which I really thought were (by their manoeuvres) either enemy's vessels or recaptures, and began to reckon up my share of prize money for them; but after chasing them for some time we found then to be Greeks, so that all my hopes were frustrated.'[55]

Even more galling for the *Pelorus* was what happened on 8 April 1814, when in a flat calm a felucca was sighted and the sweeps were got out in chase. The crew were pulling the ship herself, by means of these huge oars, for no less than eleven hours, the felucca responding likewise. Eventually she was overhauled – and turned out to be a tender to the British line of battle ship *Aboukir*. The felucca had taken the *Pelorus* to be hostile, just as the *Pelorus* had taken her for a potential prize.

In 1814 Peckston was cheered by the arrival of Lord Algernon Percy in command, for 'the Commander in Chiefs interest lies almost entirely with the Duke of Northumberland, so that if a good cruize can be found for his Lordship, he will certainly have one'.[56] But Percy quickly moved on and was relieved by Captain Hole; and although the *Pelorus* took part in the capture of Genoa, netting as Peckston hoped about £300 as his share of the prize money, she had no further individual luck. *Pelorus* returned to England in November 1814, destined probably to be laid up in ordinary, but was brought back into service for the Hundred Days, cruising in the Western Approaches between mid-April and mid-July 1815. Peckston hoped for a 'good large prize', but his hopes diminished. On 25 June he wrote that 'all hands seem in spirits at the Idea of making Prize Money', but later, dejectedly, 'we fear we shall come back to Plymouth as poor as we left it'.

He was right, and indeed found himself in dire financial straits for the next year or so, as his purser's accounts for the two previous ships took long to settle and his agents were not prepared to make advances. But he eventually prospered as a manager in the new coal gas industry.

Further down the hierarchy, among the petty officers and seamen, the written records are scanty and the history largely anecdotal. There was no doubt in the minds of some senior officers that prize money was a prime motivation for seamen. Thomas Cochrane regarded it as 'the seaman's inciting motive to engage in war'.[57] The judgement was less starkly stated in other contemporary writing, but it was unquestionably general and was implicit in the work of George Rose throughout his time as Treasurer of the Navy. Moreover, the fiction that arose out of the war, notably that of Marryat, was full of the lure of prize money for the sailor.

Such documentary evidence as has become available from the seamen themselves bears out the keen interest that was taken. Richard Greenhalgh,[58] who joined the navy in 1793 and wrote regularly to his parents in Lancashire until his desertion in 1802, was initially enthusiastic: 'We took a Spanish galloon on 14 April [1793] . . . laden with Dollers Gold and Jewels wich is thought to be the richest prize ever took . . .'. This was not only enthusiasm but gullibility: Spain was then an ally, and the letter is evidence more of lower-deck rumour than anything else. But it does show the force of prize thinking and the lure of Spanish gold. In all his correspondence, Greenhalgh never disclosed to his parents how much prize money he received and he requested money from them more often than he remitted it.

George Price, alias Green, pressed on 18 December 1803, took some months to recover from shock and chagrin on board HMS *Speedy*.[59] But by June 1804 was writing to his brother about a colleague, 'his ship is allways in harbour and this is allways at sea and sailing close to the enemys and give them a Gun as a Challenge', and a year later, 'as soon as I Git my Prise ticket I will Impower you to receive my Prise Money for We Expect something Hot and Warm very soon'. In July the *Speedy* was indeed in hot action and Price's pride in doing well was tempered both by a continuing hankering for the land ('there is a number in the Ship that Wood wish to be out of it') and by doubt about his prize money ('our Captain thinks nothing at all about prises at this time').

There is some indication that attitudes to prize money changed as the war went on. In 1793 the navy undoubtedly inherited an eighteenth-century ethos on the matter. Gain was expected and might actively be sought, even by naval officers' fitting out ships as privateers; Bartholomew James did this twice before 1800.[60] There is evidence of a fairly free-and-easy, not to say grasping, attitude to prize booty until about 1797, typified by the Jervis-Grey Caribbean expedition of 1793–4. It is probably no coincidence that Sir William Scott, who as King's Advocate would undoubtedly have given opinions about that affair, came to the Admiralty Court in 1798.

But the change in attitude that occurred from 1798 was not just a matter of law, nor even of increased governmental control as formal blockades, orders in council and licences proliferated. It also owed something to the changes in moral tone that accompanied the evangelical movement, which reached something of a peak in the régime of Lord Gambier, and even more perhaps in the perception that Britain was in conflict with a genuinely tyrannical regime, a struggle in which personal gain had to take second place to the defeat of the enemy.

Too much should not be made of this. It was a tendency, no more, and as the account above has shown it was much less perceptible at the time than it is now. In retrospect, the whole principle and practice of the prize system had begun a decline from the peak it reached in the second half of the eighteenth century, and would not survive more than another forty years, except in a much weakened form. But throughout the wars of 1793–1815 the 'fruits of our labours', in the words of the naval prayer, meant prize money, and the lure of that applied to all, even Nelson, even Collingwood. No one was immune.

NOTES

1. C. Northcote Parkinson, *Edward Pellew, Viscount Exmouth* (Methuen, 1933), p. 327.

2. Edward Osler, *The Life of Admiral Viscount Exmouth* (Smith, Elder, 1835), p. 228.

3. Parkinson, *Edward Pellew*, Pellew to Broughton, 1 May 1807, p. 375.

4. RN Museum Papers No. 1997/65, Thomas Snowden Peckston to Mary Peckston, 15 April 1813 and 6 April 1814.

5. Michael Lewis, *A Social History of the Navy 1793–1815* (George Allen and Unwin, 1960), p. 320.

6. Sir Nicholas Harris Nicolas, *The Dispatches and Letters of Lord Nelson*, vol. II (Chatham edn, 1997), p. 242.

7. Ibid., p. 179.

8. Nicolas, *The Dispatches and Letters of Lord Nelson*, vol. III, p. 43.

9. Denis Orde, *Nelson's Mediterranean Command* (Pentland Press, 1997), pp. 155–7.

10. Ibid., p. 160, Nelson to Collingwood, 13 March 1805.

11. XIII NC, p. 134; XVII NC, p. 239.

12. XIX NC, p. 151.

13. NMM DUC/20, Calder to St Vincent, 12 April 1801.

14. XV NC, p. 283.

15. XX NC, p. 113.

16. XX NC, p. 279.

17. XXI NC, p. 93.

18. XXVIII NC, p. 272.

19. Wellington to the Earl of Longford, 22 May 1815, quoted in Philip Guedalla, *The Duke* (Hodder and Stoughton, 1937 edn), p. 256.

20. Sir William Henry Dillon, *A Narrative of my Professional Adventures* (Navy Records Society, 1953), p. 237.

21. Sir Clements Markham (ed.), *Selections from the Correspondence of Admiral Sir John Markham* (Navy Records Society, 1904), p. 88.

22. See Chapter 17.

23. IX NC, p. 255.

24. ADM 51/1461.

25. XVIII NC, p. 1.

26. Ibid., p. 11.

27. Ibid., p. 17.

28. Brian Tunstall (ed. Nicholas Tracy), *Naval Warfare in the Age of Sail* (Conway, 1990), p. 259.

29. See Chapter 6.

30. W.L. Clowes, *The Royal Navy: A History from the Earliest Times to 1900*, vol. 5 (Chatham edn, 1997), pp. 193, 220–9.

31. XXX NC, p. 2.

32. Clowes, *The Royal Navy*, vol. 5, pp. 346, 361.

33. XXVI NC, p. 265.

34. David Syrett and R.L. Dinardo, *The Commissioned Sea Officers of the Royal Navy 1660–1815* (Scolar Press for the Navy Records Society, 1994), p. 111. The dates of promotion to Lieutenant and Commander are evidently misprinted.

35. XXVI NC, p. 277.

36. G.L. Newnham Collingwood, *Correspondence and Memoir of Lord Collingwood* (Ridgway, London, 1829), p. 193.

37. Edward Hughes (ed.), *The Private Correspondence of Admiral Lord Collingwood* (Navy Records Society, 1957), p. 107.

38. Ibid., pp. 248, 298.

39. HCA 2/355.

40. William James, *The Naval History of Britain*, vol. III (Bentley, 1847 edn), p. 40.

41. ADM 51/1317.

42. Sir R. Vesey Hamilton (ed.), *Journals and Letters of Sir Thomas Byam Martin*

(Navy Records Society, 1903).

43. Clowes, *The Royal Navy*, vol. 6, p. 185.

44. Vesey Hamilton, *Journals and Letters of Sir Thomas Byam Martin*, p. 291.

45. E.g., ADM 1/3896, Gostling to Marsden, 5 April 1804.

46. ADM 1/3894, 15 November 1799.

47. Thomas Cochrane, Earl of Dundonald, *Autobiography of a Seaman*, vol. I (Constable edn, 1995), pp. 175–6.

48. P. Crimmin in N.A.M. Rodger (ed.), *The Naval Miscellany*, vol. 5 (Navy Records Society, 1984), p. 293.

49. Jane Austen, *Persuasion* (Collins, 1953 edn), p. 374.

50. Ibid., p. 241.

51. Ibid., p. 207.

52. See, e.g., Sir William Henry Dillon, *A Narrative of my Professional Adventures* (Navy Records Society, 1953), *passim*.

53. See n. 4.

54. See Chapter 14.

55. Peckston, n. 4, letter to Mary Peckston, 9 July 1813.

56. Ibid., 6 April 1814.

57. Cochrane, *Autobiography of a Seaman*, vol. I, p. 54.

58. RNM 546/84.

59. D.B. Ellison, *Pressganged: Letters of George Price of Southwark* (Ellison's Editions, 1994), p. 18.

60. John Knox Laughton and James Y.F. Sulivan (eds), *Journal of Rear Admiral Bartholomew James, 1752–1828* (Navy Records Society, 1906), pp. 212, 336.

CHAPTER TWENTY-THREE

A Self-adjusting System

The title of this final chapter is deliberately provocative. Some sleepless hours were devoted to whether it should end with a question mark, but finally it was decided that if the hypothesis was sustainable, the statement should stand. First, though, it should be explained just what is meant by 'a self-adjusting system' in the context of this book.

Lt-Cdr 'Shmoo' Ellis, the charming, modest and very effective Flight Deck Officer of HMS *Albion*'s 1956–8 commission, once described flight deck operations in an aircraft carrier as a 'Roller-Bearing, Self-Adjusting Shambles'. What he meant by that unforgettable phrase was that within a flexible organization of nearly a hundred people, decisions were constantly being made and executed that resulted in the orderly despatch into the air of serviceable aircraft appropriately fuelled and armed, and their timely recovery when their missions were completed. It needed the deployment of people with a great variety of skills, knowledge and experience, and sufficient communication between them particularly in the resolution of fast-moving problems, to achieve that common goal. As Stella Gibbons wrote about the spring in *Cold Comfort Farm*, it looked chaotic, but it was better organized than you might think.

The prize system during the wars of 1793 to 1815 had many of those characteristics. Within the framework that had been laid down over centuries, there was room for initiative and modification and the framework itself could be adjusted to accommodate new developments in the strategic and economic situation. The result often did not look tidy at the time, but in the light of subsequent analysis shows much more order than chaos.

The first and most governing part of the framework was the law. This itself fell into two provinces. The first, the law of nations regarding prize, was the law administered by the High Court of Admiralty and the Vice Admiralty Courts overseas. This was the essential regulator to ensure that capture at sea did not degenerate into piracy and pillage, whether conducted by the state or by private individuals. Its very core was the requirement that no benefit could be derived from a capture until it had been condemned, that is to say adjudged lawful prize in a properly constituted court. That principle was followed by all nations, though some interpreted it more loosely than others.

Even here, however, there was in practice some flexibility. It is clear that on remote stations, where Vice Admiralty Courts were few and far between and communications in the days of sail lengthy and difficult, captors would feel themselves justified in bending the rules, making their own arrangements for the disposal of captures and praying in aid anything from operational necessity to the prevention of unrest among their crews. It appears that actions of this kind were condoned so long as they remained isolated and did not get out of hand, but those who overstepped the mark found themselves the target of investigation.

Moreover, as the war went on the law of nations, as interpreted by Sir William Scott in the High Court of Admiralty, itself became subject to considerable modification. The great watershed was reached in 1806–7, with the escalation of economic warfare begun in Britain's two-tier blockade of May 1806, continued in Napoleon's institution of the Continental System and the Berlin Decree and countered in turn by the British Orders in Council. As both Scott and the Admiralty Secretariat admitted, this brought in new principles which had to be applied in the courts and about which many influential people in Britain were uneasy. Scott managed to square his legal conscience and justify the Orders and the licence system on what might be called politico-legal grounds, and the jurisdiction of the Admiralty Court remained secure.

To some extent, however, its function as the protector of the innocent neutral was weakened. Up to 1806 the genuine neutral, carrying no enemy goods or contraband, could be assured of a fair hearing in the High Court of Admiralty. Restorations were not uncommon. The protection was not confined to cases that reached court, because captains of British cruisers knew very well the penalties that awaited the injudicious captor of a neutral, and in consequence many would not touch a vessel carrying neutral papers even if they had suspicions. *The Eenrom* case, the most complete analysed in this book, was probably near the margin. After the Orders in Council, however, latitude for cruisers was somewhat greater because the tests of innocence were more clear-cut: licence or no licence. Even then, the Admiralty Court erred as a matter of policy on the side of liberality in its interpretation of licences and cruisers were warned against over-strict interpretation of the Orders.

The other element of legal regulation was enshrined in domestic law. During the wars of 1793–1815 about a dozen major statutes were enacted covering the prize system. Some of their provisions put into municipal law the principles of the law of nations: for example, the fundamental rule that no benefit could be derived from capture that was not adjudged lawful prize, the anti-pillage rule that bulk must not be broken in the cargo of any captured vessel, the prohibition of ransom, and the control of the issue of letters of marque. Others, however, were more concerned with fair administration: composition and conduct of Prize Courts, rates for salvage, and rules concerning prize agents, recalls, and powers of attorney issued to navy agents.

The statutes also contained provisions for those things that were in the Crown's gift, both giving and taking. First and most fundamentally, there was the reiteration of the 1708 Act that signed away Crown droits to captors, notice having first been given by royal proclamation. Not far behind was the provision for head money, an important incentive for fighting the enemy and one found entirely from the exchequer. A disincentive directed at those not disposed to remain in naval service was the barring of the entitlement of any deserter to the proceeds of capture. There was also provision for the exacting of revenue for any dutiable prize goods sold and this was sometimes in practice heavy.

Again, statute law developed as the war went on. Administrative control was strengthened, particularly so far as agency was concerned. Arrangements were made seeking to make it easier for dependants to recover prize money. The rigour of the rules against personation was reinforced. All these modifications, introduced under the influence of Rose the Treasurer of the Navy, appear from the figures to have worked to the benefit of captors; the percentage of proceeds from merchant prizes accruing to the captors actually rose as the war went towards its close. This was in spite of a counter-adjustment when after 1806 a compulsory levy was imposed for the benefit of the Chatham Chest and Greenwich Hospital.

As well as the law of nations and domestic statutes, there was a host of proclamations, orders and directions that had the force of law. These would issue generally from the King or Prince Regent in Council but could, for example in the declaration of blockades, come from naval Commanders in Chief. The courts took full account of them – including, on many occasions, a discussion of their legality or the legality of their implementation – in their deliberations.

Thus the law, both international and domestic, had a decisive influence on the system throughout the war. It was not static, but its evolution was gradual and in hindsight had a great deal of logic to it. Often it may have been somewhat laggardly in responding to new situations or to newly exposed abuses, but that is scarcely a defect confined to that period or that particular branch of law.

How much did those at sea know about the legal side of the system and the adjustments to it that were constantly going on? This is a question that more than any other was the genesis of this book, and though the evidence gathered has gone some way towards finding an answer, it cannot be definitive. A short statement would be in the form 'A good deal more than might at first be thought'.

Cruising captains did frequently receive instructions on the detail of their business in the mater of prize. For example, there was a general issue of the 1805 Prize Act, all 123 sections of it. Orders in Council were similarly issued and guidance amplifying them was sent by the Secretary of the Admiralty. The *Naval Chronicle* became steadily more helpful in publishing the relevant regulations and in selecting Admiralty Court cases to report; and though it was not an official publication, it reached a very wide audience. Commanders in Chief generally confined their written or signalled instructions to time-worn formulae such as 'the protection of the trade and annoyance of the enemy' but often passed on more detailed guidance by personal contact. Instructions as to blockade were usually (not always) precise and the principles of effective blockade were generally known. Agents, whose own experience increased as the war went on, were in a good position to give advice to their naval clients on both law and procedure. There is in fact much evidence that in the war that began in 1803, naval officers were sufficiently briefed in the basics of prize-taking to know what the pitfalls were and what standard procedures to carry out.

It is rather doubtful if that applied equally to the war of 1793–1801. There is evidence that the Admiralty had to rein in over-enthusiastic captors and there are many indications of lack of knowledge of the system or even of the principles governing it. The arrival of Scott at the High Court of Admiralty may well have done something to enhance perception of the law's importance. It is not a coincidence that Horne's *Compendium* was published in 1803 after what was clearly a concentrated effort of authorship and it is highly indicative that the copy of this work in the Admiralty Library bears the bookplate of Admiral Lord Keith.

The establishment of priorities in the prosecution of the war at sea was the peculiar responsibility of high command, ultimately of the Admiralty Board but in large degree delegated to Commanders in Chief. It is not easy to detect any decisive shifts in the balance between prize-taking and fighting the enemy as the war went on, even within stations, much less over the conduct of the war as a whole. There were times when prizes were so plentiful that it would have been strategically wrong, and the height of absurdity, not to pick them up: West Indian operations at the turn of the century, the swoop at the resumption of war in 1803, the entry of Spain into the war at the end of 1804 and the outbreak of the American War in 1812. These have been described as 'pleasant days' and for the captors they certainly were.

But the core business of the Navy was always to fight the enemy and both in major battles and a host of minor actions it did that business. The combination of sanctions and incentives, in place to ensure that this priority was honoured, was a prime example of the system's self-adjusting nature. Articles of War, with condign punishments for not doing one's utmost to annoy enemies and support friends; disapprobation, at the least, from authority if high standards of courage and initiative were not displayed; frowns, if not worse, for any suggestion that prize-taking was given higher priority than fighting or protecting; faint or no praise for simple, unopposed capture: those were the sanctions. Incentives, on the other hand, were patronage and promotion for success in action, particularly if accompanied by brave conduct; fair and relatively rapid payment for warship and privateer captures, which if of major war vessels could amount to large sums of money; and head money, which was neither generous nor negligible but was sometimes the only recompense for an enemy destroyed.

The result of this balance can be seen over and over again in the histories, where particularly in the cutting-out actions against the French and their allies that increasingly dominated littoral warfare – oceanic campaigns having largely vanished after 1805, owing to British dominance – accounts can be found of a proportion of the captures being brought out for condemnation, while the remainder were driven ashore, burnt, blown up or sometimes all three. There was ample opportunity for acquiring military merit, and possibly promotion (though this became less automatic for such deeds as the war went on), but at the same time the pecuniary interest of officers and ships' companies was maintained. A similar pattern, though more oceanic in nature, can be found in the American War of 1812; captures were fairly frequently burnt, either because they were of little value or in order to cut down the requirement for prize crews, but enough were brought in to enrich the captors and maintain morale.

It should not be thought that such a balance was entirely lacking in the earlier war that ended in 1801. Many examples exist of vessels driven aground, particularly on the western lee shores of France and Spain, and there destroyed; or burnt at sea, as being of little value. There is, it is believed, a perceptible trend during the course of the wars towards the annoyance of the enemy and away from prize-taking pure and simple, but it is by no means marked and there were many variations within the general pattern. It must always be remembered, too, that the protection of trade was part of the equation: there is no indication that this ever commanded less than a high priority. Convoy was an integral part of strategy throughout the wars, and convoy duty though unpopular was conscientiously carried out.

So much, then, for the operations and the way in which the prize system sought to balance the factors involved. How did it serve those who stood to benefit from it?

The courts were of varying quality. At its height – probably in the years 1804 to 1809 – the High Court of Admiralty was a formidably efficient tribunal. With Scott at its head, Nicholl as King's Advocate, Heseltine and then Bishop as King's Proctors, Gostling oiling the wheels as Admiralty Procurator, Arden as Registrar with Jenner his deputy doing much of the work, Crickitt (albeit whingeing) in the background as Marshal, and an expert team of advocates able to take the part of captor or claimant alike, it disposed of a vast range of complex business and was very seldom reversed on appeal. Moreover, it surmounted without too much difficulty the watershed of the Orders in Council, even though it could not by its judgments mollify the most important neutral, the United States; that would have required a political, not a legal ruling and that was not in the Court's power.

The Admiralty Court's reputation for legal fairness was exemplified by correspondence between Sir William Scott and Judge Story, his counterpart in the United States; the two men had great respect for each other's learning in the law and the wisdom of their views. Its reputation for fair dealing in financial matters was attacked very seldom and then by people who were known to have made it their mission to conduct such attacks. Court fees, as analysis has shown, were generally moderate by the standards of the time; it was always possible to find a horror story and then argue from the particular to the general and this was the method employed by critics, as it has been from time immemorial in any form of polemic. But against the statistics, it will not do.

The Vice Admiralty Courts were a different matter. First, so far as fairness under the law was concerned, most conducted their affairs reasonably. It has not been possible to gather much evidence about how closely they kept in touch with the decisions of the High Court of Admiralty in London. Necessarily, communications being as slow as they were, little immediate adjustment to conform with leading Admiralty Court decisions could be expected and it is notable that many more appeal cases lay to the Lords Commissioners in Prize Causes from the Vice Admiralty Courts than from the High Court of Admiralty itself. However, the number of reversals from Vice Admiralty decisions appears to have been limited, and so far as the quality of legal decision was concerned, most of these courts did an adequate job.

It was in their financial dealings, particularly with captors, that the Vice Admiralty Courts came in for most criticism. The Malta Court might well have become notorious even without Cochrane's dramatic intervention; other, more level-headed officers expressed doubts about its management and exorbitant charges and events subsequent to 1811 showed a lack of control that invited and indeed led to financial malpractice. Similar, and almost as acute, criticism was made of two of the smaller West Indian courts between 1812 and 1815. Even though in this case much of the odium fell on practitioners who were not in fact officers of the court, reputations suffered.

But even here the system showed itself to an extent to be a self-adjusting one. The Commission set up by Sir William Scott in late 1811 did thorough work in establishing a scale of fees for all the Vice Admiralty Courts and through their careful language one can without difficulty read that they discovered many areas where costs had been unnecessarily raised. The courts went along quietly with the new scales, with only one dissentient – and he received short shrift. This falling-in with the wishes of Parliament, in themselves a response to feeling in the Navy as represented by Cochrane's catalytic actions, was quite a large step for Scott, who had run the Vice Admiralty Courts on a light rein since taking office. But it was in tune with the times, which were moving in all fields in the direction of centralized control.

That showed itself too in the work of the Navy Office. Here, from 1809 onwards, under the aegis of George Rose the Treasurer, Samuel Hancock had established himself as analyst and recorder and it was he who produced the background material for Rose's report in 1811. As Prize Officer in the Navy Pay Office, Hancock continued for many years in the best traditions of the new bureaucracy, questioning, probing, picking up mistakes and painstakingly producing results.

But it was Rose who led on policy and here again the potential of the prize system for sensible, evolutionary reform was demonstrated. He had come into office in 1807 determined to see as fair a deal for sailors as could be managed, particularly in the area of prize money. The Report could well be called the centrepiece of his policy, but it is notable that several of the reforms to which it referred had already been implemented. His quiet introduction of new legislation on agency, and more importantly his following up of individual breaches of its provisions, were models of control within the limits of the possible.

For there certainly were limits. The world of agency, the other significant element of the prize system and the one to which naval people were closest, was one which particularly in its upper echelons was long established and well entrenched, where a good deal of financial power was present and where the market in general ruled. The large firms were not just prize agents but merchants and bankers, with considerable legal knowledge of their own as well as intimate contact with the courts. Even further down the scale, the navy agents who dealt in general with the petty officers and seamen displayed considerable shrewdness and could point to the essential nature of the service they provided to men whose mobility, either through leave restrictions or inability to travel long distances overland, was restricted. Rose might have wanted to exercise even tighter control over the whole range of agency, but he was constrained by the network.

In fact, as has been shown, prize agents in Britain gave a sound service by the standards of the time. They worked hard for their basic fee of 5 per cent, making arrangements that their principals could not possibly have managed without grave detriment to the naval service. Moreover, because they had the necessary experience and contacts, they were able to make these arrangements – taking interrogatories, posting monitions, disposing of cargo both perishable and durable, negotiating any

necessary movement of prizes, auctions of hulls and stores, drawing up
and sending in accounts, paying the levies to naval charities, preparing
distribution lists and paying out prize money – in a more efficient
manner than any amateur was likely to do.

The figures in earlier chapters speak for themselves. An average return
to the captors of over 80 per cent of the gross proceeds for a merchant
prize, and nearer 90 per cent for warships, privateers and recaptures, is
the finding of my survey of nearly a thousand accounts covering the
period, themselves about 12 per cent of all those brought in. It is
believed that this sample is robust enough to meet any standard of
scrutiny. Nor can there be any serious question that the accounts were
systematically falsified. They were statutorily presented for public
inspection before payment was made, and notification of this
presentation was given in the *Gazette*. They were then subject to
verification by a magistrate or similar officer.

It can of course be contended that this agency service should have
been provided by the state. The captors were, after all, doing the nation's
work in weakening enemy commerce and war-making ability and
arguably should have had the full benefit. To this, the answer must be
that the system was of its time, and there are two elements to that. First,
prize was a matter of 'the fortune of war' and in a way was equivalent to
winning at cards or lottery: it was only natural that such luck should be
accompanied by spin-off to those who helped to generate the proceeds.
Second, it is unthinkable that in the 1790s and early 1800s such a service
would have been provided by the state without exacting its own levy – and
that might have been more than 5 per cent. So, even discounting the
relative efficiencies of a free-market or state system (and the latter,
judging by other activities of the Navy Office, might have come a poor
second best) the captors, in spite of grumbles, saw the British prize
agency as at worst a necessary evil and at best a welcome lubricant of the
system.

Once more, it is necessary to enter a caveat about the foreign stations.
Some were fortunate, or well regulated, in the matter of agency. Jamaica,
Bermuda and Halifax appear to have been the pick of the bunch; Willis
and Waterhouse in Jamaica and George Redmond Hulbert in the
northern Atlantic were efficient and by all available evidence honest
agents. Indeed, in many respects Hulbert gave better service than most of
his counterparts in Britain; and the fact that his agency occupies the
latter part of the period covered by this book suggests, along with other
evidence, that the process of self-adjustment was operating here too and
agency was responding to the pressure of opinion and perhaps also of
competition.

Other areas were not so well served. Malta once again was a central
point for criticism, and it did not come entirely from Cochrane. One of

the most cogent shortcomings of the agency system was that if not properly subjected to supervision and control, it could all too easily become a cosy relationship between agents and officers of the court, to the exclusion of the interests of the people the system was meant to serve, the captors and claimants and indeed the Crown itself. The evidence suggests that this was the state of affairs in Malta. The system had ceased to be self-adjusting and had become self-serving, with serious results that had only been partly remedied by the end of the war.

When it came to distribution of the proceeds, probably the boot was on the other foot, so far as differences between home and foreign stations were concerned. Sailors abroad tended to enjoy more leave, the opportunities for desertion being fewer, and there are examples of more regular and more certain distributions of prize money to ships on these stations than to those at home, where distribution tended to be made for each individual prize, sometimes at a considerable distance from the home port and usually to the great inconvenience of the ship-bound seaman.

The introduction of the 1808 scale of distribution was a well-meant measure which did benefit the middle range of seamen, though it is hard to find evidence of any great acclaim for it from the lower deck. It caused considerable resentment among commanding officers, who were those who suffered most, but little reaction from flag officers who probably felt they had done well for a long time and were still likely to be reasonably recompensed for their 'direction' of operations. It can be viewed as a modest and necessary adjustment in the spirit of the time, a spirit which had shifted perceptibly since the mutineers at the Nore, eleven years before, had demanded a more equitable distribution of prize money and been hanged – not indeed for that demand, which came seventh out of eight on their list, but for the fact that they by violence immobilized the fleet in the face of a present threat from the enemy in the North Sea.

Before coming to the one area where the prize system can be unequivocally criticized for failing its clients, it is necessary to say something about Droits. These were of increasing concern both in naval circles and in Parliament as the war went on. The reason was the tendency of government to embark on measures which resulted in and indeed demanded capture, while neglecting – either by oversight or design – to make in time the proclamations that would render such captures the right of the captor on condemnation. Instead they became Droits of the Crown and any proceeds to the captor were in the Crown's gift. Usually these amounted to two-thirds of the whole.

That was naturally resented by the naval service and regarded as sharp practice on the part of the government. Naval Members of Parliament were not slow to express the navy's feelings and moreover to speculate on what was happening to the money. Some said it was going to the Civil List to defray the expenses of the Prince Regent, others that it was destined for Greenwich Hospital. Neither was popular, the one because it was thought extravagant and the other because it was believed to be badly administered. After the war, the charge particularly about the Civil List turned out to have been amply justified.

Other Parliamentarians, some of them natural allies of the naval Radicals, found a different target. This was the known and well attested application of some of the Droits Fund to meet the legal expenses of captors in cases where restoration of ship or cargo had been decreed. There was some feeling that a Crown fund of this nature and extent – it had a total turnover of several million pounds – should be under the control of Parliament. This pressure was resisted and the fund remained in Admiralty hands, no doubt to the relief of the Treasurer.

In spite of the allocation of quite large tranches of the Droits Fund to matters that had no connection with prize or the navy, its application for meeting the costs of captors unsuccessful in the courts is another example of the self-adjusting nature of the prize system. The security given to captains taking prizes in good faith that they were following the principles of law and their instructions – complex, and even sometimes contradictory, though these might be – must have been of great comfort. A final sanction was reserved: the Admiralty could still withhold repayment of costs in cases where capture was considered reckless. Nevertheless, it was a far cry from the days when *bona fide* captures, disallowed because the law, or the instructions, or the nature of the prize, had been misinterpreted, could result in financial ruin for a commanding officer. The fact that security was being funded by Crown Droits completed the loop.

Finally, in this assessment it is necessary to come to an aspect of the system where it must be said to have let down its clients: the business of delay. Again, the figures speak for themselves. Nearly half the merchant ship captures took more than two years to settle. The figures were better for warships and privateers, 35 per cent, and for recaptures, 16 per cent. The general level of frustration must have been extreme. Ships' companies might have been dispersed, officers sent to new appointments; many might have died of disease, drowned or been killed in action; in the worst cases they might all be dead. Legally their beneficiaries would be entitled to their shares, but the greater the delay in such cases, the less would be the certainty that they would reach the right hands.

This was a scandal and on the evidence of this book the only element of the prize system to which that word can properly be applied. Like most such failures, it cannot be ascribed to a single cause.

First, the work of the courts was sometimes slow. This applied particularly to neutral captures, where time was allowed for appeal and proceeds could not be distributed until it had elapsed. Those who made interim payments took risks. Cases sometimes went back for further proof, and that inevitably lengthened proceedings. Sometimes cases were insufficiently prepared by agents or proctors, and that again caused delay. Judges occasionally made errors and had to backtrack. On the whole, the impression particularly of the London court is that business was despatched with reasonable speed; but the law always has its delays and the fundamental rule – *that every incident of prize must go through full judicial process* – inevitably worked against speedy settlement.

Second, the work of agents was sometimes tardy. One or two names crop up in the records that seem to have been more culpable than others, but the sample in this aspect is too small to come to any conclusion and deep analysis of the progress of suspect cases is very seldom possible from the papers available. In any event, delay in disposing of a prize was usually due entirely to circumstances. *The Eenrom* was a fortunate find for a researcher, for it did provide the necessary detail and showed how prolonged the administration of an important prize could be. In that case, of course, the governing factor was the time taken for appeal, but even had an appeal not been lodged, disposal would not have been quick.

The charge that agents and the Court colluded to ensure delay and to send cases to appeal, so that interest could be earned on proceeds already realized, remained unsubstantiated. Conspiracy theories flourish on isolated cases, and it may be there were a few, but there is no evidence of system. The courts had powers to decree the payment into court of substantial sums where sales had been made pending appeal and this would have been a potent deterrent, had it been regularly exercised. There is some evidence, particularly from Rose's Report, that it was not; the amount of money in agents' hands, and invested without much of the interest accruing to the captors, remained high.

Third, agents themselves could be badly served by their clients. Information that a prize had been taken might not be transmitted to them; arrangements for the interrogatories might be defective, in particular the right officers from the prize might not have been brought in to make the necessary answers; the presence in sight of other ships of war or privateers might not be reported; in warship or privateer captures, the number of men on board the enemy, necessary for the head money bill, might not be available; and most commonly of all, the crew lists of the captor might not be transmitted, or might not be complete. Isolated examples of all these shortcomings turn up in the records, but analysis that would apportion the degree to which they operated cannot be attempted.

On one of these self-inflicted delays, however, judgement rests on firmer ground. Joint capture was a recipe for tardy payment. The figures, robust in this case, show it took on average half as long again to settle a joint-capture account than a single-ship capture. The causes of delay were various. Most common, probably, was sheer administrative load: the need for multiple crew lists, liaison between the agents representing the various ships, co-ordinating accounts and drawing up distribution lists necessarily more complex than for a single-ship capture. Actual disputes over entitlement were less common, but there were enough to ensure serious delay in a number of important cases.

It appears the court did all it could to discourage this particular evil. Scott himself censured those who dragged out joint-capture proceedings and the officers of the court sometimes intervened to try to speed things up. A rule seems to have been established that however many agents were involved in the preliminaries, only one should render the final account, and that should have saved time. Nevertheless, the joint-capture aspect made worse what was a shameful record of delay in general.

The authorities were not blind to the evils of delay. Rose pointed them out in his report, as Nelson had years before. But they were unwilling or unable to implement measures to streamline the process. The staffs of courts, from judges on down, could have been increased; further Vice Admiralty Courts could have been set up, even in the United Kingdom; sanctions could have been imposed on agents for tardy payment; the 'in sight' rule could have been re-examined and joint-capture agreements encouraged within squadrons. There were arguments, which had some validity, against all these measures: they would either disturb or dilute a system that was legally and financially robust and well understood, even if it did not deliver in a timely way. And, of course, they would have been unpopular with the established practitioners of the system, who were not without political clout. So, with some tinkering at the edges, some exhortation and some mild sanctions, 'Delay' limped on to the end of the war, the one real failure of the prize system in terms of adjusting itself.

Yet in the last analysis, in spite of the system's shortcomings Prize was one of the major factors that kept the navy of these wars going. From the highest to the lowest it gave spice to what would otherwise have been unremitting toil and frequent danger for outrageously small reward. Its capriciousness, like that of any game of chance, was accepted in what was still a gambling age. Its inequities in the matter of distribution were the subject of not much more than grumbles, for hierarchy was embedded in the system not just of prize but of the navy and the nation. It could be a motor of social advancement, relatively often for the more fortunate officers, often enough in the folklore to lure even the humblest seaman.

How did prize measure up in national strategy? War, said Napoleon, must pay for itself. The shoreside machinery of the prize system, of course, was amply paid for; it was the proceeds of prizes that financed the fees for court officials, agents, brokers and all the other middlemen. In theory, apart from prize duties and Droits – the former modest, the latter substantial – everything else went to the captors and so could be argued not to constitute a contribution to the financing of the war.

However, that argument is erroneous. Had prize money not existed, it would have been necessary to pay a great deal more to all naval personnel – probably half as much again, in line with merchant service rates – in order to maintain a fleet with any sort of morale, without impossibly high reliance on the press gang and with a tolerably low rate of desertion. By that kind of calculation, it was worth between one and two million pounds a year, which curiously is the kind of figure that prize money realized annually. These figures are kept deliberately vague here, because data are incomplete and unreliable particularly where overseas stations are concerned.

So it may be said that over the course of the war, ship captures realized of the order of £30 million. The capture of military establishments ashore probably amounted to at least another £10 million, in the roundest terms – payable in this case of course to the army and naval forces involved. The benefit to the exchequer was, on the argument set out above, something like £40 million. By comparison, the total cost of the wars, from 1793 to 1815, has been estimated at £830 million, of which the navy's share was £334 million. It may not seem very great, but it is by no means negligible: 5 per cent of the former, and 12 per cent of the latter.

To carry on the discussion in crude financial terms, did the million and a half a year compensate the navy for the wear and tear on its ships and men in the arduous business of cruising, enforcing blockade, chasing, visiting and searching? This is a question that it is fruitless to try and answer, for that part of the navy's business was inseparable from the totality of sea control, 'the protection of the trade and the annoyance of the enemy'. It was simply one facet of a structure that included battlefleet dominance, watch on enemy bases, amphibious warfare, convoy and focal point protection.

Finally, how much damage did it do to the enemy? Many authors from Mahan to Tracy have addressed the question and this book, which has been much more concerned with the workings of the prize system than with its strategic effects, can make only a limited contribution to what is likely to be a continuing debate. However, judging from the reaction of the mighty French Empire – particularly from 1806 onwards – to this form of warfare, it was clearly regarded as much more than a gadfly. The constricting effect on trade not only of France itself but of the Empire's satraps, the loss of control on the peripheries, the impotence of both overseas and home-based officials to check breaches of the Continental System, were all weakening and galling. Eventually, the understanding with Russia cracked under the strain and the signposts all led to Moscow.

But the last word must remain for the British sailors who worked the system and, sometimes, benefited by it. All must have dreamed of prize from time to time. Many were disappointed by never taking a prize at all, a few frustrated by the law, some – fewer than often reported – cheated by the middlemen, many more saddened or maddened by delay. But the prospect always glimmered, brightening from time to time with a promised cruise or sight of an unexpected sail. The Royal Navy could not have done without it. It gave to those days, soon to vanish, a unique piquancy and flavour.

A Survey of Agents' Accounts

To provide base material for Parts Two and Three of this book, a survey was carried out of agents' accounts brought in to the High Court of Admiralty between 1793 and about 1818.

There are over sixty boxes of these in the Public Records Office, in the HCA 2/300 series. There is an average of some 150 accounts in each box. The time available to an individual researcher clearly would not permit scrutiny of every bill and it was decided to take a sample that would be robust enough to support conclusions about the average value of prizes, the difference between gross and net proceeds, the proportion of costs attributable to the various services provided to captors, and the time elapsing between capture and distribution.

The headings chosen were: Name of Prize (and Master if known); Captor; Date of Capture; Date of bringing in account; Agent; Gross proceeds; Net proceeds for distribution; and Remarks, to include whether the capture was a warship or privateer (and in these cases whether head money was paid), or a recapture, and any other unusual features.

It was clearly important to have a complete span of dates from the start to after the end of the war (some accounts were brought in even after 1818, but it was a sharply diminishing number by then). This was not particularly difficult because the boxes are grouped by the initial letter of the name of the captured ship and four boxes of, for example, the initial 'A' span the whole war. A robust sample was going to need more than four boxes and I finally decided upon seven, covering two initial letters for the period 1793–1818 and approximating to 12 per cent of the total.

Choosing the initial letters could not be entirely random. Those settled on eventually were IJ (which are grouped in the records as one letter) and N. The reasoning was that IJ was arguably skewed towards Dutch vessels and the table needed correction to accommodate Spanish ones, which N amply achieved.

Thus, while the IJs showed a high proportion of *Jonge Jans* and *Juffrouw Amelias*, the Ns had an equal bias towards *Nuestra Senora del Carmens*, and so on. As for privateers, warships and recaptures, it did not seem that the letters chosen caused a bias either way. French corsairs quite often chose an initial letter I; *Intrépide* was a favourite, but there was at least one *Incroyable* and the Spaniards weighed in with an *Intrepido Cid*. On the other hand, *Industry* was a favourite name for British merchant ships and accounted for several recaptures, while *Neptunes* and *Neptunuses* covered a wide range of categories.

The spread therefore gives some confidence that it is a representative one. This is borne out by the consistency between the figures generated by the records. Mean proceeds for captures of all three categories – merchants, privateers/warships and recaptures – are remarkably similar, box for box, with one exception, and that is the first 'N' box, where the mean figure for merchants is almost twice that generated by each of the other boxes. This is explained by the fact that Britain was at war with Spain through most of the period covered by that box and Spanish ships really were richer fraught than the generality.

In the course of investigation into individual cases with initial letters other than 'IJ' and 'N', a few short runs were made through the records round about the case being examined in detail. Thus about thirty accounts with initial letter 'G' around the time of *The Guillaume Tell* judgment were noted. They have not been included in the statistical base, because they do not cover the whole span of the war, but it is notable that they indicate no significant deviation from the figures derived from the 'IJ' and 'N' batches.

Not all the accounts are complete. Some omit the date of capture and a few even do not mention the name of the capturing ship or ships. Captured ships whose names were unidentified were entered as 'Name Unknown' under the Ns, but there were not many of these and they caused no particular problem. In the early years of the war probably 30 per cent of the accounts were flawed in the matter of dates and names, but later on their form and content improved until by 1810 or thereabouts only some 10 per cent fell short of full presentation of the circumstances of the capture. It is not believed that the deductions drawn in the book about the value of proceeds, or the delay in their reaching the captors, are seriously affected by omissions of data at this level, given that some 1,000 accounts in all were examined.

So far as the figures themselves are concerned, there is no reason to doubt their accuracy. All accounts had to be sworn before a competent authority and the legal instrument confirming this is invariably included in the record. Some accounts are much more detailed than others; in general the less experienced agents erred on the side of caution and might even include a record of the sale of every barrel of flour, while the established firms contented themselves with a one-page summary.

Most of the accounts are in sterling. Of those few that are in other currencies, approximate conversions have been made for the more common, such as hard dollars and Bermuda pounds. One or two accounts in scudies and cobbs remained unconverted and were ignored, as were a couple in star pagodas, a currency in general use by the East India Company.

Glossary

Advocate	A person with rights of audience in court; in the High Court of Admiralty, a member of Doctors' Commons
Blockade	Interdiction of all sea traffic to and from the port or area declared to be blockaded
Boatswain	The warrant officer in charge of the ship's rigging and all arrangements for sail management. He was also, under the captain and first lieutenant, responsible for discipline on board
Boatswain's Mate(s)	Assistants to the Boatswain in matters of both rigging and discipline. In flogging punishments they would deliver the lashes
Bottomry Bonds	A pledge given in lieu of immediate payment for services to a ship, entitling the recipient to rights over the ship if payment is not made within due time
Bounty	See head money
Bring To	To manoeuvre a ship so that it is head to wind. In this state a square-rigged ship was easy to control
Canister	Anti-personnel shot which was designed to spread into many fragments when fired, thus inflicting maximum casualties at close range
Captor	The ship or ships making a capture
Chasse-marée	A small French coasting craft, generally armed, often used for despatches and important cargoes
Civilian	An advocate practising in Doctors' Commons
Civil Jurisdiction	Legal authority to decide non-criminal cases
Claimant	The owner of a captured vessel, cargo or part cargo, contesting whether the property was lawful prize
Colours	The national flag of a vessel. False colours were habitually used by warships as a *ruse de guerre*, though they were expected to substitute their proper colours before opening fire. Merchant ships, however, were not expected to show false colours and one of the Interrogatories asked specifically whether any colours other than those of the ship's nationality were carried on board
Colourable	Of documents, false or dubious
Condemnation	Judgment by a properly constituted court that a vessel and/or cargo was lawful prize

Contraband	Cargo of warlike nature or use destined for the enemy
Convoy	A ship or group of ships under naval protection
Court of Arches	One of the Ecclesiastical Courts of Doctors' Commons
Cruise	Term generally applied to patrol or surveillance duty by a ship or ships. There was a strong underlying assumption that a ship 'on a cruise' would have a chance of picking up prizes while one on convoy duty would not
Cruiser, Cruizer	Any ship employed on cruising duty
Cut down Ship, Rasée	A vessel originally having two gundecks with the upper gundeck removed to improve handling and seakeeping qualities. Typically a cut-down sixty-four-gun ship would mount forty-four guns and be rated as a frigate
Cutting-out	A very commonly carried out operation in which the boats of a ship or squadron went close inshore, covered where possible by fire from their parent ships, in order to capture and bring out enemy merchantmen and/or privateers
Dogger	A North Sea coasting vessel
Droit	A legal right
En Flûte	A warship adapted for cargo carrying, with a much reduced armament. Cargo might well get in the way of the armament, further reducing fighting efficiency
Felucca	A lateen-rigged cargo vessel common in the Mediterranean
Fore-reach	To overtake a ship being chased
Freight	Money paid to the shipper or carrier of cargo. Senior officers of the navy often made considerable sums by authorizing the carriage of, or carrying, bullion or other valuable cargo in their ships
Frigate	A ship of the fifth or sixth rate, carrying generally between twenty-four and forty-four guns with a crew of 200–300 (British ships). French frigates often had somewhat larger crews
Gun Money	Bounty paid for the capture of a warship or privateer based on the number of guns carried by the captured ship. By 1793 it had long been superseded by Head Money, q.v.
Hamoaze	The entrance into the Tamar River at Plymouth. The eighteenth-century dockyard is on the eastern side
Head Money	A sum of money paid out of the exchequer to a vessel or vessels which captured, burnt or drove on shore an enemy privateer or ship of war, based on the

	number of crew alive onboard the enemy at the start of the action
Hired Armed Vessel	A ship hired from a private owner and commissioned under a naval officer, with a crew provided by the owner
Hove-to	A condition where a sailing ship is held stationary, with head close to the wind, by adjustment of the sails. See also 'Bring to'
Hundred Days	The period between Napoleon's escape from Elba and the Battle of Waterloo in 1815
Indiaman	A merchant ship belonging to the Honourable East India Company or its Dutch equivalent, the VOC. These ships tended to be very large and to carry valuable cargoes. Many were heavily armed, but their crews were neither so numerous nor so well trained as those of warships
Inn of Court	A College of Barristers, empowered to Call its members to the Bar and thereby confer on them rights of audience in the courts. There are four such Inns, dating from the mid-fourteenth century, all in London: Lincoln's Inn, The Inner and Middle Temples, and Gray's Inn
Instance Court	A court empowered to try a range of civil cases but with no jurisdiction in Prize unless this was separately conferred
Interlocutory Decree	A decision or ruling made by the court not amounting to a final judgment
International Law	Also called the Law of Nations: the generally accepted rules by which nations govern their conduct towards each other
Keeping Terms	Attendance at an Inn of Court or other learning institution for certain functions (often dinners in Hall) as one of the qualifications for a degree
Lee Shore	A shore lying in the direction towards which the wind is blowing. Particularly if the wind is strong, allowing little canvas to be set, this is a dangerous situation for a sailing vessel
Leeward	The direction towards which the wind is blowing; or a position in that direction from another vessel
Letter of Marque	A legal instrument authorizing a privateer to seize property of enemy character
Line of Battle Ship	A warship of the fourth rate or higher, carrying fifty guns or more
Lugger	Generic term for a small coasting vessel; if a privateer, the word 'privateer' was generally prefixed to 'lugger' to identify the craft as such

Master	Of merchant vessels, the person in charge of the ship's conduct and ultimately responsible for the safety and work of the ship. Of warships, a warrant officer in charge of the ship's navigation under the captain
Mate	Second in command of a merchant ship
Mercantilism	A policy aimed at the increase of wealth through protected and regulated foreign and colonial trade and national industry. In war, the policy included the frustration of the enemy's attempts to achieve similar aims
Monition	A legal instrument lodged by a captor seeking the court's judgment that a captured vessel was lawful prize
Municipal Law	The laws of an individual country, either enacted by statute or established by custom and precedent
Navigation Acts	Prime statutory instruments of mercantilism, which denied to foreign shipping the right to trade with the colonies of the state concerned
Navy Agent	A trader who entered into agreements with ratings to advance money against eventual prize proceeds. They were subject to statutory regulation from 1809 onwards
Ordinary	A ship laid up in reserve, or in care and maintenance, was said to be 'in ordinary'
Post Captain	The highest rank in the Royal Navy below that of Rear Admiral, except that for a special duty a Captain could be temporarily given the rank of Commodore and would then rank above all other Captains. To be 'Made Post' was the ambition of all officers below captain's rank
Power of Attorney	A legal instrument authorizing the recipient to conduct specified financial affairs of the signatory
Private Signal	An identification signal, usually a combination of flags, shapes and gunshots, which was meant to be known only to the ships of one side. An enemy who had acquired knowledge of the Private Signal would have immense advantage in the approach to action
Privateer	A privately owned and manned vessel authorized by Letters of Marque to make captures on behalf of the nation issuing such letters. Armament and crews of privateers varied widely, extending from small craft with only one gun to vessels mounting thirty guns or more

Prize	A captured ship or other property. The term was generally used from the moment of capture. Technically, however, it should not have been applied to a capture until it was adjudged to be lawful prize by a competent court
Prize Agent	A businessman engaged to look after the prize affairs of a ship or ships. The duties of a prize agent were regulated by statute
Proctor	The eighteenth-century equivalent of a solicitor
Purser	A warrant officer charged with the victualling of the ship's company and keeping the accounts. Pursers took financial responsibility for their operations, which gave them an incentive for making them profitable, and were often regarded with suspicion in consequence
Quarter Gunner	A rating in charge of the maintenance of four of the great guns in a ship of war. Thus a twenty-four-gun frigate would have six Quarter Gunners, staid and reliable hands who would ensure their guns were in fit condition for action
Quartermaster	In the Royal Navy, a seaman chosen for his expertise and reliability in steering the ship. A frigate would generally have three ratings so detailed. In the Royal Marines or Army, a warrant officer in charge of administration and victualling
Raking	A manoeuvre in sea fighting whereby the broadside of one ship was brought to bear against the bow or stern of the other, which ideally lay at right angles to it. This had the twin advantages that the opponent could not fire much of its armament at the raking ship, and the broadside of the raking ship could cause maximum structural damage and casualties
Recalls	Distribution of prize money to those who had missed the initial distribution
Reprisal	Originally, authorization to take property as the means of righting a private wrong. In the wars of 1793–1815, it was applied only to 'letters of reprisal', the legal instrument by which prize-taking was authorized
Retorsion	A legal process, which would in normal circumstances be illegal but which is held by its initiator to be a justified retaliation against an illegal act by the party against whom the retorsion is declared

Salvage	Money paid to a person or crew who have assisted in the recovery of a vessel and/or cargo from stress of weather or capture
Scantling	A general term denoting the sturdiness of a ship's hull. 'Light' scantlings indicate inability to sustain heavy punishment from gunfire
Schuyt	A Dutch coasting vessel
Slops	Clothing, or the makings of clothing, supplied by the navy for the basic needs of the ship's company. Colloquially, any clothes worn by sailors, therefore
Slop-seller	A tailor or trader in the main naval ports, who was often also a navy agent
Standing off and on	Sailing away from the shore for an appreciable distance, turning (tacking or wearing) and then closing the shore again, repeating the process as often as the mission dictated and generally remaining outside gunshot from the shore throughout: a standard technique for patrolling craft
Strike	To signify surrender by lowering the national flag
Supercargo	The person on board a merchant vessel in charge of transactions regarding the cargo
Tack	(1, noun) The side of a ship's sails on which the wind is blowing. Thus a ship on the port tack would have the wind on her left side, while on the starboard tack it would be on the right. (2, verb) To alter the course of the ship, and the tack on which she is sailing, by bringing the bow through the wind
Taxation	Independent assessment of legal costs
Wear	To alter the course of a ship, and the tack on which she is sailing, by bringing the stern through the wind
Windward	Towards the direction from which the wind is blowing
Yardarm to Yardarm	A conventional method of fighting a single ship action, with the broadside guns of both ships engaged, in which rate of fire and weight of metal were likely to be the deciding factors

Bibliography

PRIMARY AND CONTEMPORARY SOURCES:

Admiralty documents in the Public Record Office, particularly

ADM 1/126	Channel Fleet, 1804: outletters from Rear Adm Hon. A. Cochrane
ADM 1/400–1	Outletters from Lords St Vincent and Keith, 1799–1801
ADM 1/560	Outletters from North Sea Command, 1808
ADM 1/564	Outletters from North Sea Command, 1810
ADM 1/3657	Report by George Rose on the Prize System, 1811–12
ADM 1/3894–3903	Correspondence from Doctors' Commons to Admiralty, 1798–1815
ADM 1/3993	Outletter from Admiralty to Committee of Lloyd's, 1809*
ADM 1/4353	Secret Letters
ADM 2/1079–1083	Circulars issued by the Board of Admiralty, 1795–1813
ADM 15/2	Treasurer's Outletters
ADM 50/36	Journal of Lord Keith, 1800–1
ADM 50/93	Journal of Lord St Vincent, 1798–1800
ADM 51 series	Ships' Logs
ADM 53 series	Ships' Logs

High Court of Admiralty Documents in the Public Record Office, particularly

HCA 2/121	Consolidated Fee Book, 1809
HCA 2/240	Fair Fee Book, 1811
HCA 2/355–8	Agents' Accounts 'IJ', 1793–1818
HCA 2/359	Agents' Accounts 'L', 1804–10
HCA 2/365–7	Agents' Accounts 'N', 1793–1818
HCA 30/125	Prize Court Minutes, 1811
HCA 30/161	Droits, Miscellaneous Returns
HCA 30/466	Appeal Court Notes

HCA 30/538   Appointments of Proctors 1801–3
HCA 30/627   Miscellaneous Prize Court papers
HCA 30/1024   Comparison of Clauses in Prize Acts, 1779–1805*
HCA 42/217   Prize Court Appeal Records, 'E'
HCA 42/437–41 Prize Court Appeal Records, 'IJ'

* Courtesy Michael Dun

War Office Document in the Public Record Office
   WO 52/130   Account for captured ordnance stores

Courtesy Gillian Hughes

Duckworth papers in the National Maritime Museum, particularly
   NMM DUC/20 Correspondence of Sir John Duckworth

Courtesy Captain A.B. Sainsbury

Pellew papers in the National Maritime Museum, particularly
   NMM PEL/4   Pellew's Order Book as C-in-C Downs, 1810–11
   NMM PEL/20   Outletters from Pellew as C-in-C Med, 1811–12
   NMM PEL/22   Admiralty to Pellew, 1811–12

Hulbert Papers in the National Maritime Museum, particularly
   HUL/4   Records of Vice Admiralty Court, Bermuda, 1812–13
   HUL/7   Head Money papers
   HUL/16   Prize Lists
   HUL/42 f.3 Hulbert to Doctors' Commons, post-1815

Papers in the Royal Naval Museum, Portsmouth
   RNM 197/301   Collection of Letters written to John Wilson Croker
   RNM 546/84   Letters from Seaman Richard Greenhalgh
   RNM 442/92   Letters from John Booth, Yeoman of the Sheets
   RNM 353/1994 Certificates of Service of Edward Hatherley
   RNM 64/67   Papers of John Binney, Lieutenant 1813
   RNM 1983/1062 Accounts of Trafalgar Bounty and Prize Money
   RNM 1997/65   Papers of Thomas Snowden Peckston, Purser

Statutes concerning Prize, contained mainly in *A Collection of the Statutes Relating to the Admiralty, Navy, Shipping and Navigation* (Eyre and Strahan, 1810)

Notifications concerning Orders in Council, contained mainly in *Notifications, Orders and Instructions Relating to Prize Subjects during the Present War* (Strahan, for Butterworth and White, 1810)

The *London Gazette*
The *Naval Chronicle*, vols 1–30 (1798–1813)

Biederman. *Manuel diplomatique sur le dernier état de la controverse concernant les droits des neutres sur la mer* (Brockhaus, Leipsic, 1814). The authorship of this book is uncertain; the name 'Biederman' appears only on the spine and no other attribution is given. The book has been used only to recover the French texts of the Berlin and Milan Decrees and associated documents.
Dodson, John. *Reports of Cases heard in the High Court of Admiralty under Sir William Scott* (2 vols, 1813–28)
Edwards, Thos. *Reports of Cases heard in the High Court of Admiralty under Sir William Scott* (1 vol., 1809–12)
——. *Reports of the Leading Decisions in the High Court of Admiralty in Cases of Vessels Sailing under British Licence* (Strahan for Butterworth, 1812)
Horne, Thomas Hartwell. *A Compendium of the Statute Laws and Regulations of the Court of Admiralty relative to Ships of War, Privateers, Recaptures and Prize Money* (W. Clarke and Sons, 1803)
Robinson, Christopher. *Reports of Cases heard in the High Court of Admiralty under Sir William Scott* (6 vols, 1798–1808)

SECONDARY SOURCES:

Anson, W.V. *The Life of John Jervis, Admiral Lord St Vincent,* John Murray, 1913
Austen, Jane. *Persuasion,* Collins, 1953 edn
Bourguignon, Henry J. *Sir William Scott, Lord Stowell,* Cambridge University Press, 1987
Brenton, Edward Pelham. *Life of Earl St Vincent,* Henry Colburn, 1838
Broadley, A.M. and Barthelot, R.G. *Three Dorset Captains at Trafalgar,* John Murray, 1906
Byrn, John D. Jr. *Crime and Punishment in the Royal Navy,* Scolar Press, 1989
Camperdown, the Earl of. *Admiral Duncan,* Longmans, Green, 1898
Clowes W.L. *The Royal Navy: A History from the Earliest Times to 1900,* Chatham edn, 1997
Cochrane, Alexander. *The Fighting Cochranes,* Quiller Press, 1983
Cochrane, Thomas, Admiral the Earl of Dundonald. *Autobiography of a Seaman,* first published 1857; Constable edn, 1995
Collingwood, G.L. Newnham. *Correspondence and Memoir of Lord Collingwood,* Ridgway, 1829
Colombos, C. John. *International Law of the Sea,* 6th edn, Longmans, 1967
Coupland, Sir Reginald. *Wilberforce,* Collins, 1945
Crouzet, François. *Britain Ascendant: Comparative Studies in Franco-British Economic History,* trans. M. Thom, Cambridge University Press, 1990
—— with Chaloner, W.H. and Stern, W.M. (eds). *Essays in European Economic History 1789–1914,* Edward Arnold, 1969

—— with Erik Aerts (ed.). *Economic Effects of the French Revolutionary and Napoleonic Wars*, Leuven University Press, 1990

Derriman J.'Hired Armed Cutters in the Napoleonic Wars', *Maritime South West* No. 9, (1996), pp. 97–123.

Dictionary of National Biography

Dillon, Sir William Henry, Vice Admiral of the Red. *A Narrative of My Professional Adventures*, Navy Records Society, 1953

Duffy, Michael. *Soldiers, Sugar and Seapower*, Clarendon Press, Oxford, 1987

Ellison D.B. (ed.) *Pressganged: the Letters of George Price*, Ellison's Editions, 1994

French, David. *The British Way in Warfare 1688–2000*, Unwin Hyman, 1990

Gardiner, Robert (ed.). *Nelson Against Napoleon*, Chatham, 1997

—— (ed.). *The Campaign of Trafalgar*, Chatham, 1997

Grainger, John D. *The Royal Navy in the River Plate, 1806–1807*, Navy Records Society, 1996

Green, Geoffrey L. *The Royal Navy and Anglo-Jewry 1740–1820*, Green, 1989

Guedalla, Philip. *The Duke*, Hodder and Stoughton, 1937

Gutridge, Tony. 'George Redmond Hulbert, Prize Agent', unpublished thesis, Portsmouth Polytechnic, 1981–2

—— 'Aspects of Naval Prize Agency 1793–1815', 80 The *Mariner's Mirror* (1994), p. 46

Hamilton, Sir R. Vesey (ed.). *Journals and Letters of Sir Thomas Byam Martin*, Navy Records Society, 1903

—— with Laughton, John Knox. *Recollections of James Anthony Gardner*, Navy Records Society, 1906

Henderson, James. *The Frigates*, Adlard Coles, 1970

Hill, J.R. (ed.). *The Oxford Illustrated History of the Royal Navy*, OUP, 1995

Holdsworth, W.S. *A History of English Law*, Methuen, 1952

Howarth, David. *Trafalgar: the Nelson Touch*, Windrush, 1996

Hubback, J.H. and E.C. *Jane Austen's Sailor Brothers*, Bodley Head, 1906

Hughes, Edward (ed.). *The Private Correspondence of Admiral Lord Collingwood*, Navy Records Society, 1957

James, Admiral Sir William. *Old Oak*, Longmans, Green, 1950

James, William. *The Naval History of Great Britain*, Bentley, 1847

Kemp, Lt-Cdr Peter. *Prize Money*, Gale and Polden, 1946

Laughton, John Knox, (ed.). *The Barham Papers*, Navy Records Society, 1911

—— (ed.). *The Naval Miscellany*, vol. 2, Navy Records Society, 1912

—— with Sulivan, James Y.F. (ed.). *Journal of Rear Admiral Bartholomew James, 1752–1828*, Navy Records Society, 1906

Lavery, Brian. *Nelson's Navy*, Conway, 1989

Lewis, Michael. *A Social History of the Navy 1793–1815*, George Allen and Unwin, 1960

Leyland, John. *The Blockade of Brest*, Navy Records Society, 1902

Lloyd, Christopher. *The Nation and the Navy*, Cresset Press, 1954

—— (ed.). *The Naval Miscellany*, vol. 4, Navy Records Society, 1952

—— (ed.). *The Keith Papers*, Navy Records Society, 1960

—— *Captain Marryat and the Old Navy*, Longman, 1939

Mahan, Alfred Thayer. *The Influence of Sea Power upon the French Revolution and Empire*, Sampson Low, 1892

——. *The Life of Nelson*, Sampson Low, 1897

Markham, Sir Clements (ed.). *Selections from the Correspondence of Admiral Sir John Markham*, Navy Records Society, 1904

Marsden, R.G. (ed.). *The Law and Custom of the Sea*, Navy Records Society, 1915

Marshall, J. *Royal Naval Biography*, Longman, 1823

Nicolas, Sir Nicholas Harris (ed.). *The Dispatches and Letters of Lord Nelson*, Chatham edn, 1997

O'Connell, D.P. *The Influence of Law on Sea Power*, Manchester University Press, 1975

Oman, Carola. *Nelson*, Hodder and Stoughton, 1947

Orde, Denis. *Nelson's Mediterranean Command*, Pentland Press, 1997

Osler, Edward. *The Life of Admiral Viscount Exmouth*, Smith, Elder, 1835

Owen, Hugh. 'The Naval Sons of William IV and Mrs Jordan', 83 The *Mariner's Mirror* (1997), p. 44ff.

Parkinson, C. Northcote. *Edward Pellew, Viscount Exmouth*, Methuen, 1933

Perrin, W.G. (ed.). *The Naval Miscellany*, vol. 3, Navy Records Society, 1926

Pope, Dudley. *Life in Nelson's Navy*, Chatham, 1997

Popham, Hugh. *A Damned Cunning Fellow*, Old Folly Press, 1991

Rodger N.A.M. *The Wooden World*, Collins, 1986

——. *Articles of War*, Kenneth Mason, 1982

——. *The Safeguard of the Sea*, Harper Collins, 1997

—— (ed.). *The Naval Miscellany*, vol. 5, Navy Records Society, 1984

Roscoe, E.S. *History of the English Prize Court*, Lloyd's, 1924

——. *English Prize Cases*, Lloyd's, 1926

Rose, J. Holland. *The Life of Napoleon I*, Bell, 1920

Ross, Sir John. *Memoirs and Correspondence of Admiral Lord de Saumarez*, Bentley, 1838

Ryan, A.N. (ed.). *The Saumarez Papers*, Navy Records Society, 1968

Smith, David Bonner (ed.). *Letters of Admiral of the Fleet the Earl of St Vincent*, vol. II, Navy Records Society, 1927

Squibb, G.D. *Doctors' Commons: A History of the College of Advocates and Doctors of Law*, Clarendon Press, 1977

Starkey, David J. *British Privateering Enterprise*, University of Exeter Press, 1990

Syrett, David and DiNardo, R.L. *The Commissioned Sea Officers of the Royal Navy 1660–1815*, Navy Records Society Occasional Publication, Scolar Press, 1994

Thomas, Donald. *Cochrane*, Andre Deutsch, 1978

Townley, Lynne. 'Sir William Scott, Lord Stowell and the Development of Prize Law in the High Court of Admiralty 1798–1828, with Particular Reference to the Rights of Belligerents', unpublished thesis, University of Birmingham, 1994

——. Lecture to Middle Temple Historical Society, 24 April 1996

Tracy, Nicholas. *Attack on Maritime Trade*, Macmillan, 1991

Tunstall, Brian (ed. Nicholas Tracy). *Naval Warfare in the Age of Sail*, Conway, 1990

Tute, Warren. *Cochrane*, Cassell, 1965

Warner, Oliver. *Captain Marryat – A Rediscovery*, Constable, 1953

Index

Individuals are entered under the names by which they are most commonly known, and ranks are the highest known to have been achieved. Sub-entries are arranged in book order unless another sequence is clearly appropriate. Ships' names are in italics where ships are referred to *per se*. British warships carry no further notation; the character of other ships is specified. Law cases, which in Admiralty law commonly carry the name of the captured ship, are in **bold**. When an action or incident concerns more than one ship, only the principal vessels involved are indexed.